TA 158 .H38 1996

Hawkins, Lori.

100 jobs in technology

D1065684

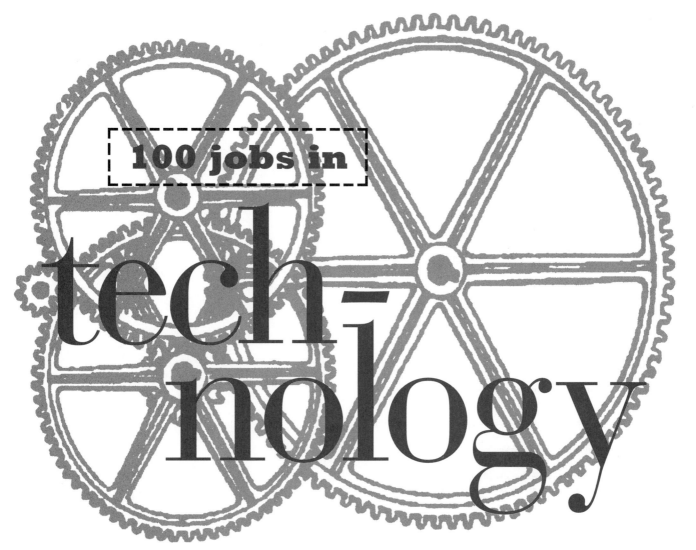

100 jobs in

tech-nology

Lori Hawkins and Betsy Dowling

Macmillan • USA

10/98

35298597

MACMILLAN
A Simon & Schuster Macmillan Company
1633 Broadway
New York, NY 10019

Book design and production by Sandy Bell
100 Jobs in Technology is produced by becker&mayer!, Ltd.

MACMILLAN is a registered trademark of Macmillan, Inc.

Library of Congress Cataloging-in-Publication Data

Hawkins, Lori.
    100 jobs in technology / Lori Hawkins and Betsy Dowling.
      p.   cm.
    Includes bibliographical references (p.).
    ISBN 0-02-861431-3
    1. Industrial technicians—Vocational guidance. 2. High technology industries—Vocational guidance. I. Dowling, Betsy. II. Title.
TA158.H38   1996
602' .3—dc20   96-36251
                                     CIP

10 9 8 7 6 5 4 3 2 1

Printed in the United States of America

To my husband, Paul Sunby.

—L.H.

*To my mother, Ruth, who has supported
me through every one of the
"100 Jobs" it's taken me to get
to where I am today.*

—B.D.

100 JOBS CONTENTS

100 JOBS IN TECHNOLOGY

INTRODUCTION

WERE MIKE NICHOLS to remake *The Graduate,* someone would give Benjamin Braddock a new password to success: "technology," not "plastics."

Once the domain of computer nerds wearing mismatched plaids, the high-tech industry is attracting more and more students and professionals. Many who graduated with nontechnical degrees are returning to school to study computer science or engineering. Some are learning on the job in entry-level positions at high-tech companies. And others are breaking out on their own, starting Internet-based businesses and multimedia shops that require fewer programming skills and more creativity.

It's easy to understand the draw. The pay is generally good, the possibilities are endless, and there's always hope of becoming the next Bill Gates. The Federal Bureau of Labor Statistics predicts that demand for computer systems analysts, engineers, and scientists will grow faster than almost any other job category in the next ten years. By 2005, 738,000 more computer-related jobs will exist than there were in 1992, the most recent year for which statistics are available.

And many jobs that ten years ago were decidedly "non-techie" are becoming so. Public relations experts, venture capitalists, salespeople, and marketing and advertising specialists are all finding new opportunities in high-tech. You don't have to write lines of software code or develop microchips to work in this industry. High-tech companies depend as much on their marketing and finance departments as on their design gurus.

While economic opportunity is a driving force behind the move to software, popular culture is also exercising its influence. Just as the Reagan era spawned business majors, and *L.A. Law* glamorized the legal profession for a few years, the icons of the information age shout high-tech.

There, Microsoft's Gates, a college dropout, built a $12.9 billion fortune selling software. And Marc L. Andressen, the co-founder of Netscape, became a multimillionaire at age 24 when his company went public with one of the biggest opening days in Wall Street history.

Part of high-tech's lure, analysts and academics say, is that it has grown from a number-crunching business tool—

think IBM in the 1980s—to serving as the base for the information and entertainment industries. This shift is opening the field to people other than traditional programmers. The Internet—especially its World Wide Web, which offers graphics and animation—and the multimedia industry—including CD-ROMs, on-line services, and games—are creating a new category of jobs.

As a result, the market for talented graphic artists, filmmakers, sound engineers, animators, writers, and marketers is wide open. And who better to fill these positions than college students who have spent the past four years writing papers using personal computers, doing research on the Internet, and spending their free time surfing the World Wide Web?

Despite the burgeoning opportunities, the odds of becoming a computer mogul, or even earning as much as a corporate lawyer or business executive, are slim. The median base salary for an entry-level software programmer is $31,000, according to a survey conducted by the Software Publishers Association.

Still, many entering the high-tech world are less interested in their earning potential than in the technology's potential. Rather than stock options or security, they seek creative jobs that involve cutting-edge technology.

And although, in the age of downsizing, high-tech can't promise job security, those drawn to the field can count on an interesting ride.

—Lori Hawkins

1. Account Executive at an Advertising Agency

SPECIALIZING IN TECHNOLOGY ACCOUNTS

description: As an account executive representing high-tech clients, it's your job to help mastermind and execute ad campaigns, which include everything from thinking up slogans to overseeing direct mailings. You'll work with the company's product managers and other executives to create a budget and the message the company wants to convey. Then you'll sit down with creative directors, designers, and copywriters to come up with a strategy. Once the company has signed off on the campaign and the artists have designed the materials, it's your job to get the information out—from placing ads in trade magazines to sending information about products to potential customers.

Helping a start-up company achieve profitability by increasing its market share can be extremely rewarding. But this field doesn't offer total job security. At some agencies, if a big client goes to a competing agency, the account executives who worked on that campaign can consider themselves unemployed.

salary: If you're new to the field, you'll probably begin as an account assistant and earn in the low $20,000 range. Account executives with several years of experience and a good track record can earn anywhere from $35,000 to $50,000 a year. An account exec who handles a number of high-profile clients can earn more than $100,000 annually.

prospects: As technology becomes more complex, the need to explain it in a detailed but comprehensible manner has increased. At the same time, the Internet and the World Wide Web are creating new advertising mediums. That has greatly increased the demand for ad agencies with high-tech expertise and account executives who specialize in technology accounts.

qualifications: A bachelor's degree in business or liberal arts is required. Most agencies want a few years of experience, either in the print world or in some area of marketing. Writing skills are very important because you'll be writing both proposals and ad copy.

characteristics: This is a stressful business. Technology changes so quickly that companies are constantly upgrading their products, and they are under pressure to get them to market before their competitors do. Those kind of deadlines often require working seven days a week and well into the night.

Jay Bower *is an account director for an advertising agency that specializes in high-tech marketing in Westport, Connecticut.*

- -

How did you get the job?

Jay Bower earned a degree in philosophy from Colgate University in upstate New York, and landed his first job at the retailer Walden Books. The job involved working in every department of the company. "It was a great introduction to the book and publishing industry," he says. "I learned not just who does what, but how it all comes together."

He then went to a publishing house in New York to work as a product manager, which involved selling books and educational products to teachers. But a ten-percent staff cut left him out of a job.

His experience managing products had prepared him to help advertise them. He got a job offer from an ad agency that specializes in high-tech marketing, and took it. "This was a job that required working directly with product managers, and

here I had been one myself," he says.

He didn't, however, have much technical experience. But what Jay found was that the companies needed help explaining in an understandable way what their products did. "These products are really as much consumer products as is toothpaste," he says. "People want to know how it's going to make their life better, and it's my job to explain that."

> SURF THE WORLD
> WIDE WEB, READ
> COMPUTER
> MAGAZINES LIKE
> WIRED, AND
> CREATE YOUR OWN
> WEB PAGE.
> - - - - - - - - -

What do you do all day?

Jay's week typically begins with a call from a client who has a new software program and the need to come up with a strategy to promote it. He'll request a copy of the software and set up a meeting with the product manager to discuss the ad campaign. He then touches base with the creative director to alert him or her as to what's coming up.

Meanwhile, there are several other projects in various stages of development. For one, Jay needs to discuss a certain feature of the product with the software programmers before he can draw up a direct mail piece to promote it. Another ad campaign involves using a Web site on the Internet to market the equipment. In that case, Jay oversees the text and graphics that are posted on the Web.

He also has several conference calls with creative directors and the client to discuss

progress. "We might talk about what type of art we could use to represent them on their Internet home page, and ask them, 'What image is you?'" Jay says. "Then we go back and figure out how to incorporate it."

Jay also oversees the budget of each campaign. If the campaign goes over budget, he's the one held accountable. "I always work closely with the production people to make sure we're on target."

Where do you see this job leading you?

Jay wants to continue working with high-tech companies. "There's nothing more interesting to me," he says. "People who work at these companies really feel like they're on the next frontier. That's different than anyplace I've ever been."

Jay has seen colleagues move from ad agencies to their clients. One friend just became a vice president of marketing at a high-tech start-up.

2. Animation Development Coordinator

description: After the production of the movie *Toy Story,* a lot of attention was given to the use of computers in animation. While not all producers of animation plan to use computers to the extent that Industrial Light and Magic did to create the character Buzz Light Year, many networks are beginning to use various computer-aided animation techniques such as nonlinear editing, animatics, and digital ink and paint.

As is typical of any change, there is a need for someone to foster it. In this instance, someone needs to research the different products on the market, determine what should be purchased, install the products, and train staff members to use them. Because this is such new territory, the title for this position can vary from company to company, but it is generally something along the lines of animation development coordinator or manager.

salary: This job pays in the range of $30,000 to $50,000 a year.

prospects: The job market in animation has been on the rise for the past few years as many networks have added animated productions to their programming schedule. While the job of animation development coordinator may be difficult to obtain, many networks are hiring employees in the area of prime-time animation.

qualifications: While it is not necessary to have a degree in computers for this type of position, knowledge of computers is helpful, especially as they relate to video and traditional animation.

characteristics: People in this business are very creative, artistic, and personable. They are usually interested in cartoons, toys, and action figures that many adults have long since forgotten. However, they must also be organized and responsible enough to keep on top of scheduling and getting the job done.

Eric Calderon *is an animation development coordinator for a major cable network based in New York City.*

How did you get the job?

Eric Calderon got his job as animation development coordinator by seizing every opportunity he came across. He began working for the company in a variety of temporary jobs, one of which happened to be as the assistant to an executive producer of animation.

While working in this capacity, Eric noticed a script on his boss's desk and asked if he could read it.

That evening, Eric stayed late to read the script, which later became an animated series. The next day he returned the script to his boss, along with some notes concerning the script's plot and story development.

"He loved it," Eric says, recalling his boss's reaction. "He looked at me and he said, 'You know, there are so many things in development that I need to read and look over. I could really use a second set of eyes.'"

This led to Eric's promotion to development assistant, a permanent position with the network. While working in this capacity, Eric developed several successful projects, and his hard work was rewarded with a promotion to his current position.

What do you do all day?

Eric is responsible for evaluating new technology that will be used in the animation department, as well as for acquiring new talent for that department within the network.

When he first started there, Eric was immediately aware that there were no computer facilities; everything in the animation department was done traditionally with ink and paint. Once he moved into the position of development coordinator, he began to investigate the different types of technology available, and eventually implemented the department's shift toward a digital studio.

While the animation is still done with ink and paint, many of the techniques that are used to enhance the production are digital. For example, along with the digital studio came the advent of the animatic—basically a digital storyboard. Using an animatic, proposed animated productions can be viewed on a video monitor with the sound track playing beneath it. In the past, storyboards were shown on separate frames or boards that allowed producers to view a drawing as someone told them what was to happen to the character. With an animatic, producers are able to get a better idea of what a cartoon looks like before it is actually animated.

Other digital techniques have allowed the producers to add special effects to animation. For example, Eric says that by using the Macintosh software program Photoshop, special lighting effects were added to the art in a series of books, which were done predominantly with watercolor and acrylic paint in the past.

Currently, Eric is researching digital pencil test machines which allow a person to shoot traditional artwork on video. Once he acquires this equipment, he will familiarize himself with the product before conducting sessions to train other employees.

Where do you see this job leading you?

Eric would like to stay where he is and eventually take on more responsibilities. "Hopefully, the projects I do will get bigger, and eventually, I will become a development director for a larger community of people."

> ANYONE INTERESTED IN BREAKING INTO THIS FIELD SHOULD START BY CONTACTING TRADITIONAL ANIMATION COMPANIES SUCH AS DISNEY, FOX, USA NETWORK, MTV, NICKELODEON, ABC, CBS, AND JUMBO PICTURES. ALSO, <u>ANIMATION MAGAZINE</u> IS A GOOD PLACE TO LOOK FOR JOB ADVERTISEMENTS.

3. Biotechnology Researcher

description: A biotech researcher is a sort of high-tech explorer. These researchers fuse biology and technology to create medicine and treatment processes as well as medical devices.

The promise of biotechnology has resulted in an explosion of start-up companies in recent years that have raised millions of dollars from investors. Although medical experts—and investors—are excited by the possibilities, most start-ups have yet to deliver. Working for a fledgling biotech firm can be both exciting and fulfilling, but it can also be risky. If a company fails to develop a product after a few years, investors sometimes back out, shutting down the firm. When a company does have a breakthrough, the rewards include both the high-dollar financial returns and the personal satisfaction of helping create a new treatment or device.

Researchers are involved in developing the product, as well as in seeing it through clinical tests and bringing it to market. Currently, many researchers are focusing on genetic engineering, which experts believe has the potential to change the way diseases and illness are treated.

salary: A recent graduate could start in the mid-$20,000 to low-$30,000 range. A researcher with experience and a master's degree could earn $50,000 a year. Senior researchers can earn double that, depending on the company.

prospects: A lot of money is still flowing into biotech, which has resulted in hundreds of biotech start-ups. But it is cyclical, and when investors become pessimistic about their returns, money dries up, and so do companies. Companies are concentrated in a handful of cities. These include: Raleigh-Durham, Boston, San Francisco, and San Diego.

qualifications: The level of education required depends on the level of research being done. Some companies have positions for people with bachelor's degrees doing lower-level work. Others hire only Ph.D.s. Popular majors for people going into this field include biochemistry, molecular biology, chemistry, and chemical engineering.

characteristics: You have got to be able to deal with the idea of job insecurity. You also need to be self-motivated, because in many cases you're exploring an area that has never been looked at before, and it's up to you to set the pace.

Todd Talarico *is a biotech researcher at a biotechnology start-up in Raleigh-Durham, North Carolina.*

How did you get the job?

Todd Talarico studied chemical engineering at Pennsylvania State University. After finishing, he worked as a chemical engineer. But the field that really interested him was biological research. "This was in the mid-'80s, when genetic engineering was a big topic," he says. "I thought it sounded exciting." He went back to school, this time at North Carolina State, where he earned a Ph.D. in microbiology. He did postdoctoral work at a large pharmaceutical research conglomeration. Then it became time to choose between a career in academia or one in industry.

"I got a call from a headhunter who knew of a small start-up that needed someone with a broad background who could do engineering as well as basic science," Todd says. Leaving the large company was a tough decision. "I knew it could go under in six months," he says. But he decided to go for it.

"The thing that really interested me was that I would be responsible for everything from start to finish," he says. "I knew I would learn a lot more and be more involved in development." Although the financial risk was much greater, there was also the possibility, with the right product, of hitting the jackpot.

What do you do all day?

Todd's company studies chemicals that have a therapeutic effect on toxic shock syndrome,

arthritis, and chemotherapy patients. Half of Todd's day is spent doing research experiments, tracking down data on various processes, and doing testing.

He also does a lot of research in the library, and meets with vendors and manufacturers to keep up to speed on new technology that could assist his company's work.

Todd also trains other researchers, and he has participated in some trials using animals and people. "I was there when they injected people the first time," he says. "That's when I felt we were really accomplishing something."

Working at a start-up involves both stress and long hours. Todd works about 70 hours a week, arriving at 7 A.M. "Sometimes I feel like I'm locked at work," he says. "I wish I had more time to spend with my family."

> IF YOU'VE GOT A LIBERAL ARTS OR A TECHNICAL BACKGROUND, CONSIDER GOING BACK TO SCHOOL FOR ANOTHER UNDERGRADUATE DEGREE IN SCIENCE. MANY SCHOOLS OFFER NIGHT COURSES.

Where do you see this job leading you?

"I know I don't want to be a paper pusher. If I'm not hands-on, I'm not happy," he says. Although he wants to stay in biotechnology, he doesn't see himself working for a fledgling company forever. "My next job," he says, "will be with a larger company that has more stability."

4. Book Designer

description: John Grisham may use a word processor to write his best-selling novels. By the same token, the artist who designs his book covers may very well use acrylic paints. But it requires more than the talents of both artist and author to put art and words into a form that can be printed into a book. This task is saved for someone skilled in the technology of book design.

Book designers use various pieces of computer equipment to scan images at a high resolution, manipulate text, and place them both into the format you see in the finished product. This job requires knowledge of printer capabilities and design, as well as computer programs and equipment.

The bulk of a book designer's work is spent sitting in front of a computer tweaking the art and text. However, the job of a designer often encompasses more than paying attention to the details of a book in the making.

Designers are usually called upon to read manuscripts before publication so that they will be able to get a feel for the book's character. This allows them to choose the appropriate font and colors for the book. Having a feel for the book is also important when choosing an artist to depict the author's work, which is a job often left to the designer.

salary: You will most often start out in this industry as a design assistant, and could expect to make somewhere in the neighborhood of $18,000 to $20,000 a year. However, as you move up the ranks to become a junior designer and eventually a designer, you should earn upwards of $30,000.

prospects: While jobs can be fairly easy to find in this field, the highest concentration is in New York City, where the larger publishing houses are located.

qualifications: A bachelor's degree, ideally in design, is required in this field. It would also be helpful to have some advanced course work in English or literature.

characteristics: Most book designers are detail-oriented and organized. They also have the ability to work well with people, and generally have a love for books.

Ethan Trask *is a design assistant for a major publishing company in New York City.*

How did you get the job?

Ethan Trask first became interested in book design when he watched a close family friend at work in her art studio where she illustrated books. "It was just amazing to me. I knew I never wanted to become an illustrator, because I do art on my own, but I don't necessarily do illustrations. But I was interested in how they made the books. I've always loved books. I like books as an object."

In college, Ethan's love for books led him to work toward a degree in literature. After graduation, he headed up to New York to find work in a publishing house. His first job was as a production assistant at Random House. There he learned an enormous amount about the printing process, but, perhaps more importantly, he began to learn about design. One of the book designers there recognized Ethan's interest in design, so she took time to show him some of the computer programs used in book design. Ethan then took a college course in basic design that allowed him to further familiarize himself with some of the computer programs used in book design. The knowledge he gained from the course allowed him to put together a portfolio that he used to secure a job as a design assistant in children's books at Simon & Schuster.

> **THE BEST RESOURCE FOR SOMEONE SEEKING A JOB IN THIS INDUSTRY IS THE _LITERARY MARKET PLACE_, WHICH IS A DIRECTORY OF PUBLISHING HOUSES. ALSO, _PUBLISHER'S WEEKLY_ CONTAINS JOB LISTINGS FOR PUBLISHING JOBS.**

What do you do all day?

Because Ethan works in children's books, which are, for the most part, heavily illustrated, his job is more focused on working with art than anything else.

Ethan is usually working on anywhere from five to eight books at a time. It can take as long as a year for a book to go to print once the publishing process has begun, so he will begin working on any given book no later than six months before it is scheduled to publish. Within this time period, he will work with the illustrator to come up with a concept for the art that will be used. Oftentimes, this can involve deciding on a scene in a novel that will be used on the book's cover, or choosing the medium in which the art work should be done. Once these decisions have been made, the artist will have five weeks to complete the work. During this time, Ethan will begin preliminary designs for the book, such as designing the title. After the art on a book is turned in by the illustrator, there are sometimes corrections to be made. It is important that Ethan be familiar with the book at this point so that, for example, a book's main character will not be described as having blonde hair and blue eyes in the text, but be depicted as having black hair and green eyes on the cover. When every detail has been sorted out, Ethan can begin scanning the art work, placing it on the page, and putting it on a computer disk to be sent to the printer. After a book is sent to the printer, it will come back to Ethan for more corrections before it is finally printed in mass and sent out to stores.

Where do you see this job leading you?

Ethan plans to continue to move up the ranks as a designer. Someday, he hopes to work as an art director for children's books at a publishing house where he will take on the responsibility of managing a group of designers.

5. Cable Network Digital Systems Analyst

description: With all of the new forms of technology being developed for the broadcast industry, just keeping up with what's on the market can be a full-time job. That's why some cable television networks have opted to hire digital systems analysts who determine what products are best for the corporate community in all areas, ranging from word processing and graphics production, to digital media such as Internet activity and digital video systems.

It is often the job of the digital systems analyst to maintain the high-end equipment once it has been acquired and to keep track of what is new and how it's implemented. Perhaps the most stressful part of a digital systems analyst's job is tending to emergency situations. If the equipment malfunctions, it is up to the analyst to get it up and running so that the broadcast divisions will be minimally affected.

salary: The salary in this position is in the range of $40,000 to $60,000 a year.

prospects: Because not all companies have as much money for research as they do to put into other functions such as production, these jobs are few and far between. The best place to look is in larger companies such as Viacom, HBO, Showtime, and Disney.

qualifications: A college degree is preferred for this type of work. Although computer science could be helpful, in order to steer your knowledge toward computers used in the entertainment industry, a degree in multimedia is preferred.

The best way to make yourself a likely candidate for this type of position is to gain as much knowledge about as many computer platforms as you can. A good way to do this is to work on the help desk at a large company that is likely to use more than one computer platform.

characteristics: The one trait everyone in this industry is likely to share is a curious nature. In order to work with computers in this capacity, you must be inquisitive and have a determination to find answers to computer-related problems. You must also be able to integrate technology and research to provide solutions.

Robert Stewart *is a digital systems analyst for a major cable network.*

- -

How did you get the job?

Robert Stewart studied at Massachusetts College of Art, where he earned a degree in industrial design and multimedia. During college, Robert worked at a nightclub as a roadie, testing and setting up audio and lighting systems for major-label bands. This allowed him to gain experience with the integration of computers, video, and sound.

Shortly before graduation, Robert started his own business, creating graphic work with the computer. In his business, he developed CD covers for bands, as well as business cards.

After school, Robert spent eight months job searching. He finally landed a job as computer systems coordinator for a publishing firm, where he soon realized the environment was not conducive to his career goals. After another long job search, a headhunter was able to find him a long-term temporary position working as a consultant at MTV. From this position,

MTV hired him permanently, and he eventually was made a digital systems analyst.

What do you do all day?

A lot of what Robert does during his day consists of researching the market and testing hardware configurations.

"The problem with technology is that it updates itself so quickly that while you are into that newest technology development, your new technology is already old," Robert says.

He estimates that he subscribes to and reads about 20 different magazines, most of which are computer publications; the rest deal with advertising, graphics, and production techniques. Robert says he also spends a lot of time doing research on the Internet. It is also his responsibility to fix malfunctioning equipment and to find equipment for a needed function. Sometimes, he may assist in the setup of special events such as the *MTV Music Awards.*

While all of Robert's responsibilities are important, emergency support is the one that

> **WORKING YOUR WAY INTO THIS INDUSTRY COULD BE DIFFICULT, BUT THE FIRST STEP WOULD BE FINDING OUT WHO'S WHO IN THE BUSINESS. LOOKING THROUGH TRADE JOURNALS SUCH AS MAC USER, ON-LINE DESIGN, AND INTERACTIVE AGE IS A GOOD PLACE TO START.**
> - - - - - - - - - -

holds the most potential for stress. Emergencies may come up once or twice a week, and they vary from the fairly simple problem of a failed hard drive, to something more extreme like a crashed digital video system. But no matter what the problem may be or how urgent its repair is, Robert says the most important thing for him to remember is not to get caught up in the situation.

"I just had a call yesterday from somebody who creates on-air promotions. They said, 'I'm getting this green fuzz on my

screen. What do I do?' We went over it on the phone, and I didn't have a machine in front of me that was identical to theirs, so I just had to use the knowledge in my head to be able to fix it. It took 15 minutes to fix. Even though it's an emergency to them, you don't go into panic mode until you can't figure it out," Robert says, adding that even if he's having trouble finding a solution, he always keeps the user calm.

Where do you see this job leading you?

As far as future goals, Robert has his sights set on management in the area of research and development. However, he is also toying with the idea of starting his own development production house.

6. CAD Manager

description: As a CAD (Computer Aided Designs) manager for an architectural firm, you could be doing anything from setting up hardware, software, or network systems, to training staff to draw on the computer, which can be a difficult task. The biggest challenge is making the transition between drafting by hand and drafting on the computer. On the computer, systems get layered over each other. You can highlight electrical, structural, and plumbing elements, and you can experiment with lighting designs. Manual drawings take a lot longer, and you can't change variables nearly as quickly. As a CAD manager you could also find yourself managing information services and analyzing elements including design, size, color, and the heating systems of the buildings you are designing.

salary: Experienced CAD managers earn salaries ranging from $40,000 to $90,000 annually. An entry-level CAD architect with a bachelor's degree in architecture and one to two years CAD experience can start at anywhere from $28,000 to $35,000.

prospects: Most firms only need one CAD manager. Because more firms are converting to CAD systems, however, the demand for CAD skills is growing rapidly. While architectural firms have felt the fluctuation in the economy over the last few years, those applicants with CAD knowledge have had an edge over other architects.

qualifications: Qualifications required of a CAD manager used to be a general background in computers and a B.A. and an M.S. in architecture. "Now one needs to cross-pollinate," says Patrick Mays, a CAD manager for an architectural firm, "using the CAD or CAM [Computer Aided Manufacturing] skills in conjunction with a degree in electrical, mechanical, structural, or geotechnical engineering."

characteristics: A CAD manager needs to be well organized, a good educator, and a diplomat. "They cut through a lot of departmental rivalry as they coordinate many parts of a company—from marketing and accounting, to production and client interface," Patrick Mays declares.

Patrick Mays *is a CAD manager for an architectural firm in San Francisco.*

How did you get the job?

Patrick Mays was working for an architectural firm in Washington, D.C., when he was recruited by a firm in California. "I was known as an architect who knew about computers—a rare combination at the time," says Patrick. "I worked both ends of the spectrum, as an architect designing buildings and as a construction manager." He has a B.A. and an M.S. in architecture, and studied naval engineering, horticulture, and CAD.

For the first 15 years of his career, Patrick drafted for an architectural firm. His personal interest in technology led him to computer programming as part of his naval architectural work, where he also taught himself architectural computing. His success as a CAD manager stems from this combination. "With an interest in technology and a background in architecture, I knew how to make that marriage work," says Patrick.

What do you do all day?

As CAD manager, Patrick organizes data, runs back-ups, plans strategies, creates schedules, and does whatever it takes to keep up to 15 architects and 45 consultants working on several projects simultaneously. A constant challenge is figuring out ways to integrate new CAD systems from older manual systems and to train staff accordingly. "You can't train others until they're more proficient in 2-D drawing," says Patrick.

Meetings can be quite a challenge. As project manager, Patrick recently facilitated a meeting at a research lab his firm was renovating. "In attendance were the clients, facilities managers, cost estimators, and mechanical, electrical, structural, and environmental engineering consultants," he says. "That's many perspectives looking to you to keep their best interest at heart."

Patrick interacts with CAD managers and MIS directors from many kinds of firms. They

> **PROJECTS THAT REQUIRE JUGGLING MULTIPLE TASKS ARE GOOD PREPARATION FOR CAD MANAGERS.**

all handle a lot of graphical data and need to keep up with the changes in technology. With such large files and complex data structures, he enjoys pushing the limits of the computer software and hardware. It also brings him great pleasure to openly exchange ideas and information with other like professionals. "Even between other architect firms, I don't see the usual competition," says Patrick. "Each firm has its own strengths, and they share the technology available."

Patrick likes to help direct vendors in the industry in producing truly useful products, from software, to hardware, to texture of paper. "Yes, architects still use paper," he adds.

Where do you see this job leading you?

"I take great pleasure in being on the cutting edge of technology," Patrick says. "I'm in an ideal position to keep up with changes." Architects still do a lot in 2-D, but he predicts rapid changes. "The next technological challenge is to be able to efficiently send drawings electronically to other offices," Patrick notes.

Most CAD managers advance within the managerial system. Although it's an atypical move, Patrick will probably become a principal in the firm.

7. CD-ROM Producer

description: Computers have always been used for both entertainment and educational purposes, but within the past ten years—through the introduction of CD-ROMs—the computer's capacity to both educate and entertain has grown tremendously. A CD-ROM enables a computer to display intricate graphics in conjunction with sound, digitized video, animation, and text. This allows for a variety of programs that can, for example, teach computer users how to communicate with sign language or take them on a tour of the San Diego Zoo from their living room.

Creating any CD-ROM is a multifaceted task and requires the work of numerous editors, authors, designers, and programmers. All of these people, however, would be incapable of manufacturing a CD-ROM without a producer to create the concept.

salary: This is typically a freelance job, and the amount of income realized is directly related to the amount of work found. A CD-ROM producer working year-round could expect to make anywhere from $40,000 to $70,000 a year.

prospects: Because CD-ROMs are fairly new, most companies have a fluctuating workload and can't afford to take on employees such as CD-ROM producers full-time. Most producers have found the best way to find work and gain credentials in this field is to do freelance or contract work. Freelance projects will last anywhere from six to fourteen months.

qualifications: While some companies may seek employees who have a bachelor's degree in graphic arts or computer science, a liberal arts degree is also desirable, as long as it is coupled with some experience in technology. Someone wanting to be a producer should have experience in one or more aspects of the industry—animation, programming, graphic arts, or film producing. One way to get this experience is to work for a developer in the entry-level position of production assistant.

characteristics: CD-ROM producers must be good communicators. Because they are coordinating the efforts of numerous people with different skill sets, they must also be diplomatic and able to handle multiple tasks simultaneously.

Lisa Brand *is a CD-ROM producer at a major publishing house in New York City.*

How did you get the job?

As a literature major, Lisa Brand spent a lot of time writing papers on the computer. At the time, she had no idea how useful computers could be in helping to enhance her work for her minor, which was art.

After college, Lisa's interest in art led her to an internship at the Eastman Kodak Center for Creative Imaging. The school, which focused on helping people in the visual arts to learn how to use computers in their work, allowed Lisa to become familiar with a wide range of the software applications being used in the industry. The knowledge she gained and the contacts she made at the school enabled her to begin work as a freelance graphic designer. Her freelance work soon led to a full-time job as an interface designer for Voyager Company, a CD-ROM publisher. But after having worked at the company for a year, Lisa became discouraged with the industry and decided to go to graduate school to study film production.

But no sooner had she given up than the industry began to show signs of advancement. "At that point, there was a lot of hype, but there wasn't much to back it up. That was just a few years ago, and the industry has really evolved since then. It's a much more exciting place now."

During her year in film school, Lisa continued to freelance for fear that she would fall behind in her knowledge of an industry that was moving so quickly. After she began working as a project manager for animation at MTV, she decided to leave film school and pursue a career in interactive technology.

After she completed her project with MTV, she landed a job working on a long-term project for a major book publishing house in New York, where she is currently producing a CD-ROM in the children's interactive department.

What do you do all day?

At the onset of any new project, Lisa spends a lot of time meeting with everyone who is going to be taking part in creating the CD-ROM. Most of these meetings, which include editors, authors, and technical people, will be spent conceptualizing the finished product. Once there is a consensus, it is time for the work to begin.

Lisa starts by writing a script that will be followed by everyone who is working on the project. The script—which contains information about the product's content, from the details of the user's navigation, to technical requirements—is treated as a set of blueprints.

During the actual production of a CD-ROM, Lisa makes day-to-day decisions about the animation, programming, and other aspects of the CD. She also coordinates the efforts of everyone working on the project, apprising them of its progress and making sure that everyone is doing his or her part to keep the project on schedule.

Where do you see this job leading you?

Ultimately, Lisa would like to start her own business, developing interactive software for children's museums and foundations.

> **PERHAPS THE BEST WAY FOR SOMEONE TO FIND A JOB IN CD-ROM PRODUCTION WOULD BE TO GET ON-LINE AND SEARCH THE JOB LISTINGS FOR NEW MEDIA. LISTINGS CAN BE FOUND ON THE WORLD WIDE WEB'S MONSTER BOARD AT HTTP://WWW. MONSTER.COM.**

8. Central Intelligence Agency Engineer

description: For the CIA, technology is a national security issue. The goal is to stay ahead of the rest of the world when it comes to the use and development of technology for government intelligence. To that end, the CIA employs hundreds of engineers and scientists to develop technology that will help it collect, process, and analyze intelligence. That involves both in-house research and development and acquiring technology from the private sector that can be used by intelligence specialists in the field.

As the agency has become less clandestine, its science and technology arm has become an important one.

The deputy director for science and technology is responsible for understanding where technology is headed on a worldwide basis and for steering engineers and scientists toward doing groundbreaking work in those areas. The director also spends a lot of time working with staffers and committees on Capitol Hill to educate them on high-tech trends and fighting to keep the budget off the chopping block.

salary: This is one of the best-paying branches of government service. Engineers right out of college start in the high $30,000s to low $40,000s. Senior intelligence people can earn well over $100,000.

prospects: A fast-changing world and a revolution in technology have spurred the CIA to change its focus and operating style. The shift to bringing in new high-tech talent means that opportunities are very good. The CIA has launched an aggressive recruiting plan in an effort to increase its staff in areas including information technology, computer engineering, and computer science.

qualifications: Entry-level engineering and science positions require a minimum of a bachelor's degree. Senior jobs require advanced degrees in engineering or physical science.

characteristics: Working for the CIA isn't for everyone; you've got to believe in the work you're doing. Since a lot of projects involve classified information, you've got to be good at keeping quiet about your work. You have also got to be a good communicator—in many cases you'll be working closely with people in other parts of the intelligence community who need to understand what you're doing.

Ruth David *is deputy director for science and technology at the CIA in Washington, D.C.*

- -

How did you get the job?

"I was convinced in high school I was going to be a math teacher," Ruth David says. "I went to a small school in Kansas where we assumed 'engineering' meant driving trains." A physics professor at her community college convinced her to go into science, and she eventually transferred to Wichita State University, where she earned a bachelor's degree in electrical engineering.

Her first job was at Sandia National Laboratory in Albuquerque, New Mexico. As part of the job, the government sent her to Stanford University, where she earned a master's degree in engineering. She returned to the lab, where she developed technology for defense-related projects. Three years later, Sandia sent her back to Stanford to earn a Ph.D. After returning to Sandia, she was put in charge of developing strategies for the lab in the area of information technology.

When the CIA position

> **THE CIA RECRUITS STUDENTS AT COLLEGE CAMPUSES ACROSS THE COUNTRY. YOU SHOULD BE WILLING TO ACCEPT AN ENTRY-LEVEL POSITION AND BE READY TO MOVE—POSSIBLY OVERSEAS.**

opened up, Ruth was Sandia's nominee. She interviewed for the job and got it. "There were a couple of reasons I got the job," she says. "First was my background in information technology, and the other was that I had led government organizations through some fairly dramatic changes in terms of restructuring and downsizing. Those skills were needed in this position."

What do you do all day?

"I'm in the office at 6 A.M. so I can catch up on reading and e-mail before meetings start," Ruth says. Meetings usually take up most of her day. She spends time briefing Capitol Hill committees on the directions in which her department is moving. She also meets with her managers and scientists to discuss new technology and how it can be integrated into existing programs. "A lot of what we're doing now is developing strategies and plans for the future," she says. "Like every government agency, we've gone through several years of downsizing, and that's continuing. We've got to make decisions about what we can stop doing so we can invest in new ideas."

She also focuses on leveraging existing technology from private companies, which saves her engineers from reinventing the wheel. Ruth is an avid trend watcher. "It's not imperative that we be on the cutting edge in every area, but we have to understand how technology drives our ability to collect and process intelligence," she says. Ruth spends a lot of time traveling around the world to meet with intelligence agents to discuss their needs and how technology being created by her group can help meet those needs.

After a typical day which includes 14 to 16 hours of meetings—sometimes with no time for lunch—Ruth often heads for an evening dinner engagement downtown where she mingles with Capitol Hill's movers and shakers.

For Ruth, the long hours are canceled out by the rewards. "I like having the ability to have an impact in an area which I believe is very important to our country."

Where do you see this job leading you?

"At the end of a certain number of years, I'll have to look around and see where can this take me," she says. Until then, Ruth wants to continue to steer the CIA's high-tech course.

9. Chief Technology Officer

description: Chief Technology Officers serve as their company's high-tech visionaries. It's the CTO's job to help chart the company's technology course over the next two to three years. The CTO focuses on long-term strategies, which are developed by talking with customers about their changing needs and by studying market trends and new technology. Their plans suggest steps the company should consider to stay ahead of the curve and the industry trends it should anticipate. CTOs may also look for technology and start-up companies to purchase.

But that's only half the job; the other half is lobbying and selling the company's developers on the ideas. Having a grand plan doesn't guarantee that the rest of the company will support it. Because most company officials and developers are preoccupied with the products that are generating revenues right now, convincing them to invest in the future isn't always an easy sell. But CTOs don't mind trying because they know that their ideas are just as important to the future of the company as is any technology the company is currently developing. CTOs at large companies often have a budget that they can use to fund some of their ideas. At smaller companies they are likely to be at the mercy of their colleagues.

salary: This is a senior position, so salaries usually start at $125,000 and increase according to the size of the company.

prospects: The CTO is a fairly new concept, although as tech companies pay more attention to long-term vision, many are creating CTO jobs. The positions are most common at companies doing advanced research and development. Despite the increase in the number of these positions, these aren't easy jobs to get. They require years of business and technical experience, and are usually open only to people with senior-level experience.

qualifications: You will need about 15 years of experience in high-tech, with a background in both business and technical matters. A proven track record of guiding a company is also valued.

characteristics: You have to be good at selling your ideas. Being persuasive and persistent are key to making an impact in this position. You also have to be a good listener because a lot of your ideas will be based on observations drawn from conversations with customers and industry analysts.

David Ladd *is the chief technology officer at a company that develops voice mail systems in Milpitas, California.*

How did you get the job?

After earning a master's degree in computer science, David Ladd got a job as a software engineer. He worked his way up in management, then left to launch his own voice mail company. The son of an entrepreneur, he always dreamed of owning his own business. "My partner handled the marketing and sales, and I was the technical guy," he says. Their company became a $100 million industry leader, and they eventually sold it to a major electronics company.

When he was offered the position of chief technology officer, David chose to stay. "I had enough of dealing with the day-to-day operations," he says. "I liked the idea of looking ahead."

> DON'T SPEND ALL YOUR TIME IN ENGINEERING. GET EXPERIENCE IN MARKETING AND FINANCE AS WELL. ALSO GET SOME EXPERIENCE WORKING WITH CUSTOMERS; YOU WILL BE INTERACTING WITH THEM ON A DAILY BASIS.

What do you do all day?

The first thing David does when he arrives at the office at 8:30 A.M. is check his e-mail and voice mail. Next, it's a meeting with marketing, and then with engineering to discuss current projects and future plans. He then often sits down with a customer who has stopped by for a visit. "I spend a good deal of time in front of customers, presenting where I see the world going and checking with them to see whether they agree," he says.

David spends the rest of the day working by himself. He does his own market research on the Internet, and he reads many trade magazines to keep up with high-tech trends. He also devotes a lot of time to writing reports explaining his proposals, which involve everything from acquiring a start-up, to focusing more energy on an emerging technology. "I clarify my ideas a lot better if I write them out first," he says. After putting them in writing, David shares his ideas with colleagues, who usually include the chief information officer, and marketing and engineering managers. "Then I call a meeting to discuss my report, and I ask if they're ready to fund it," he says.

It's not always that easy, though. Getting his busy colleagues to hear out his ideas is a challenge. "It can be tough to get their attention," he says. "Sometimes you just want to say, 'Come on, guys, this is the right thing. I'm convinced of it.'" He has made an impact already, however. In addition to helping shape the direction the company's engineers take toward new product development, he has helped the company acquire two start-ups.

Where do you see this job leading you?

David wants to continue to help his company anticipate trends and new technology. "As long as I feel like I'm having an impact, I plan to keep doing this," he says. At some point, he may consider doing private consulting for companies for which he serves as a board member.

10. Commercial Industrial Resource Analyst

description: Resource analysts manage projects in commercial industrial conservation. Their focus is to identify more efficient ways to use energy and water resources. They do this by conducting a resource audit of a commercial or industrial building to study the building's energy and water uses. With spreadsheets and computer modeling, they determine how a company can use its resources more efficiently and cost-effectively. They help the customer to implement these measures, and they inspect to see that the measures were installed properly. A resource analyst could be employed by a public or private utility, an architectural or engineering firm, an energy service company, or an equipment vendor.

Some medium- to large-size private companies, such as high-end grocery store chains, banks, property management companies, and department stores, are beginning to see the benefit of having their own resource analyst on staff.

salary: Commercial analysts start at about $25,000 and top out at $70,000 as an office manager. You can break into the energy field with less education as a residential analyst and earn anywhere from $22,000 to $45,000.

prospects: If you keep your energy conservation skills upgraded, you'll have an easier time finding a job, but the market is a little tight.

qualifications: Technical energy and conservation skills used to be enough to carve out a successful career. With reduced conservation funding by utilities, however, a business background is useful. You will need a degree in energy management, engineering, architecture, or environmental science.

characteristics: Networking both personally and professionally with colleagues in the industry will help you advance your career. Analytical thinking is also imperative for this work.

Michael Laurie *is a resource analyst.*

How did you get the job?

Michael Laurie has a two-year degree in energy management and a recently-acquired M.B.A. He started in residential and commercial construction, did sales and installation of insulation and windows, and worked his way up to residential analysis with a public utility doing audits and public education. He later did oversights of several utility companies' residential conservation programs. Then, he did entry-level commercial/industrial inspections and audits and worked his way up to more complex audits and project management.

Concern for the environment brought Michael into his current position through the back door. "I wanted to do more than just protest harmful environmental practices," he says. "I became proactive to help develop the positive alternative solution to some of our environmental problems."

FOR MORE INFORMATION, CONTACT ASHRACE (AMERICAN SOCIETY OF HEATING, REFRIGERATION, AND AIR CONDITIONING). IN ADDITION TO SETTING THE STANDARDS FOR THE INDUSTRY, ASHRACE DEVELOPS TECHNICAL MANUALS FOR EQUIPMENT, PROVIDES TRAINING, AND HAS LOCAL CHAPTERS ALL OVER THE COUNTRY. (SEE RESOURCES, PAGE 212.)

What do you do all day?

Michael works with modeling and spreadsheet software that simulates the resource usage of a particular building. He works by himself or in a team to audit and inspect buildings, to analyze resource-consuming equipment (lights, heating and cooling equipment, and controls), and to summarize his findings. "I teach others, manage projects, review other people's work, develop marketing materials, study the latest in efficient technologies, and organize lots of information," he says, laughing at how consuming his work is.

Michael works for a company that provides residential, commercial, and industrial energy analysis to a wide range of customers. Although his hours are flexible, Michael finds himself in the office 70 percent of the time, 60 percent of which is spent at the computer analyzing the costs and savings associated with energy usage.

Where do you see this job leading you?

Michael hopes to integrate energy, water, and waste audits into a complete resource analysis package. His aim is to carry the skills he has developed in energy conservation into a broader arena of other resource-efficiency work. "My goal is to be hired to go into a building and give it the royal efficiency treatment of auditing its energy, water, and materials usage," he grins. "The technology exists. Now comes the arduous task of changing public perception."

11. Computer Book Author

description: Whether a book tackles a broad topic or a specialized one, the author's job is to explain new technology in a way in which both novices and veterans can learn something.

It doesn't take a contract wtih a mega-publishing company to get your work published; a number of small publishing houses that focus on high-tech topics have sprung up in the past few years.

Writing about technology—be it a book translating jargon or one explaining the Internet—can take months of research. When the research is complete, the writing begins, often under deadline. Some books go through several rewrites before the publisher is satisfied. Thorough research and good writing don't necessarily guarantee a long shelf life; in such a fast-changing industry, there's always the danger that the book will be outdated by the time it arrives in stores.

salary: You might earn anywhere from $5,000 to $100,000 depending on the size of the market your book is targeting and the size of the publishing firm. Authors usually receive an advance, which can be anywhere from $2,000 to $20,000. At the halfway point, they are paid a similar portion, and they receive the final payment when the book is completed. Royalties typically range from 8 to 15 percent of sales.

prospects: Bookstores are devoting more shelf space to books about technology, and publishers are responding with more titles. Still, trying to pitch an idea to a book publisher is not easy. This is an extremely competitive industry, and even most published authors rarely have the luxury of writing full-time.

qualifications: Most publishers consider strong writing skills to be more important than an in-depth knowledge of the book topic. You will need to have a range of writing samples—such as magazine or newspaper articles—that show off your abilities. Research experience is also very helpful.

characteristics: You have got to be good at organizing your time, especially if the book isn't your full-time job. Working from home on your own time requires self-discipline.

Scott Taves *is the author of a book about games on the Internet.*

How did you get the job?

As a college student studying journalism and philosophy, Scott Taves began writing about arts and entertainment for his school paper and for magazines. After graduating, he started a business in Chicago that handles marketing and publicity for European record companies in the United States. He still continued, however, to write for magazines, including reviewing computer games and music for *Wired*.

He was approached by a small publishing company about writing a book about music on the Internet. "By the time I got back to them, they had given it to someone else," he says. "So they asked if I'd be interested in writing about games on the Internet." It was

an offer that Scott couldn't refuse. "Every writer wants to do a book, and here was an opportunity where I had experience in the right area," he says. "I knew it would be a crunch, but this was an opportunity that I would be really silly to turn down."

What do you do all day?

Scott had four months to research and write the book. During the day, while he was running his business, Scott squeezed in six to seven hours on the Internet looking for interesting sites to profile.

In the first two months of his Net travels, he found 400 sites, including interactive chess games, CD-ROM war games, and Web pages containing long lists of gaming strategies. "I had WordPerfect running at the same time, and whenever I found a place I liked, I'd mark it and do a rough review." He also had to download all the graphics and visual images from the Internet to illustrate the book.

Finding time to write the book was more of a challenge. "Because I have two small chil-

dren and a day job, I was writing every evening from 9 P.M. till 1 or 2 in the morning."

After Scott finished the manuscript, his editor gave it an initial read, and then Scott and his editor went through once more to proofread every section. Finally, it was production time. "Sometimes it seemed like it would never come together, and it felt really good when it finally did."

Where do you see this job leading you?

"There were a lot of frustrating moments learning how to organize the book and get it together," Scott says. "But now that that first painful book is over, I'd like to write another."

Scott wants to focus on high-tech topics. "I love working with computers, and to me, there's nothing more exciting than buying a new piece of computer equipment."

Many technology authors continue to freelance for magazines and newspapers between book projects.

12. Computer Chip Designer

description: Chip designers create the brains of computers and other electronic devices. A chip, which is a tiny piece of silicon with an integrated electronic circuit embedded in it, is what stores memory in your computer. Designers develop chips from scratch, as well as make existing chips stronger, faster, and more powerful. Chip manufacturers such as Intel, Samsung, and Advanced Micro Devices sell their chips to computer and electronics companies. Other companies, such as IBM and Motorola, develop chips for use in their own products.

It can take more than two years to turn a concept into an actual computer chip. First, micro-architects dream up how the chip will behave, and then circuit designers figure out how to turn the idea into the real thing. Once the design is completed, a prototype is created. Designers then spend months, and often every waking minute, testing the chip and tweaking it to get optimum performance before it is rolled out and plugged into computers.

salary: A designer just out of school with a bachelor's degree could start at $35,000 a year. With a Ph.D., starting salary would be about $40,000. Chip designers with several years of experience earn $60,000 to $80,000. Salaries for designers with specialized skills can reach $100,000.

prospects: Computer chips are popping up in everything from car door openers to boom boxes, and there are simply not enough qualified people to design them. Chip makers are aggressively recruiting college seniors. With the right educational background, you should have little difficulty finding a job in this field.

qualifications: Most chip designers have at least a bachelor's degree in computer science or electrical engineering. It's more difficult to break in with another type of engineering degree, but it can be done. It's possible to get a job right out of college with no work experience.

characteristics: Much of the chip design process is done as a team, so you need to like working closely and sharing ideas with other people. You have also got to be an analytical thinker and a good problem solver. Hours can be very long and irregular, especially when the design process is coming to a close.

Gian Franco Gerosa *is a chip design manager for a major chip manufacturer in Austin, Texas.*

How did you get the job?

"I knew from the time I was in seventh grade that I wanted to do something involving engineering," Gian Franco Gerosa says. "I was always interested in how things work and what makes them do what they do." Gian received a Ph.D. from Ohio State University in solid state physics. He spent three years doing chip design at Intel in Portland, Oregon. When he learned his project was being cancelled, he began exploring out-of-state possibilities. "I had friends who had come here to Austin from Intel, and they suggested I look into working here," he says.

The job was his for the asking. "I was a shoo-in," he says. "They were starting a new design, and needed someone with my exact skills. It was a match, and we packed up and moved south."

What do you do all day?

There are 40 people in Gian's design group, which is broken up into teams that design, build, and test the computer chips.

Gian arrives at work at 8:30 A.M., but there are no set hours. "You cannot just turn this job off at 5 P.M. and go home," he says. "If you're hot on the trail of a solution, you're glued to the tube until you get it right, whether it's 7 or 8 or 9 in the evening."

Mondays, Tuesdays, and Wednesdays are usually spent meeting with team members to discuss projects and to brainstorm on new design approaches. "Thursdays and Fridays are my play days," he says. "That's when I set aside some quiet time and focus completely on design work." Occasionally he pulls a late night. "I can lock myself in my office and work until 2 in the morning."

Gian's work depends on the stage of the design process that his team is in. The last few months are chaotic. "We have no life during that time," he says. "Our spouses complain, we don't see our kids, we're at work all weekend," he says. But once the deadline is met, there's a chance to recuperate. "Everyone has poured their hearts out on the project, and then they have a chance to take it easy."

Gian also meets regularly with Apple Computer, which is the primary customer of the chips his team designs. "Tomorrow, I'll be in California to see how they use our design," he says. "We'll talk about performance issues and what we can do to help them with any problems they might be having."

Where do you see this job leading you?

Gian is happy where he is. He would prefer to stay involved in chip design rather than move up in management. "I do need to do design work. I just need the fix," he says.

13. Computer Chip Manufacturing Technician

description: Manufacturing technicians ensure that the multimillion-dollar equipment that makes computer chips stays up and running. They also integrate new machinery into production lines and write documentation to describe every step of the process.

Technicians work with manufacturing engineers to make changes in the process if a customer has a specific chip requirement. They also stay in close contact with the operators who work on the production lines and work with engineers to figure out ways to improve the yield of flawless components. Technicians evaluate new chip manufacturing technology, and help cross-train other employees on new equipment. Piecing together the manufacturing system is like putting together a puzzle, and technicians say that's one of the draws of this job. It involves a lot of problem solving and, when something goes wrong, quick thinking. No two days are alike, and a technological revolution in the chip manufacturing process guarantees that the high-tech systems, and the challenges, are constantly changing.

salary: Entry-level jobs start at about $11 an hour. Experienced technicians with the right skill set can earn $30 an hour, which translates into $62,000 a year. Thanks to overtime, chip technicians often earn more than engineers.

prospects: With several chip manufacturing plants, called "fabs," opening in the next two years, the opportunities in this field have never been better. Fabs typically employ hundreds of manufacturing technicians.

qualifications: A minimum of a two-year associate's degree in electronics is required. Most companies are willing to train employees, but to be successful, you need to possess particular skills. An understanding of mechanics and hydraulics, and skills in comparative analysis are important. Good technical writing skills are needed because this job involves writing a lot of process documentation.

characteristics: You have got to pick up new technology very quickly, have an eye for detail, and be a good troubleshooter. A lot of the equipment you'll be working with doesn't come with a manual, much less instructions on what to do if it malfunctions. This job involves a lot of overtime, so you need to be flexible.

Lee Bryant *is a chip manufacturing technician at a chip plant in Austin, Texas.*

How did you get the job?

Lee Bryant worked for his father's automotive shop, but when the business hit hard times, Lee got a part-time job at a chip plant as an operator using mechanical equipment to scan components. "I knew I didn't want to work with cars the rest of my life because it's such a dirty job, but I loved mechanics," he says. "It wasn't until I got this job that I learned I could make money doing this kind of stuff."

Lee worked as an operator for a year before he realized that if he wanted to move up to a technician's job, he was going to have to take the initiative. "Since my experience was working for a family business, I didn't realize you had to ask for a promotion; they don't come to you. When I figured it out, I went in and applied." He got the job and a lot of on-the-job training. "I think I really lucked into this job. It's very stable, and you can make a lot of money at it," he says. "The best part is I learn every day, and I know that's not something everyone can say."

What do you do all day?

Lee arrives at work at 7 A.M. and immediately surveys the equipment. "We're in a continuous state of upgrading, which means we've always got a new system of some sort to deal with," he says. Because they are working with cutting-edge equipment, there are often bugs that Lee and his colleagues must isolate and fix. "Since everything is so new, a lot of the manuals aren't as complete as they should be," he says. "We're pretty much on our own when it comes to servicing them." When new equipment arrives, Lee teams up with manufacturing engineers to pull it into the process. When a customer changes the specifications of its components, they spend the morning making adjustments that will change the design.

New equipment means writing technical documentation that explains to the technical team how it works and how it interacts with other types of equipment. Technical writing is one of Lee's favorite parts of the job. "I like figuring out how something works and writing it

> COMPUTER CHIP PLANTS ARE CONCENTRATED IN SPECIFIC AREAS OF THE COUNTRY, SO TO GET A JOB IN THIS FIELD, THE FIRST CONSIDERATION IS OFTEN LOCATION. KEEP IN MIND THAT THOUGH MANY POSITIONS ARE ADVERTISED AS REQUIRING EXPERIENCE, MANY COMPANIES ARE WILLING TO TRAIN.

in a way that anyone can pick up and understand," he says.

When he's not putting out a fire, Lee checks out new equipment that his company's vendors want technicians to evaluate. "They need to know what we like and what we don't like," he says. "And we get the scoop on the latest technology."

There's not a lot of downtime during his 12-hour day. "We get very few waiting moments," he says. "I'm on my feet all day long. But that's the way I like it. The day never drags."

Where do you see this job leading you?

Lee's dream job is to open a marina, and he is already selling jet skis as a sideline. But he has no immediate plans to leave his job. "I like the challenges that every day brings, and I think that I'd really miss that."

14. Computer Corporation Media Spokesperson

description: When a trade press reporter wants the scoop on a company's latest product, it's the media spokesperson who fields the call.

The spokesperson writes news releases, sets up interviews for the press, pitches stories to reporters, and extinguishes false rumors before they take on a life of their own. Because the job involves representing the company at trade shows and other high-profile events, a spokesperson spends a lot of time outside the office and out of town.

Working as a corporate spokesperson differs from working for a public relations firm because, instead of having five or six accounts, you're solely devoted to acting as the company's voice. This can have its drawbacks: When a negative story hits the front page, it's often the spokesperson who is held accountable by company officials.

salary: If you're just out of college, you can expect to start at less than $25,000 a year, with mid-level positions earning in the low- to mid-$30,000s. An experienced spokesperson for a major corporation can earn well above $50,000. The larger the company and the city, the higher the salary.

prospects: Most high-tech companies consider media coverage key to their growth, and as they expand, so does their media relations department. Even small- and medium-size businesses hire media specialists to write press releases and answer reporters' questions.

qualifications: A bachelor's degree in communications is a plus, but not mandatory. If you want to work for a high-tech company, knowledge of the particular industry is important, but not required. Most companies are willing to train new, promising job candidates.

characteristics: Because you're responsible for answering questions that could have a major impact on the company, you've got to be articulate and good at thinking on your feet.

Kris Wilen *is a press relations specialist for a computer manufacturer in North Sioux City, South Dakota.*

How did you get the job?

As a communications major at Morningside College in Sioux City, Kris Wilen began working at a small advertising shop as a copywriter and graphic artist. After graduating, she moved to Denver, where she earned a graduate degree in communications from the University of Phoenix and spent two years doing public relations for the Denver Center for Performing Arts.

She moved on to a couple of large advertising agencies, where her accounts included McDonald's and Pepsi Cola. When she decided to return home to Sioux City, she took a job in a computer manufacturer's marketing department. But she missed contact with the public. "I didn't feel I was getting enough action," Kris says. "I

> INTERNSHIPS, EVEN IF THEY'RE UNPAID, ARE A GREAT WAY TO GET YOUR FOOT IN THE DOOR. IF YOU WANT TO BE A SPOKESPERSON FOR A PARTICULAR COMPANY, BUT THE ONLY JOB THAT'S AVAILABLE IS IN ANOTHER DEPARTMENT, GO AHEAD AND TAKE IT—MANY PEOPLE START IN OTHER DEPARTMENTS AND WORK THEIR WAY OVER.

wasn't meeting new people, and I missed traveling and interacting with the press." She began lobbying the public relations manager for a position. "I just kept telling him about myself," she says. "I didn't have

any computer experience, but I had focused on consumer products, and that's what a computer is." Her persistence paid off, and she was given the job.

What do you do all day?

Much of the day is spent writing news releases, sending out press packages, and talking on the phone with journalists from publications ranging from highly specialized trade journals, to magazines like *Better Homes and Gardens.*

When reporters come to North Sioux City to write sto-

ries, Kris arranges all the interviews and photos, and acts as the local tour guide. She recently arranged a photo shoot for a *Wired* magazine article and escorted the photographer there.

To keep up with new products, she meets frequently with her marketing staff. And then there's travel, which takes Kris to Microsoft's headquarters in Redmond, Washington, and to trade shows in Los Angeles and Mexico City. She's now handling press relations for non-European foreign countries, and she's crossing her fingers that this will lead to more trips.

Where do you see this job leading you?

Kris hopes one day to open a small public relations firm. "I'd like to be able to see a project through from beginning to end again," she says. "At a small firm, you have more control and it's more hands-on."

15. Computer Designer

description: Computer designers create the tangible parts of the computer, which include printers, disks drives, modems, and speakers.

Computer designers work with technology vendors and with marketing and manufacturing teams to design products. Customer demand for a new technology—such as a more lightweight notebook computer—can be reason enough to build a new machine. Computer designers take those specifications and work together to create a product plan. They build a prototype, test it, test it some more, make changes, and finally move it to the assembly line.

Designers describe the process, which usually takes nine to twelve months, as the closest a person can come to giving birth without being pregnant. It's that ability to create something from nothing that inspires designers. On the downside, hours can be very long, and when you spend months pouring your heart into a product that bombs, it can be devastating.

salary: Designers with bachelor's degrees usually start in the $40,000 range. With a master's degree, starting salary begins in the $50,000s. A really good designer can earn well over $100,000 a year.

prospects: This is a fast-growing field. The highest demand is for people with backgrounds in electrical, mechanical, and power-supply engineering, and in computer-aided drafting design. In addition to large computer makers, hundreds of smaller companies that build computer clones also need designers; sometimes these firms offer the best opportunities for those just starting out.

qualifications: Although companies do hire recent grads with bachelor's degrees in engineering, you might have to start in an entry-level support job and work your way up. Large companies usually want those with master's degrees.

characteristics: Designing computers involves a lot of teamwork, so you need to like working closely with other people. You have got to be a very technical thinker, and you must be willing to put in long hours for weeks at a time.

David Altounian *oversees the design of portable computers at a leading computer company in Austin, Texas.*

How did you get the job?

"I was one of those kid hackers growing up," David Altounian says. "Not a bad hacker, but one who said, 'Here's a computer, I'm going to get inside and figure it out.'" David studied electrical engineering while working as a software test engineer. After working for several companies, he signed on at Compaq Computer, where he spent three years as manager of industry marketing, which focused on new technologies.

He left to work at Motorola on one of its most challenging products—the personal digital assistant, or PDA. A PDA is a handheld computer that combines the power and flexibility of a desktop computer with the convenience of a small electronic organizer. The technology has yet to catch on, and it was a disappointment for those who invested so much time and ener-

gy in the project. "It's as if you were writing a book, and at the end of the day someone burned it all," David says.

He left to join a major computer company as marketing director for portable computers. The company, which had experienced difficulty in the notebook computer area, needed someone who could jump-start the group. "They were under a lot of pressure, and they needed someone who could pull people together," he says. Today he oversees the entire process, from hiring designers and engineers to participating in the actual design.

FOR MORE INFORMATION, CONTACT THE INSTITUTE FOR ELECTRICAL AND ELECTRONIC ENGINEERS. (SEE RESOURCES, PAGE 212.)

What do you do all day?

David arrives at work at 7:30 A.M. and meets with marketing and engineering team leaders. His day depends on what stage of product development his group is in. Right now, his company is focusing on designing a notebook computer, and David and the team leaders discuss issues like who will buy it and how much it should cost. If marketing surveys show that customers want a different palm rest, it could have a major impact on the design of the notebook. Designers take all those factors into account.

David also meets with designers to discuss schedules and deadlines, and what can be done to stay on track. Once development work begins, designers use a "breadboard," which is a thin board made of fiberglass or plastic with little holes arranged in a grid. Using the breadboards, designers create prototypes of circuit boards by wiring chips, resistors, and other electronic parts onto the board by hand. When the prototype is finished, they test it to make sure it works. If it does, it

is translated into a drawing using computer-aided design tools. A computer prototype is created, and the testing and redesigning begin. "The best part is watching it move from a rough design to a computer," David says.

David also spends a lot of time traveling abroad. "We design them here, but we build them overseas, so I go over for a week every five weeks to meet with our manufacturing partners."

Where do you see this job leading you?

David wants to continue to be involved in computer notebook design. "Notebooks are an interesting place to be right now," he says. "The technology is changing so fast, and we're using it to do new things that never would have even been possible a year or two ago."

16. Computer Game Animator

description: Animators create the characters, the backgrounds, and the 3-D graphics that make up computer games.

This is a job that requires a wild imagination and strong artistic and technical skills. Often, an animator is given nothing more than a rough idea of what a character should look like, and is turned loose to bring it to life.

Unlike many positions in multimedia design, animators enjoy a good degree of creative control.

The work schedule varies according to the stage of the game. Early in a project, hours are fairly predictable. But when deadline for shipping the game approaches, and the project manager suddenly demands that the hero eject safely from his jet fighter rather than explode, you can expect to pull an all-nighter.

There's no guarantee that a million-dollar computer game will be a hit. Small game development houses are where many beginners get started, but they don't offer a lot in the way of job security. While major gaming companies can absorb the losses when a game doesn't sell, one flop can put a start-up out of business.

salary: Pay varies widely, depending on experience and the company. Rookies might start at $12,000, with seasoned animators earning as much as $100,000.

prospects: The computer industry has seen explosive growth, and experienced animators are in strong demand. In many cases, animators who possess the skills that a game developer needs can write their own check. Because of the shortage of animators, most gaming companies are willing to train artists who show promise.

qualifications: Formal art training, especially in animation, gives you an advantage. A portfolio containing samples of your artwork, even if it doesn't involve animation, is a big plus. The top priority for most companies is creative talent. It's common for game developers to give animation and drawing tests to applicants in order to evaluate their skill.

characteristics: In addition to creativity, you will need to work well under intense deadlines. Because a lot of design work is done in teams, you need to be able to collaborate with others.

Cyrus Lum *is director of advanced technologies at a computer gaming house in Austin, Texas.*

How did you get the job?

"I always loved art, drawing, and animation, but I didn't think I could ever make any money doing it," Cyrus Lum says. So he went a more traditional route, studying industrial engineering at San Jose State in California.

During college, he took a part-time job at a computer game maker. "I got paid to play the games and see if I could make them crash," he says. The company had an art department, and Cyrus brought in some samples of his animation work. The art department put him to work moving artwork from one computer system to another, and he got a firsthand look at how developers put games together.

After graduating, Cyrus went to work full-time doing original animation and artwork. "I realized this was what I should be doing," he says. Cyrus eventually took a job as chief artist at a five-person start-up that created games for the 3DO computer game machine, and worked for another company as a modeler and animator.

By that point, his work was drawing attention in the gaming industry. He considered doing animation for a movie studio, but decided that the lack of creative control would drive him crazy. "The director, the producer, and the art director come up with the idea, and they have a very set idea of how it should look," Cyrus says. "You wouldn't even be able to make the ears on a rabbit a little longer because it might screw up another part of the production. I decided to stick with games, where the animator is the one with the creative input."

When a leading computer game maker in Austin offered to make him director of imagery, 3-D production, and animation, Cyrus accepted.

> **WORK ON CHARACTER DESIGN AND ANIMATION ON YOUR OWN TO BEGIN BUILDING A PORTFOLIO.**

What do you do all day?

Usually when he arrives at work at 9 A.M., he grabs a soda and sits down with each person in his department to see how his or her work is progressing. Most mornings are spent having meetings and phone conversations with programmers, game designers, and other artists to coordinate various parts of the project they are working on.

Then he holds a class for new trainees, where he teaches them how to use animation tools and assigns them exercises that they spend the afternoon practicing.

When the administrative work is taken care of, Cyrus retreats to his office to work on the animation he's contributing to the project. When a deadline is approaching, late nights are common, and a week before D-day, he might be at work until 3 A.M. "During the big rush, you put in whatever hours it takes," he says.

Where do you see this job leading you?

"I'd really like to start my own multimedia development house someday," he says. Cyrus has seen other animators and game developers go from working for large gaming houses to opening their own development shops, where they can pick and choose projects that interest them.

17. Computer Game Programmer

description: Computer game programmers write the software code that makes a game run. Although the players can't see it, the code is what determines the way the game looks and feels.

Programmers usually go to work after the direction of the game has been mapped out. They may spend six months writing the underlying code, or the infrastructure, of the game. When that's built, game designers enter the picture. It then becomes a back-and-forth development process, with designers kicking back the code for changes and the programmers tweaking various parts of the game. It can take anywhere from six months to two years to complete a game.

You don't have to be a gaming whiz to thrive in this business, but most development companies like to hire people who love games because they tend to have a better understanding of what separates mediocre ones from standouts.

salary: A first-time programmer at a small start-up can start in the mid-$20,000 range. A veteran programmer with a leading gaming company can earn $75,000 or more a year.

prospects: Gaming companies complain that they can't hire talented programmers fast enough. You might have to relocate—gaming companies are concentrated in cities such as San Jose, Austin, Boston, and New York.

qualifications: Many successful entertainment software companies were founded by gamers who never went to college. This is a job in which skill is far more important than schooling. Talented kids who grew up writing their own software games often are recruited right after high school. Others enter gaming after doing software programming in the business sector. Before knocking on doors, it helps to have some work samples.

characteristics: You have to not mind working erratic hours. When a deadline is approaching, you may be working 15 to 20 hours straight. Also, because many gaming companies fail, you have to be willing to take a risk. If the game you spent 18 months developing is a flop, you could find yourself unemployed.

Michael Abrash *is a game programmer at a software development house in Richardson, Texas.*

- -

How did you get the job?

Michael Abrash wrote his first program, a Space Invaders game, when he was 14. While working on a master's degree in energy management at the University of Pennsylvania, he got involved in a research project for the department of energy. It turned out the part he liked best was the computers. "My wife and I spent all our savings to buy an IBM PC so I could write games," Michael says. "I got one big check and stopped taking my school courses."

He was a computer programmer for several computer companies before joining Microsoft. There, he oversaw graphics for the Windows NT operating system. With 15 people reporting to him, he had little time for programming. He had corresponded for some time with the

> **IT'S A TOUGH ASSIGNMENT, BUT YOU WILL NEED TO KNOW COMPUTER GAMES TO GET A FOOT IN THE DOOR OF A GAMING COMPANY; PLAY THEM, LIVE THEM, BREATHE THEM. KNOW WHAT'S HOT, AND HAVE YOUR OWN IDEAS AND DESIGNS READY TO PRESENT.**
> - - - - - - - - - -

founder of Id Software, the creator of the game Doom and one of the country's most successful computer gaming companies. When the founder was in Seattle, he visited Michael and offered him a job programming games. "I was ready to program and do purely technical stuff, rather than deal with personnel issues, which I was doing at Microsoft. I needed a change, and this was an opportunity to get back to where I wanted to be." Michael took the job, and he and his family left Washington for Texas.

What do you do all day?

From home, Michael logs on to his computer and checks his e-mail before heading to work. When he gets in, he fixes the bugs he had found in the software the day before. Then, he spends the day at the computer writing software and testing existing code. His days are agenda-less. "There is no structure to the day," he says. "We all do our own thing." Fellow programmers sometimes take time out to challenge each other to Doom matches, but Michael, who is not an avid gamer, usually sits out the competitions.

Programmers occasionally meet with artists and game designers, but for the most part they work by themselves.

At the end of the day, Michael returns home and spends time with his wife and daughter. Once they've gone to sleep, he does more programming. Though Michael often works 60 hours a week, being able to do some work at home helps offset the hours.

Where do you see this job leading you?

Michael is happy to be back at straight programming, and he plans to continue pushing the envelope in game development.

18. Computer Help Desk Technician

description: The advent of computers in the workplace has allowed employees to complete daily tasks with more efficiency than ever before. However, when a computer goes on the fritz, no one saves time. Most large companies combat this problem by keeping a staff of technicians in the office who will be able to respond to computer problems at a moment's notice so that the least amount of time will be wasted on computer glitches.

It is not unusual for a computer help desk technician to show up at a job and find an employee frantic or on the verge of tears. This is often the case when the employee has spent hours working on a project that appears to no longer exist in the computer files. Computer help desk technicians need to be knowledgeable both in computer software and hardware. These technicians will also need to be able to come up with solutions quickly, as employees are often in a rush to get back to their work, but can't do so until the computer problem has been sorted out.

salary: The salary in this field will vary greatly depending on the region in which you live and the type of company in which you are employed. Someone starting out in this type of work could expect to earn a salary in the $20,000s, but within five years you could expect to make somewhere in the range of $50,000.

prospects: The job market for computer technicians is still very healthy, although some companies have turned to hiring consultants to do this kind of work.

qualifications: A bachelor's degree in a computer-related discipline—preferably computer science—is what most employers are looking for in a prospective employee. Employers also desire someone who has experience working in the field, whether it be from a part-time job or from an internship.

characteristics: For the most part, people working in this field are very interested in and knowledgeable about computers. But perhaps more importantly, they must be able to work well with people.

Alex Belov *is a computer help desk technician.*

How did you get the job?

During Alex Belov's freshman year in college, he secured a job working on the computer help desk at the student newspaper. As a computer science major, the benefits this job brought for Alex were twofold: he was able to earn both money and experience.

He worked in this job for a year and six months before he was recruited by a growing computer company looking for technicians. The company was tied into a help line used by people who had bought the company's computer equipment. Alex, along with other technicians in the company, would take phone calls from people experiencing problems.

He worked in this job for a little more than a year before he found a job working on the help desk at Time Warner. He is still working there today.

What do you do all day?

In an average day, Alex spends very little time in his cubicle. The calls for help can start coming in as early as 9 A.M. Sometimes, he will find a message on his voice mail when he comes in, so he will have to go out on those calls first thing.

The majority of the calls Alex receives deal with problems a user is having with the software. For the most part, these problems stem from the user's limited knowledge of it. However, there are other times when the calls are of a more serious nature. For example, Alex was recently called by a user whose hard drive had failed. Alex was able to recover data from a

THESE POSITIONS ARE MOST OFTEN ADVERTISED IN THE NEWSPAPER CLASSIFIED ADS. THERE ARE ALSO DIFFERENT TRADE MAGAZINES, SUCH AS <u>MACWORLD</u>, THAT PUBLISH JOB ADVERTISEMENTS.

- - - - - - - - - -

damaged hard drive using some software designed for data recovery. However, in a more serious failure, he might have been required to take the hard drive apart in order to retrieve data from the hard drive. A process such as this could take more than a day.

Where do you see this job leading you?

Alex would like to continue working in this field and hopes to eventually move to a position where he would take on greater responsibility.

19. Computer Learning Center Owner

description: Learning centers teach both kids and adults how to use personal computers and software. Some owners conduct the classes themselves, while others hire teachers. As the owner, you'll schedule the sessions and plan the curriculum, as well as recruit students and manage the business. Many learning center operators also teach computing skills at schools and private organizations like summer camps.

Working with kids and helping technophobic adults become comfortable with computers can be very rewarding. On the other hand, starting a business is always a risky proposition. Hours are long, you're constantly looking for students, and you've got to invest a lot of money in the latest and greatest computers and software. As one owner puts it, if parents see that your computers don't have the bells and whistles that the one in their den has, they're not going to pay you to teach their kids.

salary: Several national learning center chains sell franchises, which cost about $100,000 to open. It usually takes at least a year to become profitable. With a strong clientele and a full schedule of classes, you can make anywhere from $45,000 to $85,000 a year.

prospects: Private learning centers are growing fast because parents are making computer literacy a priority for their kids, and many public schools can't afford to offer top-notch equipment or training. At the same time, adults who want to improve their computer skills are also boosting enrollments.

qualifications: Because this job combines teaching and running a business, you've got to be good at both. A technical background and experience in marketing and sales are ideal.

characteristics: Working with kids and parents takes patience. Seeing a lucrative market, many computer stores and vocational training centers are getting into the act, making this an increasingly competitive business. To attract customers, you'll need to be persuasive, enthusiastic, and good with people.

Harvey Lewis *owns a computer learning center in Wellington, Florida.*

How did you get the job?

Harvey Lewis had worked as a controller for a bank in New York for 25 years when he was laid off. "I saw an ad in *The New York Times* about a computer learning center franchise for sale, and it got me thinking," he says. "I liked working with kids, I had an M.B.A. and an understanding of management, and I was a techie. I thought, 'This is it!'"

The franchise was also a good excuse to move exactly where he wanted: Florida. Harvey bought the rights to the Palm Beach County branch, said goodbye to New York, and headed south. He rented a small space in a neighborhood shopping center, invested thousands of dollars in computers and software, and opened for business. Finding students took time, but through word of mouth and advertising, Harvey has built a loyal customer base.

What do you do all day?

Harvey's first love is working with kids, but it's business matters that take most of his time.

> THE SMALL BUSINESS ADMINISTRATION HAS OFFICES AROUND THE COUNTRY THAT OFFER SEMINARS AND ONE-ON-ONE HELP FOR FLEDGLING ENTREPRENEURS. REFER TO THE GOVERNMENT SECTION OF THE PHONE BOOK FOR YOUR LOCAL BRANCH NUMBER.

"It's about 80 percent sales and marketing and 20 percent teaching," he says. He hires teachers according to class schedules, which vary from month to month.

During a typical day recently, Harvey called parents about a new summer school program, met with school administrators about on-site training sessions, and taught a class when a teacher couldn't make it. He also worked on a new class curriculum and balanced his books.

Harvey is constantly looking for new niches. "In one case, I convinced a children's sports camp to let us do computer training," he recalls. "I said, 'It's hot out! The kids need to have something to do inside when they're ready to take a break.'" The camp leaders agreed, and Harvey's center has taught computers there for the past three years.

To keep up with the latest technology, Harvey spends his free time reading computer trade magazines and surfing the Internet. And he takes time out to visit with his students and watch their progress. "When you see a 65-year-old man who once couldn't turn on a computer now use an on-line service to send e-mail to his friends," he says, "that's the biggest enjoyment."

Where do you see this job leading you?

Harvey hopes to open additional franchises in Florida. Most of his colleagues also hope to expand. He does know one former learning center owner who went to work as a technician at Microsoft.

20. Computer Products Project Manager

description: Much like a software or hardware engineer, project managers are responsible for the development of computer products. However, project managers work on a much broader scope than engineers. For example, an engineer working on a word-processing program may be responsible for developing the program's spell-check function, but the project manager would decide how the spell-check function will be incorporated with the rest of the program's components. The manager also makes decisions about how the product's other components will be developed, when each component will be completed, and how much money is needed to complete the project. Much like a conductor leads every member of an orchestra into a grand crescendo, the project manager leads programmers and engineers into the completion of a product. To do this, he or she will typically dole out to individual engineers the responsibility of writing code for the product's many different components. The project manager will then work closely with each engineer to ensure that the individual components will work together when combined in the final product.

salary: Typically, the salary of a project manager depends on the amount of experience he or she has in programming. Someone with about five years of experience can make upward of $65,000 a year, while someone with ten years of experience can earn as much as $100,000 annually.

prospects: With the current growth of the computer industry, there are plenty of jobs available for software engineers. Project manager positions aren't found as frequently, but the best way to come across one is to first work as an engineer.

qualifications: Not only is it necessary to have a degree in a computer-related field or in electrical engineering in order to get hired as a project manager, but two to three years of experience as a software or hardware engineer is also a requisite.

characteristics: Project managers must be organized because they have to manage both their own workload and that of others. It is also important that they be approachable and good-natured so that the people working for them will feel comfortable asking for help on projects. At the same time, project managers must be able to enforce deadlines and demand quality work from their workers.

Tom Eck *is a computer project manager for the Associated Press.*

How did you get the job?

When Tom Eck was in college, he had aspirations of becoming a chemist, but about a year before graduation he changed his mind. While working closely with one of his professors who was interested in computers, Tom found that his interests had shifted from petri dishes to disk drives.

"I realized toward the end of my junior year that I was much more interested in computing than I was in chemistry," Tom says. So after receiving his bachelor's degree in chemistry, he went right back to school, this time to get his master's in computer science.

While working toward his master's, Tom began gaining experience in the field of computers by opening his own consulting business. Following graduate school, he worked on various temporary assignments that he found through consulting agencies. One of these temporary assignments led to full-time work as a senior software engineer for the Associated Press. After working in that capacity for about a year, Tom was promoted to his current position of project manager.

> PERHAPS THE BEST WAY TO FIND FULL-TIME WORK IN THIS FIELD IS TO START OUT WORKING TEMPORARY ASSIGNMENTS THROUGH A RECRUITING OR CONSULTING AGENCY. THESE TYPES OF AGENCIES USUALLY ADVERTISE FOR CONSULTING POSITIONS IN TRADE MAGAZINES SUCH AS <u>PC WEEK</u> AND <u>BYTE</u>.

What do you do all day?

Tom says he likes to start off his day writing code. "If I am going to be doing any programming, I try to get that done in the morning because I'm just more fresh," he says.

He usually spends a couple of hours in front of the computer writing code before he walks around to talk to each one of the members in his project group. For the most part, he is just checking to see that they are on schedule, but sometimes there will be a specific problem with which he will help out.

A lot of Tom's day is spent in meetings. He will meet with all the other project managers at least once a week to discuss new assignments and the progress of ongoing projects. He also periodically meets with managers of other departments, such as marketing, where the discussion centers around new pieces of software and their release dates.

This busy schedule is not the only thing that keeps Tom on his toes at work; most of what keeps his interest is the type of technology he works with. Tom says that being a part of a large, forward-thinking organization such as the Associated Press gives him the advantage of staying in the forefront of advances in the industry.

"Technically, we are doing interesting work, and I am given challenging things to work on. I'm also given a pretty wide range of freedom, so I am able to explore certain things that I might not be able to under a different type of organization."

Where do you see this job leading you?

Tom hasn't really decided on where he will go from here, but he says it would be possible for him either to continue working at the Associated Press and move up into higher management, or to move on to a different company as a project manager or consultant.

21. Computer Sales Representative

description: A computer maker's sales force is responsible for selling and shipping its products to customers, which might include businesses, computer dealers, and resellers.

When a company invests in a computer system, it can mean big sales and consequently a big commission for the person doing the selling. A sales representative must know the computer line inside and out because buyers will want to know everything, from how a particular feature works, to whether the computer can be integrated into the company's existing system. Finding customers involves hours of making cold calls which many times go nowhere. It can take months of phone conversations, meetings, and product demonstrations to develop a lead. And even then, there's no guarantee you'll sell even a mouse.

Getting a customer to sign on the line is just the beginning. The goal is to build long-term relationships that mean continued sales and support.

Sales is a highly competitive business, and income is based on commission. Successful reps are well compensated, but those who don't reach the goals set by their company won't last long.

salary: Depending on the commission system and how well you do, you might earn anywhere from $5,000 to $100,000 a year. Sales representatives with established customers can make $70,000 to $100,000. This is a field where salary isn't based on experience; you can land the biggest account the company has ever seen during your first week as a sales rep.

prospects: Computer makers have experienced enormous growth in recent years, and the market for computers both at home and at work is robust. As companies expand, so do their sales forces. Because many companies don't require sales experience for entry-level positions, this is a relatively easy field to break into.

qualifications: Companies expect job candidates to be knowledgeable about the industry and the product. Since sales is such a people-oriented profession, personality also comes into play. Recruiters look for job candidates who display enthusiasm and drive.

characteristics: Because it's up to you to build contacts and make sales, you've got to be highly self-motivated. Resilience is also important; when a deal you've spent months putting together falls apart, you've got to be able to start from scratch.

Lyndon Hanson *is a regional sales manager at a marketing firm in Boulder, Colorado.*

How did you get the job?

"I came out of school not really knowing what I wanted to do," Lyndon Hanson says. After earning an M.B.A. from the University of Colorado, he took a job as a sales rep for a computer company in Solana Beach, California. He soon realized that sales suited him well. "I like people, and I'm not the type of person who would be happy sitting at a desk all day and not talking to anyone."

And there was another motivator: "Sales is a good way to make good money," Lyndon says. Because earnings are tied directly to individual performance, there's no limit to the amount of money a person can earn in a year.

Lyndon eventually decided he wanted to live in Boulder, and took a job at a fast-growing computer company there. Getting established in a new city was a challenge. "I was selling a machine no one had ever heard of, against some of the biggest companies in the world," he says. "I had to build relationships with people and give them a reason to buy from me.

"It took 18 months before I built up clients and was making the amount of money I wanted to make."

What do you do all day?

"A lot of people think sales is playing golf and taking people to lunch, but that's the farthest thing from the truth," Lyndon says.

He spends two to three hours a day on the phone following up on leads from customers and a network of industry sources. He is currently concentrating on selling computer systems to law firms nationwide. He discovered the niche through a cold call to a large law firm in Denver. Lyndon landed the business, and the company was so pleased that it has recommended him to several other firms across the country.

Since only 40 percent of his business is from repeat customers, a lot of his time is devoted to looking for leads. "My business has progressed," he says. "I've built up a strong network of people who help me find places to put my computers."

Still, only a small percentage of tips pans out. And because his salary is based on commission, the pressure to make sales is always there. "If I don't sell," he says, "there's no paycheck."

Where do you see this job leading you?

Lyndon would like to manage a sales force so that he could mentor new sales reps. Most people he's worked with have either moved into management or stayed in sales, which can be more lucrative than being a manager.

> DO EVERYTHING YOU CAN TO RESEARCH A COMPANY IF YOU WANT TO WORK THERE. WRITE AWAY FOR ANNUAL REPORTS, RESEARCH RECENT NEWS STORIES ABOUT THE COMPANY, AND LEARN ABOUT ITS PRODUCTS.
> TRY TO SET UP INFORMATIONAL INTERVIEWS SO YOU CAN GAIN INSIGHT INTO WHAT SKILLS THE COMPANY LOOKS FOR.

22. Computer Science Professor

description: Large universities usually prefer that computer science professors divide their time between teaching and research. Typically, that involves teaching two classes a semester, complete with labs and office hours, and spending the rest of the week working on an ongoing research project. Professors often teach a lower-division class, such as computer programming, and a graduate-level course, such as advanced software design.

Becoming a professor requires a doctoral degree, and getting tenure takes six to eight years of teaching and research work. Some schools stress research and being published, while others, usually smaller colleges, encourage professors to mentor students. Many professors cite the satisfaction they receive from teaching the next generation of high-tech pioneers. Others are drawn to academia because of the opportunity it provides to pursue research.

At top computer science departments, getting tenure is extremely competitive. But people who fail to be tenured at large universities can usually obtain tenure at smaller schools.

salary: Salaries for assistant professors start at about $40,000 a year, and tenured professors at large universities can earn $70,000 or more annually. Many universities have endowed chairs which pay $100,000 or more a year. Not surprisingly, large universities and small elite schools pay more than small state colleges.

prospects: Getting a position at a leading school has become very competitive in recent years. Schools have begun to seek professors with specialized skills, such as a Ph.D. with an emphasis in operating systems. There are still many opportunities at smaller schools and at state universities. If you're willing to work at a college that's off the beaten track, you shouldn't have a hard time finding a position.

qualifications: You need a Ph.D. and, depending on the school, some research work under your belt. Some schools, particularly those with leading computer science departments, look for specialists. Others, especially those with small departments, prefer generalists.

characteristics: You have got to enjoy teaching and working with students from a variety of different backgrounds and interests.

David Cordes *is a professor of computer science at the University of Alabama in Tuscaloosa, Alabama.*

How did you get the job?

When David Cordes graduated college with a degree in computer science, he decided to go back to school. "I realized I didn't know everything there was to know about computers," he says. David then earned a master's degree from Purdue University, where he worked as a teaching assistant, and completed his Ph.D. at Louisiana State University. Having grown up in academia—his father is a professor of chemistry at the University of Alabama—David knew he wanted to teach. "I liked the idea of working with students and having an influence over what they learn," he says.

And so the job search began. "I sat down and wrote to 20 schools across the South that I thought would be interesting

places to work for," David says. "Some contacted me, and others said, 'Thanks but no thanks.' The University of Alabama was the best offer I got, and I took it." Two years ago he received tenure.

What do you do all day?

David gets an early start, thanks in part to his two young daughters. On Mondays, Wednesdays, and Fridays, he and other faculty members meet at 6 A.M. to play basketball, and he usually gets to his office by 7:15 A.M.

On Tuesdays and Thursdays, he teaches an 8 A.M. class in systems programming for sophomores and juniors. Later in the day, he teaches a senior software engineering course. He and another professor are also overseeing a group of doctoral students in Ph.D.-level software engineering.

After his morning classes, he

FOR INFORMATION ON BECOMING A PROFESSOR, CONTACT THE AMERICAN ASSOCIATION OF UNIVERSITY PROFESSORS. (SEE RESOURCES, PAGE 212).

keeps office hours, during which any of his 70-plus students can stop in to chat about assignments or get help if they are stuck.

David tries to spend Monday, Wednesday, and Friday mornings doing research work. His afternoons are often tied up with more student visits and faculty meetings.

David gets home around 5:30 P.M. "I play with the girls until 8 or 8:30, and then I get back on the computer and tinker some more."

Where do you see this job leading you?

David plans to remain in academia, but he's not necessarily tied to the University of Alabama forever. "My wife and I had never lived anywhere for more than three years until we came here," David says. Once a professor receives tenure, it's not difficult to make a lateral move to another university. "We haven't decided yet where we'd like to end up."

23. Computer Trade Magazine Reporter

description: Covering an industry that experiences dramatic change on a seemingly daily basis means that no two days—or stories—are exactly the same.

Trade reporters cover breaking news, write about new products, and explain technology trends that affect both business and consumers. Reporters usually focus on a particular area, such as microprocessors or software. Most trade publications are published weekly, which gives reporters only a few days to write often three or four in-depth highly technical stories. Meeting a deadline frequently requires long hours and unpredictable schedules.

The industry is extremely competitive. Successful reporters develop reliable industry sources and a thorough understanding of the technology they're covering.

salary: Reporters start in the mid-$20,000s, and those with experience can earn $40,000 or more a year. Specialized writers make significantly more.

prospects: While daily newspapers have been folding, the number of high-tech trade publications has skyrocketed in recent years. A shakeout appears to be occurring, with some magazines laying off reporters and editors. The industry's long-term future looks bright, however, and overall employment prospects are good.

qualifications: Some tech reporters have strong science and engineering backgrounds; others were liberal arts majors with limited technical knowledge. The most important factors are good writing skills and an ability to learn quickly.

characteristics: Much of the background information that tech reporters get from companies is loaded with jargon, and you have to be willing to ask what might seem like stupid questions in order to translate it into English. High-tech companies are also famous for "vaporware," or news releases on products that are more dream than reality. A good reporter reads between the lines and is skeptical enough not to get swept away by breathtaking claims that are, in fact, fantasy.

Gabrielle Mitchell *is a reporter for a weekly computer trade magazine in San Mateo, California.*

How did you get the job?

As a literature major focusing on premodern drama at the University of California at Santa Cruz, Gabrielle Mitchell clearly didn't set out to cover the computer industry.

While in college, she did an internship at a weekly newspaper, and after graduating, she worked at a weekly covering local politics, restaurants, and food. After a year, ready to make more money, she began looking for work at other publications.

In an interview for a reporting position with a leading computer trade magazine, Gabrielle was asked how she would go about tracking down a rumor about a new revolutionary computer. "I said, 'I'd call a public relations person and ask about it, and if they stalled, I'd know there was more information there, and I'd track it down,'" she recalls.

She got the job.

Gabrielle thinks she was hired because, although she didn't have technical expertise, she convinced the editors through her writing samples and her interview that she was an aggressive reporter who was willing to work to get the story.

"I admitted I didn't know a lot about computers, but they were willing to give me a try because they saw I wanted to learn," Gabrielle says.

For the first six months, she says, "I was like a big sponge. There was so much to learn—terms, products, companies, channels of distribution—and I just tried to ask questions, listen a lot, and soak it all in."

> **TRY TO OBTAIN INTERNSHIPS AND FREELANCE WRITING ASSIGNMENTS— ANYTHING TO GET SOME CLIPS WITH YOUR NAME ON THEM.**

What do you do all day?

Gabrielle, who covers entertainment and education products and on-line services, spends a good chunk of her day on the phone, touching base with sources and following up news tips. She also uses e-mail, on-line services, and electronic bulletin boards to see what people are talking about. "It's a great way to pick up on trends," she says.

Touching base with sources is key, even when there's no news. "You have to take the time to call those people and chat, even if you're not working on a story, because when there is a story, you want them to tell you," she says.

She usually meets with software vendors a few times a week to keep up with the latest offerings. Wednesdays and Thursdays are usually dedicated to writing. Once her Thursday afternoon deadline is over, her downtime is spent reading to catch up on new technology.

"You really have to keep up with the changes, because if you don't, you're going to miss a story," she says.

Where do you see this job leading you?

Gabrielle eventually would like to be an editor. She's also interested in all the new editorial opportunities being created online. "For anybody in the tech field, that's an exciting place," she says.

Computer trade magazine reporters often go on to do public relations for computer companies. Gabrielle knows one former reporter who is now a technology analyst at a major marketing firm.

24. Consumer Product Research and Development Engineer or Designer

description: Research and development (R&D) involves dreaming up new products, figuring out how to make them, and testing prototypes. R&D engineers are responsible for seeing the process through from the idea phase to the time the product is put on store shelves. Often, engineers start with nothing more than a list of company requirements—ranging from features it must include, to recommended size, cost constraints, and government regulations that need to be taken into account. From there, engineers go to work to develop a prototype. Working as a team, engineers think up ways to incorporate new features into the basic design. When it receives the thumbs up from company officials, a prototype is created and tested. After some more changes, the product is put into mass production and, ultimately, shipped to stores. Engineers usually continue to track the product, evaluating its sales performance and adding improvements based on customer feedback.

R&D engineers say satisfaction comes from turning a concept into the real thing. But it can also be disappointing when consumers snub a product you've devoted months to creating.

salary: Entry-level positions start in the mid-$20,000 range. Experienced developers who have a track record of successful product design can earn $60,000 to $80,000, and more if they are overseeing the project.

prospects: Increased global competition has spurred many corporations to put more emphasis on research and development, making this a field with a lot of opportunity.

qualifications: You need at least a bachelor's degree in engineering or in one of the sciences. An internship that involves engineering will help you get your foot in the door. Many companies hire electrical and mechanical engineers right out of college.

characteristics: Turning a list of requirements into something tangible requires a lot of creativity and imagination. If your coffee machine is the same as the rest, what's the point? That's where the ability to look at things with a fresh eye comes in. Disney calls its R&D engineers "imagineers." And to excel, that's what you have to be.

Jill Gantos *is a housewares product designer for a large consumer products company in Ada, Michigan.*

How did you get the job?

Jill Gantos picked packaging engineering as her major at Michigan State University because it was a way to combine her interests. "I've always been interested in engineering, but I also wanted to do something creative," Jill says. Designing packaging required both. While a student, she did a six-month internship at a pharmaceutical company, where she worked to ensure that packaging would help products arrive undamaged.

After graduating, Jill was hired by a pharmaceutical company in Fort Worth, Texas, where she focused on package design. A call from a headhunter in Michigan brought her back to work for her current employer as a packaging engineer. She later decided to move to housewares product development. "I liked the idea of being involved in the development process from beginning to end," she says. In addition, working in R&D presented Jill with the opportunity to be a product leader, which would have been unlikely in packaging.

What do you do all day?

Jill's day depends on where she is in the R&D process, which has four basic steps: concept phase, development, testing, and product launch. Often, R&D makes a model of the product and conducts market research to see whether consumers like the product's size and shape. Based on the findings, Jill and her team rework the features.

Once the product is in the prototype stage, Jill's team puts together a test plan to verify marketing claims. When, for example, her company plans to promote a new home water treatment system as easy to operate, Jill pulls together a panel of testers to make sure that's true. She also sends the product to an outside lab to make sure it meets government regulations. In the event that the product doesn't pass the tests, it's back to the drawing board for a redesign.

Once the product is ready to launch, Jill follows it as it makes its way through production and to consumers. Customer feedback is taken seriously, and adjustments are made accordingly. "We're involved in every step, and I really like that," she says. "In a lot of places, you work on the concept and throw it over to the manufacturing engineers. Here, we get to watch it all the way through."

Jill travels regularly to meet with international affiliates. So far, her work has taken her through Asia.

USE THE LIBRARY AND THE INTERNET TO FIND COMPANIES THAT DESIGN THE KINDS OF PRODUCTS YOU'RE INTERESTED IN DESIGNING. MANY COMPANIES LIST JOB OPENINGS AND REQUIREMENTS ON THEIR WEB SITES. INQUIRE ABOUT INTERNSHIPS AND CO-OP PROGRAMS, WHICH OFTEN TURN INTO FULL-TIME JOBS.

Where do you see this job leading you?

Jill wants to stay in research and development. "I just want to do more of what I'm doing."

25. Cyber Cafe Owner

description: Cyber cafes are coffeehouses that offer access to the Internet along with lattes and cappuccinos. The first cyber cafe opened in the San Francisco Bay area in 1991, and since then dozens more have sprung up nationwide. Cafes offer up the latest multimedia CD-ROMs, which customers can test out by popping them into a nearby machine. In addition to charging for coffee and a connection to the Internet, some cafes sell computers and software. Most cyber cafes have instructors on hand to help novices get on-line, and some offer Internet classes.

Launching a cyber cafe requires a bigger financial investment than an ordinary restaurant because, in addition to counters and cash registers, you've got to install top-of-the-line computer systems with high-speed Internet connections. Start-up costs range from $75,000 to $100,000. And, because customers won't pay to rent equipment that isn't the latest and greatest, you'll be spending a lot on computer upgrades. Because this is such a new idea, also expect to devote a lot of time and money to advertisements and special promotions.

salary: Like any restaurant, it can take several years to become profitable. Keeping the business going during that time requires deep pockets. But in a good market, cyber cafes can bring in profits of more than $100,000 a year.

prospects: This could either be the next hot entertainment concept or a short-lived fad. The number of cyber cafes expanding into other cities suggests that owners are making money, but whether people will continue to pay to explore the Internet at a cafe remains to be seen.

qualifications: You will need to have a good understanding of computers, computer networking, and the Internet. But in addition to being a techie, you've got to be able to run a business, from balancing the books to managing your employees.

characteristics: This is a risky venture, so you must be willing to risk failure. Long hours—most cyber cafes open early and close late—mean you've got to be willing to postpone a social life for a while.

Thomas MaGee *owns a cyber cafe in Ft. Lauderdale, Florida.*

How did you get the job?

Tom MaGee graduated from the State University of New York with a dual degree in economics and political science and became a trader on the New York Stock Exchange. After three and a half years, he felt that his job would eventually become obsolete. "The Internet is eliminating the need for traders," he says. "It's a dying business." Tom, who had been a computer hobbyist since high school, mentioned his disenchantment to his childhood friend Glen Bocchino, who lived in Florida. "I told him I was ready for a career move. I needed a change of pace, and wanted to go into business for myself," Tom says.

The two put together a proposal for an Internet coffee bar and decided to go for it. Tom quit his job, moved to Florida, and joined Glen and another friend to plan the cafe. The three partners pooled their savings and invested $30,000 to

> BECAUSE YOU ARE RUNNING A CAFE AS WELL AS A COMPUTER SERVER, IT HELPS TO HAVE RESTAURANT EXPERIENCE OR A PARTNER WHO IS FAMILIAR WITH THE INDUSTRY.

furnish it with six multimedia personal computers, coffee machines, tables, and bar stools. Doing most of the work themselves, they transformed a 1,400-square-foot former lawyer's office into a hip, high-tech coffee bar.

What do you do all day?

Tom arrives at work by 9 A.M. He starts brewing a pot of coffee, and gets customers set up at computers. That often involves giving a crash course on the Internet and acting as a World Wide Web tour guide. "Computers are so impersonal, and that's really intimidating to people who are new to them," Tom says. "We show people they can have fun."

His customers are mostly in their 20s to 40s, but the cafe also draws teenagers and senior citizens. Tom spends the morning talking with customers about new Web sites, introducing them to the latest software, and helping users get logged on.

Eventually, one of his partners arrives to relieve him, and Tom concentrates on the business end of the cafe—paying bills and ordering coffee and computer equipment. He is also working on an advertising campaign and is negotiating with radio stations to run a series of promotions.

Although Tom skips out earlier, the cafe stays open until 5 A.M. and has a large crowd of late-night regulars. "People like to be on the Internet at all hours," Tom says, "and we want to accommodate them."

Where do you see this job leading you?

Tom and his partners hope to open more cyber cafes in South Florida over the next two years, and to eventually expand to the southeastern region of the country.

26. Cyberlibrarian

description: Librarians are getting wired. In addition to putting local citizens on-line, librarians are digitizing collections for delivery over the Internet to local, national, and global users. Patrons at libraries across the country can surf the Internet from public terminals. And librarians are using the Internet to get visitors information that is stored on other sides of the world.

Libraries are increasingly hiring high-tech librarians who bring with them Internet skills and computer programming experience, which is put to work doing digital searches and teaching visitors how to navigate the Internet. Cyberlibrarians also develop sites on the World Wide Web to offer archive information and to interact with library patrons.

salary: Salaries vary depending on the size of the library. Big-city libraries and university libraries offer the best pay and benefits. Entry-level positions start in the mid- to upper $20,000 range. Experienced librarians with extensive technical skills can earn $50,000 or more at major libraries.

prospects: Large cities and university towns offer the best opportunities for high-tech positions because they are putting a lot of emphasis on digital services. Libraries in small towns or in cities that don't have a large high-tech base are years behind and have few openings for someone who wants to focus on technology.

qualifications: You will need a master's degree in library science and experience doing database and Internet searches. Basic programming skills are also a big plus because a growing number of libraries are creating their own Web sites.

characteristics: Because this is such a new area for libraries, you'll probably end up creating your own job. Creativity and the ability to follow through on projects are important skills to have. You'll also need to be able to sell your cause, because this is an idea that is just catching on, and not everyone on your staff may be as enthusiastic as you are about emphasizing technology.

Nancy Wildin *is a librarian specializing in the Internet at a public library in Seattle, Washington.*

How did you get the job?

"I got hooked on computers 15 years ago, and I've always been intrigued and fascinated about their potential for library services," Nancy Wildin says. "I discovered the Internet four years ago, and I knew it was a dream come true for librarians."

Nancy, who has a degree in library science, began to explore the possibilities of the Internet while doing business librarian work at a public library in Seattle. The job involved working with small businesses and entrepreneurs to help them find financial information, statistical and market reports, and import and export data. The Internet proved to be an excellent resource. But in addition to using it to retrieve information herself, Nancy wanted to educate small businesses and other library visitors about the on-line world. She began teaching Internet classes and pushing to offer free Internet service at the library.

Her next goal became setting up an Internet Web site to link libraries across the state and to provide information to patrons. "I looked around at what was happening on the Web, and I said, 'Hey, we've really got to do this,'" she says. "I kept asking and asking, and finally they recognized it was needed and said go ahead and do it." So Nancy turned her attention to developing Washington State's public library Web site.

What do you do all day?

Nancy spends a lot of time talking with librarians around the state about what information they want to post on the site and deciding the best way to present it. Nancy wanted to be able to build the Web pages herself, so she took a class to learn the programming language. "I spend as much time as I can in front of the computer doing programming," she says. "I love to play around with different page layouts. I'm not a technician though. When

> **FOR MORE INFORMATION, CONTACT THE AMERICAN LIBRARY ASSOCIATION. (SEE RESOURCES, PAGE 212.)**

there's a glitch, I still have to call for help."

Nancy envisions a site that will allow people from anywhere in the state to have access to community information, and she is working with local organizations across the state to begin creating databases. "It's going to take a while to ferret it out, but when we do, it's going to be a great resource," she says.

Nancy is wrapping up a newsletter she will send to public libraries throughout the state that asks how they use the Web and whether they need training. "We're at the information-collecting stage," she says. "When we get a feeling for where libraries stand, we can come up with a strategy on how to bring everyone up to speed."

She still teaches Internet classes in the library. "People just need an introduction," she says. "Once they see how easy it is, and how much fun, they're off and exploring."

Where do you see this job leading you?

Nancy's top priority is getting the Web site going. "Technology changes so fast, we're just trying to stay a few steps ahead," she says. "In a year, the Web might be completely different, and we'll have to be flexible enough to adapt."

27. Data Retrieval Specialist

description: Many company officials use auditors' and accountants' reports to gauge the financial health of their companies, and they make earnings and sales projections based on those numbers. Many of the figures are extracted from extensive computer databases that require a high level of expertise to operate. Enter the data retrieval specialist.

This job involves working with the auditing or finance department of a company to cull information from databases and electronic archives. Although the common perception of a database is a highly ordered system that offers up information with the stroke of a computer key, many database systems are simply a free-form collection of information from which extracting financial data is like pulling teeth.

Data retrieval experts spend hours and sometimes days searching for a particular piece of information—be it sales figures for a particular day five years ago or storewide layaway plan balances. Often, retrieval specialists write software programs designed specifically to extract the data.

salary: Pay depends on the size of the company, the part of the country in which you're working, and your experience. The average annual salary for a data retrieval specialist with a few years of experience is $40,000 to $50,000.

prospects: Companies have become much more reliant on their computer systems in the past five years, and this field has expanded accordingly. Many companies are realizing that to use their systems efficiently, they need experts who understand its inner workings. That has made this a fast-growing job category.

qualifications: The standard college background for this job is a bachelor's degree in computer science or information systems. Some people start in auditing or finance and move into this area. Regardless of a person's major, computer programming skills are very important. You also need to know database programming languages and be knowledgeable about database systems.

characteristics: It helps if you are the kind of person who can't take no for an answer. As you search through files for information, you'll run into blocks and dead ends. A lot of determination and self-motivation are necessary to thrive in this job.

Ron Hudson *is an electronic data processing auditor for a large retail chain in Detroit, Michigan.*

How did you get the job?

A business major at Indiana University, Ron Hudson planned to go into accounting. During college, he worked part-time as a stocker for a large retail chain, and when he graduated, the company hired him as an auditor at a store in Raleigh, North Carolina. He stayed there for two years before being named assistant manager of the field audit department. As an

auditor, he had taken computer training courses, and had a knack for troubleshooting. "I've always been the one in our department that everybody came to when they had computer problems," he says.

After several years working in auditing, Ron was ready to learn something new, and he was hoping to use his computer skills. "When I heard about this position, it just seemed like something I'd be good at," he says. Ron proved to be well suited to database investigations. "I really enjoy programming, and it feels like a major accomplishment when you write a software program that gets the information you want," he says.

What do you do all day?

Ron arrives at work at 7 A.M. and immediately checks his e-mail. He usually juggles five or six different projects, and digs into the most pressing one. One recent morning, that meant working to retrieve

records of rent payments the company's stores have made to landlords. "They really need this one, so I'm doing everything I can to track it down," he says. That means making changes to a software program that he hopes will pull up what he needs.

In the meantime, the manager of the store audit department has asked for the receivable balances for all stores. "I'm writing a program to get that information from the cash and sales database, but I can't get it all as soon as they want it."

Ron is also looking for files of invoices from vendors that the company has not been able to match with receipts. His boss needs to know the number of receipts and the vendors and

stores involved.

In between, Ron helps auditors who have questions about how to find various information that they need. He also spends a lot of time on the phone talking to other departments to see if they can offer any clues as to where the data that he needs might be.

Because of his computer expertise, Ron has taken on an extra assignment—training field auditors in how to use new laptop computers. He is working individually with auditors to get them up to speed and—because they spend most of their time on the road—providing coaching over the phone. At about 5 P.M., Ron calls it a day and heads home.

Where do you see this job leading you?

Ron hopes to move into a job within his company that would allow him to do software programming full-time. Because the company is open to employees making job shifts, Ron is optimistic he'll get a chance. After all, that's how he got into programming in the first place.

28. Director of On-line Service

FOR NONPROFIT GROUPS

description: As a director of a nonprofit on-line service provider, you'll work with civic groups, social service associations, and government agencies to provide them with Internet service, train them how to do on-line data searches, and help them set up home pages on the World Wide Web.

In addition to possessing technical expertise you need to be an astute businessperson: keeping a nonprofit service like this on its feet requires both financial savvy and fund-raising skills. This type of on-line service provider generally relies on state government support, grants, and private donations.

salary: Nonprofit on-line service providers pay much less than commercial services. Fees are based on a sliding scale, with most groups paying about $150 a year, versus the $250 to $500 that a private company would spend for similar service. Executive director salaries start in the mid-$20,000 range and increase depending on the size of the service. In contrast, a director of a commercial, for-profit Internet provider might start somewhere in the $40,000 range.

prospects: Although they aren't growing as quickly as commercial providers, nonprofit services are springing up in many cities. Because a city typically has only one such group and the number of paid positions is limited, salaried jobs are competitive. Still, the opportunities are increasing rapidly.

qualifications: A college degree is generally required for directors, but the area of study isn't important. You need to be familiar with computers and the Internet, and will need accounting and finance experience. You will be spending a lot of time educating groups about the Internet, so you need to be patient and a good teacher. Drumming up support for your group requires someone who isn't afraid to ask for money. Organization is also important, because you will be overseeing hundreds of Internet accounts; if too many groups fall behind in paying for their Internet subscriptions, your service will fall apart.

characteristics: An entrepreneurial spirit is a must. This is a new idea in many communities, and just like with a start-up company, its survival depends on your skills and your vision. Mastering the art of persuasion is also important, because you'll be charged with convincing nonprofit groups to invest in the Internet, and donors to subsidize it.

Tamara Blaschko *is director of a nonprofit on-line service provider in Minneapolis, Minnesota.*

How did you get the job?

After graduating from college with a degree in art history, Tamara Blaschko got a job as a publicity assistant for an art museum. She moved around over the next 10 years, holding jobs including public relations director for a theater company, executive director for a women's art collective, and legal secretary at a public defender's office. She was working as a development director for a community radio station when she heard about an opening at a nonprofit group that provides Internet services and training to community groups and government agencies.

Tamara was drawn to the position because she sees the Internet as an innovative way to help nonprofits. "The cost of publishing and distributing paper materials can cost thousands of dollars," she says. "You can put the same information on-line and reach people all over the world. Many nonprofits aren't aware of this great

> START BY GETTING EXPERIENCE WORKING FOR A NON-PROFIT ORGANIZATION. MOST GROUPS WELCOME VOLUNTEERS, AND MANY ARE LOOKING FOR HELP GETTING ON THE WEB. BECOME AN EXPERT ON THE INTERNET BY SURFING ON YOUR OWN AND READING ALL YOU CAN. INTERNET BULLETIN BOARDS AND JOB-RELATED WEB SITES ARE ALSO GOOD RESOURCES FOR JOB HUNTERS.

resource, and I wanted to introduce them to it."

Her first job for the group involved raising funds and managing volunteers. She helped drum up more than $200,000 to get the program off the ground. Eventually, she began asking for a title that reflected her responsibilities. Her business cards now carry the title "director."

"For the first time I'm combining my nonprofit work, which I love, with my computer knowledge," she says.

What do you do all day?

Tamara spends the morning working at home. At 9 A.M., she checks her e-mail and then listens to her voice mail. "For the next two hours, I'm on the phone talking with nonprofits that have questions or technical problems," she says. If a group is having technical difficulties that she can't solve over the phone, she dispatches someone to take a look. She spends the rest of the morning working on grant applications, and heads into the office at 1 P.M.

The afternoon is a blur of decisions, discussions, and negotiations. Right now, Tamara is negotiating a $10,000 contract to provide the city with Internet service. She also is in the process of putting the city's Catholic schools on-line and is working with the Minnesota Teachers Federation to set up an on-line homework help site where students could post questions and get help on their studies. "If they couldn't figure out a math problem, they could ask for help, and college student volunteers would respond." She is also working with several nonprofit groups to help them put Web sites on the Internet.

In between, there is a lot of administrative work, from budgets to deciding whether to order new modems for the Internet service. After work, Tamara often attends community events, where she meets potential subscribers.

Where do you see this job leading you?

Tamara is thinking about leaving the world of nonprofits to become an independent Internet consultant. "So much is going to change in the next five years, and I want to be a part of it," she says.

29. Electrical Engineer

description: Just about any piece of equipment that plugs into a wall or runs on batteries was designed in part by an electrical engineer. EEs design electronic circuits and the equipment that uses them. Some EEs work on the tiny chips that serve as the brains of the products, while others focus on integrating those chips into the products.

Electronics companies, the government, and the military depend heavily on electrical engineers, but virtually every industry relies on EEs for the technology that keeps its businesses running. Electrical engineers like to say they take ideas and turn them into something real. For most, that is what makes this job so rewarding.

salary: An engineer fresh out of college can expect to start at $40,000 a year. Engineers with several years of experience can earn $55,000 to $60,000 a year. Top EEs with specialized skills can top $90,000. High-tech companies typically pay the most, while military and government positions pay significantly less.

prospects: There are usually more job opportunities in private industry, particularly in high-tech companies, than there are in the government, though this fluctuates depending on the economy. Congress' mood toward funding research projects, which varies from year to year, greatly affects the job outlook for government and military jobs.

qualifications: You will need at least a bachelor's degree in electrical engineering. Some companies require master's degrees or even doctorates, depending on the technology. But many good corporate and government jobs are open to engineers with bachelor's degrees, and many recruit engineers while they're still in college.

characteristics: You have to like problem solving, and you have to be good at it. Excellent math skills are also a must. Although some people think of electrical engineers as antisocial, many engineering jobs involve working closely in teams, so you've got to be able to deal well with other people and to express your ideas clearly.

Ray Cravey *is an electrical engineer at a high-tech start-up in Albuquerque, New Mexico.*

How did you get the job?

"I was always interested in computers as a kid, but I didn't know anything about electronics or engineering until I got to college," Ray Cravey says. "I discovered it in a physics class, and I knew it was for me." He declared himself an EE major and graduated from Texas Tech with a bachelor's degree. During the summer of his senior year, he worked for a California company that specializes in pulse power, which involves converting regular electrical current into high-energy pulses. He loved the field and decided to specialize in it.

Ray eventually went back and earned a master's degree, and he worked for five years at a government lab in California working with pulse power. "At that point, my wife and I had a couple of children, and we wanted to get closer to our family in New Mexico," he says. He applied for a job doing research and development at a small start-up in Albuquerque. "They were looking for people who were energetic and who could bring some experience into the company," he says. "I filled those requirements."

Moving to the start-up was part of a plan Ray formulated in college. "I had made the decision that I was going to work at the same place for two years and move on," he says. "I felt like if you stayed somewhere any longer, you would get too settled and end up in a rut." He stayed at the lab in California three years longer than he intended, but he feels that moving on was the right decision. "It was hard to leave, but I knew there were things I wanted to accomplish, and I knew I would be able to do that here."

What do you do all day?

What Ray's day is like depends on what phase of a project he is in. When he first gets a product proposal, he spends weeks, and sometimes months, involved in problem solving and design. Once the design is completed, the product is fabricated. "Testing is the exciting part," he says. "Once it's built, you get to see if what you designed actually works." If it doesn't, Ray and his team go back to the drawing board. "You expect it never to work the first time," he says. "You're doing something that no one has done, so you can't read up on it. It's up to you to figure it out on your own, and that can involve some false starts." If it does work, they do extensive testing and write detailed reports on their findings.

His company depends on contracts, and Ray spends a good deal of time writing work proposals. "It's my job to say 'Here's my idea for the best way to do it and here's how much that will cost.'"

Where do you see this job leading you?

"That's a real dilemma," Ray says. "I really love my job, and it's hard to imagine doing anything else. But my company had layoffs not long ago, and I'm wondering if it's time to make a career change." The layoffs have prompted him to reevaluate his priorities and to consider moving to a more established company. "I've got a family, and in some ways it seems like job stability is more important than job satisfaction at this point. If you're young, it doesn't matter if you get laid off, but when you've got other people depending on you, it does."

FOR MORE INFORMATION ON ELECTRICAL ENGINEERING, CONTACT THE INSTITUTE FOR ELECTRICAL AND ELECTRONIC ENGINEERS. (SEE RESOURCES, PAGE 212).

30. Electronics Technician

description: While electrical engineers design circuitry, electronics technicians make sure it works. When something goes wrong with a circuit, technicians act as investigators, isolating the problem and coming up with solutions. That often involves working with the engineer who designed it to make modifications and testing it again to make sure it's functioning properly.

Technicians also design circuit prototypes—using either real materials or a computer model—to test out the design. They meet with customers to discuss their needs, and if the design doesn't include all the customer's product requirements, the technicians will either make changes themselves or instruct the engineers on what's needed.

Helping a product move from a computer design to the real thing is one of the rewards of being an electronics technician. Because technology is always changing, so is the work, making no two projects the same.

salary: Annual salaries start in the low- to mid-$20,000 range. With a few years of experience, electronics technicians can earn $40,000 or more a year.

prospects: The government, which has traditionally employed a large number of electronics technicians, has been cutting back in recent years because of a decrease in weapons contracts. Demand in the private sector, however, is increasing. The fast-growing semiconductor industry, for example, employs a large number of technicians.

qualifications: A two-year associate's degree in an area such as electrical engineering technology is a minimum requirement. Computer programming and troubleshooting skills are also necessary. Some companies prefer these with a couple of years of experience, while others hire employees right out of school.

characteristics: You have got to be organized and able to meet tight deadlines. You also need to have a heavy interest in electronics and in making things work.

J. Gregory Hughes *is a senior technical associate of electrical engineering technology at a lab in Albuquerque, New Mexico.*

How did you get the job?

Greg Hughes graduated from Youngstown State University in Youngstown, Ohio, with a degree in electrical engineering technology.

After graduating, he went to Florida. His job hunting there resulted in dead ends, though, and he was determined to find a good job where he could put his skills to work.

Then he got a call from a government lab in Albuquerque, New Mexico, that wanted to interview him. Greg spent hours studying up on the lab. He memorized the facility's square footage, the number of employees, and the types of projects it handled. "That was the key part of getting the job," he says. "I had a three-hour interview, and they knew I really wanted it because I had taken the time to learn everything I could about them."

He wasn't hired immediate-

> **CONCENTRATE ON HONING YOUR COMPUTER-PROGRAMMING AND TROUBLE-SHOOTING SKILLS, AND DON'T SHY AWAY FROM CLASSIFIED ADS IN THE NEWSPAPER. EVEN IF YOU DON'T HAVE THE PRECISE SKILLS THE COMPANY IS LOOKING FOR, MANY COMPANIES ARE WILLING TO TRAIN.**

ly, however. The lab had a hiring freeze, and no one knew when a position would open. During that time, Greg turned down another offer from a computer company in New Hampshire. "I felt it was worth taking a chance on, and I'm glad I went with my instincts," he says. Three months after his first interview, he got a call telling him he had a job in New Mexico.

What do you do all day?

"I've always been fascinated by electronics, and in this job I get paid to play with high-tech toys," Greg says.

He spends a lot of time looking for flaws in software and circuit design. That involves running simulations on a computer, as well as meeting with colleagues who have done similar work. "We do a lot of comparing notes," he says. "If I'm having problems getting something to work, chances are someone else will have some ideas on what's going wrong."

For the most part, Greg sets his own work schedule. "I don't have anybody really structuring my day, and I like that," he says. "It would be hard to have someone sitting over me saying, 'Do this, do that.'" Greg's hours also suit him. He works Mon-

day through Friday from 7:30 A.M. to 5 P.M., and has weekends and every other Friday off.

Where do you see this job leading you?

Greg wants to continue working for the lab, where he uses cutting-edge equipment to develop products that take technology a step further. "There are a lot of guys with my degree sitting around stuffing circuit boards all day," he says. "I feel fortunate that I found a job that allows me to invent, think, and develop."

31. Entertainment Software Writer

description: Writing an entertainment software title is similar to writing a screenplay. Although the gaming company usually has a general idea of the characters, it's the writer's job to develop their personalities and the plot. But unlike a movie, software offers a range of different plot twists that, depending on which choices the player makes, can result in completely different story lines. So instead of writing one story, you're writing dozens.

Most software companies hire writers on a freelance basis. After sitting down with the project manager to discuss the direction of the title, the writer is cut loose to write a script. Often, the company will have nothing more than a character around which it's the writer's job to build an adventure game. This means inventing other characters and thinking up ways to let the user interact with the game.

When the script is finished, the writer works with the project manager to tweak and rework the story, before the final version is passed on to the development team.

salary: Most writers are paid per script. The amount varies, depending on the size of the software company and the track record of the writer. Established companies pay about $50,000 for a script, and a successful writer can easily do four or five titles a year and still have plenty of downtime.

prospects: The explosion of entertainment software titles, which includes educational programs and games, has created a strong demand for people to pen them. But this is a highly competitive business. Cold calls rarely work; veterans suggest taking an entry-level job at a company that makes the kind of programs you want to write and learning the business from the inside.

qualifications: Your educational background doesn't matter in this business—your writing skills do. Companies will want to see samples of your work—published or unpublished.

characteristics: You have got to like being alone, because you will be doing most of your work at home in front of a computer. You also need to be very detail oriented; in addition to coming up with a game's twists and turns, you have to paint a vivid backdrop and develop three-dimensional characters.

Laurie Bauman Arnold *writes software titles from her home in Redmond, Washington.*

How did you get the job?

After high school, Laurie Bauman Arnold started college in California, "but I decided it was not my calling." She got a job at a production company, mounting slides for business presentations, and worked her way up to production manager. Eventually, Laurie was asked to head the company.

Laurie accepted the job, which involved writing and producing videos focusing on interactive corporate training programs. "When I had my son, I decided I needed to get out of production because I felt that it was just too grueling," she says. Laurie then did freelance writing for companies that had been her clients, and wrote some screenplays, which she has yet to sell. Then, a friend, who had talked about creating a CD-ROM game based on the char-

acter Sherlock Holmes, called her. "He had always said that as soon as he could raise the money to do it he would want me to write it," Laurie says. "Well, he got the money." As Laurie helped design and write the CD-ROM, she realized that she had a knack for it.

Her husband's job took their family to the Seattle area, which is home to a large number of software development houses. In a nearby town, some friends who were involved in launching an entertainment software start-up hired Laurie to write scripts.

> **CONSIDER TAKING A JOB AS A RUNNER AT AN INTERACTIVE MULTIMEDIA COMPANY AS A WAY TO LEARN THE BUSINESS.**

She still works for them, and she also writes for a number of other leading software companies.

What do you do all day?

"In the morning, I grab a cup of coffee, step into my (home) office, sit down at the computer, and start writing," Laurie says. Though she does most of her work from home, before signing on to a new project, she meets with producers at their office. Often, they leave the entire story line up to Laurie, which is fine with her because it gives her a lot of freedom. That's what happened with a recent title about the French character Madeline, the subject of a number of children's books. "They said, 'We want you to do an interactive Madeline,' and that was the extent of their input," she says.

Laurie came up with a story in which Madeline helps a neighbor who is about to be evicted. Madeline and her

friends put on a puppet show to save the day. Laurie added puzzles and games that allowed kids to design the puppets and the puppet stage and to make invitations.

Laurie writes four to five scripts a year. Working independently allows her to pick and choose projects and to work the hours she wants. "I have two kids, so I work 9 to 5 and take the summer off," she says. "When I first started, I worked all the time because I was afraid no one would ever call me again. But I've learned to relax. The phone always rings again."

Where do you see this job leading you?

Laurie recently got a job writing a script for an animated Saturday morning television show, and would like to do more television work. She plans to continue to write software titles.

32. Environmental Engineer

description: An environmental engineer cleans up past mistakes and plans new facilities designed to avoid mistakes in the future.

Private environmental consulting firms are often hired by state and federal government to determine the best way to clean up contaminated industrial sites. An environmental engineer might be called in if, for example, a manufacturing plant has buried toxic waste that has begun seeping into the water supply. The engineer would assess the site, present a plan for cleaning it up, and help to oversee the cleanup process.

Environmental engineers are also utilized to design and oversee construction of facilities such as water and sewage treatment pile lines, pump stations, and plants.

This job involves a lot of fieldwork. Rather than sit in front of a computer all day, environmental engineers spend a lot of time doing biological and chemical studies and working with regulators, clients, contractors, and the public, which in many cases is footing the bill for cleanups and new facilities.

salary: Engineers can expect to start at $35,000 to $40,000 a year. The average mid-level salary is about $60,000, while salaries for those in top management can exceed $200,000. Pay is based on experience and, in some cases, on the amount of work an individual brings in.

prospects: In the late 1980s and early 1990s, growth was explosive and demand for engineers was high. But growth has declined from 10 to 15 percent a year to about 5 percent. The industry is more crowded, and breaking in isn't as easy as it used to be.

qualifications: A minimum of a bachelor's degree in engineering or geology is necessary, and a master's degree is sometimes preferred. Some firms hire engineers right out of college, while others prefer to hire those with a few years of field experience.

characteristics: You will be meeting with clients and making presentations, so you need to be comfortable speaking in public and working closely with other people.

Gary Meyerhofer *works as a regional manager for a national environmental engineering firm based in Sacramento, California.*

How did you get the job?

In high school, Gary Meyerhofer's best subjects were math and science. He had an older brother who was an engineer, so when the time came to pick a major, engineering was what came to mind. He studied civil engineering at Loyola University in Los Angeles, and earned a master's degree in environmental engineering from the University of California at Davis.

After teaching for a year at the University of Wisconsin, Gary signed on with a national environmental consulting firm in the San Francisco Bay area.

He spent the first few years out in the field overseeing the construction of water treatment facilities. Eventually, he focused on planning treatment facilities and got involved in marketing. He moved into management and now oversees a staff of 100 engineers.

What do you do all day?

Gary spends a lot of time meeting with prospective clients to discuss proposals, which can include new water treatment plants, facility expansions, or cleanup projects.

If his team is working on a new treatment plan, Gary is involved in creating drawings, calculating cost estimates, and coming up with a schedule for

> **MAKE CONTACT WITH PEOPLE WHO WORK AT ENVIRONMENTAL CONSULTING FIRMS BY CALLING FOR AN INFORMATIONAL INTERVIEW. STAY ABREAST OF ENVIRONMENTAL ISSUES AND CHANGING LAWS BY READING AS MUCH AS YOU CAN.**

construction. He also meets regularly with clients to update them on their projects.

If the cost estimate turns out to have been too low, Gary's the one who sits down with the client and explains why it's going to cost more than they expected. "I'm in the middle of one right now," he says, "and it's terrible."

Depending on how many proposals are in the works, Gary will work anywhere from 50 to 80 hours a week.

Where do you see this job leading you?

Gary hopes to continue managing projects for his company and moving up in the ranks.

Many environmental engineers move from fieldwork, to project design, to management. Project managers sometimes end up going to work for the companies for whom they have done consulting work.

33. Environmental Risk Assessor

description: An environmental risk assessor is a sort of eco-doctor who diagnoses environmental problems, develops treatments, and monitors the healing process.

Assessors working for a government agency, such as the Environmental Protection Agency, study factors such as bacteria, viruses, and electromagnetic fields to determine whether they pose a danger to public health. An assessor can decide whether a product will go to market or a manufacturer will be shut down.

Assessors are also employed in private industry. An assessor working for a company that, for example, makes chemical substances would analyze all the steps involved, often using computers to simulate the process.

The assessment would reveal during which steps an explosion could occur, which errors could cause an environmental disaster, and at which points in the process employees are most at risk. Assessors also suggest changes that could be made to prevent a catastrophe.

This job puts you on the cutting edge of new environmental technologies and lets you use them to combat risks to public health. It's not a job without controversy, however. Assessors are a sort of intermediary between the science and the political communities, and often end up being resented by both sides. There is a lot of debate about what role risk assessors should play and how their work should be applied.

salary: Pay ranges from $50,000 to $100,000 a year, depending on your education, your experience, and whether you are working for a private company or a government agency.

prospects: As manufacturing becomes more complex and the potential for toxic disasters rises, private companies are increasingly adding assessors to evaluate the risks of new, advanced technology. The government has also expanded the role of assessors, although that funding is never guaranteed.

qualifications: Most environmental risk assessors have degrees in some area of science or engineering. A few years of lab work experience is mandatory because a lot of this job involves scientific research, and you need to be up on the latest advances in environmental technology.

characteristics: Your findings won't always be well received. You have to be able to stand up and defend your assessments, even when your own employer doesn't like what you have to say.

Terence Harvey *is director of a federally-funded risk assessment center in Cincinnati, Ohio.*

How did you get the job?

After spending six years as a veterinarian in Chicago, Terence Harvey took a job at the Food and Drug Administration in Rockville, Maryland, that involved studying drugs, medical devices, and food additives for government approval. The job provided vital lab experience for his career in risk assessment. "If you're going to review somebody else's data, you ought to know how to do some of it yourself," he says. "You don't need to spend years in the lab, but you need the experience."

Eventually, he moved to the private sector, joining a large chemical company's biotechnology division. His group developed BST, the chemical that increases milk production in dairy cows.

"At that point I was a technology junkie," he says. "I like to go where the new stuff is happening. After we got worldwide approval for BST, I wanted to keep moving."

He was drawn to environmental science. "It's the least understood science, and the most important one to society," he says. "It's a challenge because it's so slippery. Environmental issues aren't black and white. It's the uncertainty that was attractive to me."

He left the private sector to become the director of a government-funded environmental risk assessment center. "You make less money with the government, but there's more opportunity to make a difference," he says.

What do you do all day?

Terence spends a good deal of time meeting with politicians and government officials to drum up support for his center. "We need their money, we need their interest, and we need to be one of their priorities," he says. "That's a hard thing to get in science today."

He is also the co-author of most of the center's research projects, which involve studying and researching issues that pose environmental hazards. He and his team determine the extent of danger and the best way to solve the problem.

Terence is currently involved in a study of the danger that mercury poses in recreational fishing. He and his team will ultimately present their findings to the government.

Where do you see this job leading you?

"I've sort of had a grand career plan that involves spending a third of my career in public service, a third in the private sector, and a third in academia so that I can share what I've learned," he says. He plans to spend another 10 years in environmental risk assessment and then move on. "

> ALTHOUGH GOVERNMENT JOBS GENERALLY DON'T PAY AS WELL AS THOSE IN THE PRIVATE SECTOR, THEY CAN OFTEN BE MORE REWARDING. BE PREPARED FOR JOB INSTABILITY IF YOU WORK IN AN AREA THAT HAS STRONG PARTISAN LEANINGS.

By then, I'll be tired of fighting the politics," he says. "My next stop is at a university."

34. Fast Static RAM Product Engineer

description: Most computer applications that involve a heavy amount of number crunching require the use of Fast Static RAM, a component that enhances memory. This device allows the computer to store a portion of code for quick access. Fast Static RAM is a very complex device, and its development necessitates the cooperation of numerous people who will work on areas such as design, process programming, debugging, and marketing.

Rather than be in charge of one aspect of this memory device's production, a Fast Static RAM product engineer steers a product through production from start to finish, playing a small role in almost every part of the product's creation. For example, the product engineer may be involved with the design of these memory devices, although he or she won't be the principal designer. In this capacity, the product engineer is able to gain experience in every facet of making Fast Static RAM, ranging from design and semiconductor manufacturing, to programming, testing, and marketing.

salary: This position can pay anywhere from $30,000 to $70,000 a year, depending on your level of experience.

prospects: With a growing number of businesses and individuals purchasing computers, the demand for engineers has grown over the past few years, creating a fertile job market.

qualifications: Someone going into this field will need at least a bachelor's degree in either electrical or electronics engineering, physics, or some sort of material science. Experience working in the field, which can be gained through an internship or a co-op program, is also helpful.

characteristics: Fast Static RAM product engineers need to be able to work under pressure, be well-organized, and be able to work well with people. Perhaps most importantly, they must be versatile and able to shift their concentration from marketing to programming at a moment's notice.

Tim Chesnut *is a Fast Static RAM product engineer for a semiconductor products manufacturer in Texas.*

How did you get the job?

After Tim Chesnut got his bachelor's degree in electrical engineering, he was eager to get a job working with semiconductors. But at the time, the job market was slim, and he didn't have much luck. Tim decided to take the most logical step—going back to school to get his master's degree.

However, about a year after he had enrolled in graduate school, Tim was offered a position working as a Fast Static RAM product engineer with a major semiconductor products manufacturer in Texas.

> OTHER THAN THROUGH AN INTERNSHIP OR A CO-OP POSITION, WHICH CAN OFTEN TURN INTO A FULL-TIME JOB, THE BEST PLACE TO LOOK FOR THIS TYPE OF JOB IS ON THE INTERNET. TRY THE CAREERPATH WEBSITE AT HTTP://WWW.CAREERPATH.COM.

What do you do all day?

Because the job of a Fast Static RAM product engineer covers a plethora of tasks, Tim almost never does the same thing every day. However, some of the tasks require that he perform the same skills, which include analyzing data, programming, and project planning.

Because many of the company's fabrication plants are overseas, Tim spends a lot of time communicating with them via e-mail. Occasionally, he must travel out of the country to work with a fabrication plant.

Tim also spends a lot of time in meetings with the numerous people in the office who are working on the product. He must meet with designers, programmers, device engineers, process engineers, production controllers, and marketers. This aspect of Tim's job is what he likes best. "There's a lot of variety, and you are not just focused on one job. Someone in this position gets a real good flavor of the other types of positions."

Where do you see this job leading you?

Tim doesn't have any plans to leave his position. He says he likes working in an atmosphere where he is constantly learning about new technologies and is able to take on more challenging products as the technology develops.

35. Field Systems Technician

description: Companies rely on field systems technicians to develop software applications for internal use and to keep the software and hardware the company uses up and running.

As technology, business, and customers change, so must the software that a company uses to track sales, ordering, and receiving. Field systems technicians are constantly tweaking the software system—and sometimes doing complete rewrites—to keep it up to date.

Field technicians work with department managers across the company to ensure that their computer systems are doing their jobs. Some field technicians also oversee training of employees who use the company's computer system.

salary: Entry-level technician positions start at about $25,000 a year, while project managers can earn between $50,000 and $80,000 annually.

prospects: Companies complain they can't fill these positions fast enough. As they rely more heavily on sophisticated software systems, the role of the field technician is becoming one of a company's key resources.

qualifications: A college degree in computer science or some form of engineering is usually a must. Software programming skills are very important, but so is an understanding of how businesses operate. Being an ace programmer isn't enough; you have to understand how a company works and how it uses computers to meet its needs.

characteristics: Pressure might as well be a part of the job description. You have got to be able to switch back and forth between writing software programs and working with people in the field who are having problems with their computer systems. You have to be a good listener; when employees tell you what they need their computers to do, it's up to you to take that knowledge and turn it into software.

Dave Cooper *is a project manager of field systems and technology for a retail chain based in Vernon Hills, Illinois.*

How did you get the job?

Dave Cooper has a degree in business. He started at his company as a mainframe computer programmer. "I basically learned how to program through the help of others and by teaching myself," he says. "I also attended a lot of classes." From this position, he moved to the technical staff. Working in different departments gave him an overall understanding of how the business was run. And working with the company's computer hardware and software educated him on the business' technical side. Dave never let the fact that he sometimes didn't have the exact technical skills needed for a position stop him. "Just because you don't have the skills doesn't mean you won't get the job," Dave says. "The key is to be a fast learner." As a technician, he learned to fulfill the needs of employees in the field by using technology. "Before you can create a soft-ware program, you have to understand exactly who's going to be using it, and how," he says.

As Dave moved around, he picked up a range of skills that made him a candidate to manage the staff. "Over the years, I gained the right experience in programming, in technical work, and in managing people," he says. When he was offered a job as project manager of field systems, he took it. But unlike some management jobs, his position hasn't removed him from the field. He still develops software applications, and he works with district managers around the region to learn about their problems and how his department can help.

What do you do all day?

Dave spends a lot of time with the phone glued to his ear. He takes about 100 calls a day, about a third of which are from store managers, a third from other employees, and another third from computer vendors trying to sell him new equipment.

Although he doesn't particularly enjoy dealing with telemarketers and other hardware and software peddlers, part of his job is keeping up with the latest technology. So he listens, and he reads a lot of high-tech magazines and trade publications.

> IT HELPS TO HAVE EXPERIENCE IN THE COMPUTER PROGRAMMING FIELD. MANY COMPANIES LIST THESE TYPES OF JOBS IN CLASSIFIED ADS AND ON THEIR WEB SITES. COMPANIES LIKE APPLICANTS WHO ARE WILLING TO WORK LATE HOURS AND ON WEEKENDS.

In addition to helping develop new software, Dave oversees the process of getting it installed, which includes extensive testing. "In a matter of seconds you can take your whole company out of business, and we just can't let that happen," Dave says. "We're big on testing and quality control, and that has saved us a number of times."

Dave's favorite part of the job is making the company more productive. "I like finding ways to do things more efficiently," he says. "That's pretty much what my job is—keeping people productive and making sure the technology works for them."

Where do you see this job leading you?

Dave wants to continue overseeing field operations. He believes there is a lot his department can do to help employees get more out of technology.

36. Film Editor

description: Along with a slew of other professions, film editing has of late been transformed by technology. Film editors today rarely spend their time behind a projector splicing film. Instead, they sit behind a computer holding a mouse in one hand and a script in the other.

This change has brought about concern from some in the industry, but for the most part editors have begun to realize that one click of the mouse is a much easier way to pull up footage than sifting through canisters of film. Some editors even say that this instant access allows them to feel as if they are working more closely with the film.

This job combines artistic ability with technology. It is considered exciting, from the aspect of both working with the latest technology and creating entertainment that receives a large amount of attention from the public.

salary: An editor's wages depend largely on the type of film he or she works with and on his or her level of experience. Documentary films typically pay about $2,000 a week, while feature films often pay editors $5,000 a week or more. An editing room assistant with less experience may earn $500 or $600 a week to work on a documentary film and about $1,000 a week for work on a feature film.

prospects: With the entertainment industry going strong, there will continue to be a wealth of jobs in digital film editing. However, breaking into this field can be difficult. The best way to find these jobs is through a contact, and the best way to make contacts is through film school.

qualifications: While film school is not a requirement, more and more people who are serious about going into film editing are taking the academic route because it is a great way to make contacts and to find out more about the industry. However, it is experience in the cutting room that employers most desire.

characteristics: In order to work on a film from start to finish, film editors must have patience and diligence, but more importantly, they must have a passion for film. It is this passion that will keep them sitting in a dark room hour after hour during the editing of a film.

David Ray *is a film editor based in New York City.*

How did you get the job?

David Ray first started working on films in his home country of England, where he created company-sponsored educational films. When he became more serious about film making, he moved to New York and got a job managing filming equipment for the graduate school of journalism at Columbia University. Although this work furthered his experience in the industry, it did not provide him with any contacts.

David later met one editor whom he called almost daily until a job as an assistant to an editor finally came his way.

He worked as an assistant to various editors for about 12 years before he was eventually hired as an editor for the movie *All That Jazz.* Since then, he has edited numerous other films and television series.

What do you do all day?

Whether David is working on a television series or a feature film, he may spend some time on the set watching a shoot. However, he will spend much more time working in front of a computer, viewing the scenes and cutting them together.

Each scene is filmed numerous times from different angles. For example, in a scene that consists of two characters, there will be at least three "takes" where the camera focuses on just one character. There will also be three other takes in which the camera focuses on that character's counterpart. David views all six of these takes and uses portions from each to create one scene. He starts by clicking on each take with his mouse so he can view them—with sound—on the computer. He then chooses which segments he wants to use and then cuts the film together.

While the actual cutting is done simply by hitting the scissor icon on his Macintosh computer, David says knowing when to cut is important. "The skill is in the timing. You develop sort of a feeling for it."

Often, David's job is made more difficult by the conditions in which the film was shot. For example, if there is an airplane flying overhead during one take, he will have to work around the noise. If an actor forgets a line, he will have to deal with that as well. But perhaps one of the biggest challenges David faces in his job is at the beginning of every film. "You've no idea how things should be put together or what the placement should be. You have a rough idea because you have the script, but the script is just type on a white piece of paper. Once you get it out in the open, there's scenery, there's color, there are actors creating nuances with these words that you could have never anticipated in advance. The whole thing is different and the scene takes on a real life of its own."

Where do you see this job leading you?

David doesn't see editing as the pinnacle of his career in film. He would eventually like to move into the role of director.

37. Firmware Engineer

description: To the general consumer, the difference between firmware and software seems slight, but to those who create the products, the contrast is vast. If you were to purchase a computer program such as Microsoft Windows, you could use the software on any number of IBM-compatible machines, but if you were to purchase a Nintendo game—firmware—you would only be able to use it on a Nintendo machine. The advantage of designing firmware over software lies in the fact that firmware is designed for specific hardware, and therefore can be optimized for better overall performance. When software engineers design programs for generic platforms such as IBM computers, on the other hand, they must make allowances for slight differences in the range of hardware on which the program will be used.

As a firmware engineer, you could find yourself writing code for any of the various products that currently contain firmware, such as the computer that controls a car's ABS brakes or the personal organizer that keeps track of appointments and phone numbers.

salary: Firmware engineers just starting out in the field can expect to make a salary of about $35,000. With annual raises of about three to five percent, these engineers could be making as much as $50,000 after five years. To get beyond this figure, an engineer would probably need to move into a management position.

prospects: Currently, the job market for firmware engineers is good, mainly because the number of products using firmware is on the rise.

qualifications: A bachelor's degree in either computer science or a related field is required for anyone wanting to break into this industry. Although experience working with computer networks is helpful, it is not necessary.

characteristics: Firmware engineers are usually very analytical in everything they do. When something isn't working, rather than rely on gut instinct, a firmware engineer is more likely to chart out a logical path of repair before making any moves.

Kevin Smith *is a firmware engineer on the East Coast.*

How did you get the job?

After Kevin Smith received his bachelor's degree in computer engineering from the University of New Hampshire, he started scouring the classified ads in the newspaper. He soon found himself moving to Colorado to work as a components purchaser, where he tested computer hardware and determined whether it should be purchased by his company.

Although the job was within his field, it lacked the design side of engineering that Kevin desired. After six months, he moved back east to look for a more satisfying position.

Kevin soon found work as a firmware engineer for a large networks management company in the Northeast. This position offers him diversity in his assignments and allows him to deal with both software and hardware issues. For Kevin, the opportunity to develop new products and watch them move from a concept phase to a production phase is the most enjoyable aspect of his work.

What do you do all day?

As a firmware engineer, Kevin tackles large projects that may take him anywhere from six months to a year to complete. Typically, he will work with a group when he is developing a firmware program. If a task is unusually large, the group will break off with individual assign-

> **PERHAPS THE BEST RESOURCE FOR SOMEONE TRYING TO FIND A JOB AS A FIRMWARE OR SOFTWARE ENGINEER WOULD BE THE JOB LISTINGS IN LOCAL NEWSPAPERS, IN TRADE PUBLICATIONS, OR ON THE INTERNET, OR THROUGH CO-OP PROGRAMS SET UP BETWEEN SCHOOLS AND INDUSTRY.**
> ----------

ments. Once those assignments are complete, they will meet again as a group to make sure that the project is cohesive.

While Kevin is deep into a new project, it is not unusual for him to be confronted with questions surrounding a finished project that is in the "maintenance" phase, which takes place during the first year after a product has been developed. Sometimes, Kevin will be required to interrupt his work on a current project to write code that will change the way a project in the maintenance phase is functioning.

Where do you see this job leading you?

Kevin hopes to progress to some sort of management position, such as a project leader, in which he would still be working with the design of firmware.

38. Freelance Digital Pre-press Graphic Artist

description: A freelance digital graphics artist usually works for commercial printers and publishers—working most often with their art directors or creative directors. Most work is done on Macintosh computers, creating images that have been designed for books, magazines, brochures—or almost any kind of publication. You could be doing desktop publishing, which involves relatively simple layouts of graphics and text, or working with very complicated color files that can be held only on huge removable hard drives. The more complicated files take hours of manipulation in programs such as Illustrator, Photoshop, Quark, PageMaker, and FreeHand.

Most freelancers in this field have previously held positions as graphic artists to develop technical skills and have developed a professional network of clients and contacts.

salary: A degree from a two-year technical program could initially earn you about $12 per hour. Skills acquired with a four-year degree could earn you up to $16 per hour. After a few years in the field, you could command over $20 per hour.

prospects: Work for digital graphic artists is plentiful. With the advent of greater computer graphics capabilities, many companies are taking on preliminary graphic design work and desktop publishing in-house and hiring out to freelancers the more technical, digital pre-press phase. Further, many of the same technical graphic skills needed to produce books and magazines are also used for digital production of CD-ROMs, interactive videos, and laser disks. If you can keep up with the technology, you'll always be employed.

qualifications: A strong facility of the basic graphics programs is essential. Most entry-level people have at least a two-year technical degree in communications, computer science, or graphic imaging and printing technology. A four-year degree in visual communications or computer graphics would also prove valuable.

characteristics: Attention to detail is mandatory, as is a proven technical knowledge of programs.

Hilary Culhane *is a freelance digital pre-press graphic artist based in Washington state.*

How did you get the job?

Hilary Culhane got into the field about 15 years ago—before computers were heavily used. "I started out as a craftsperson in the printing industry," Hilary says. "As technology advanced, I realized the limitations of my own skills and of the equipment available to me." To keep up with changing technology, she went back to school for a four-year graphics arts degree which included computer graphics, writing, computer science, systems design, and programming.

When Hilary emerged from college, she reentered a much more technical field as a digital operator. "I heard about a teaching position at a trade organization meeting," says Hilary, "so I went for it. Now, in addition to freelancing, I am teaching computer graphics part-time at a community college."

Hilary feels there are a lot of

> ATTEND TRADE MEETINGS; THEY CAN BE INVALUABLE FOR FINDING JOBS AND ACQUIRING INFORMATIONAL RESOURCES. AND DON'T BE INTIMIDATED BY THE OLD-BOY NETWORK THAT IS SO PREVALENT AT THESE MEETINGS.

resources available to people who know where to look. "I do freelance graphics and get most of my jobs from the freelancing call-board at the college." This board is open to the public. Most schools have a career placement office that posts jobs—some of which are available to the public.

What do you do all day?

Currently, most of Hilary's freelance work is for a magazine. She scans color images, finishes up file creations, outputs them to color proofs, and corrects the color digitally—all necessary steps to prepare the files for the

printer. "The steps get more exacting and more technical the closer they get to the printing phase," says Hilary. "That's where the real expertise comes in.

"At the magazine, I work with the art director as a liaison between the editorial staff and the production staff," Hilary explains. "I'm somewhat of an interpreter who can speak both languages." She sometimes works with the printers on specifications of a particular press. "Because so many nontechnical people are dealing with file creation, a lot of file information comes to me missing or unreadable," Hilary says. "Most files

need a serious cleanup before going to the printer."

She also deals with hardware issues such as the network between the computer and the film outputting device, the computer not having enough memory, customer files freezing the computer, and viruses. "Your value increases with your technical proficiency," says Hilary.

Where do you see this job leading you?

Hilary's goal is to teach full-time rather than do production work. Her second choice would be to manage printing production. "In my experience, the printing and publishing industry is a predominantly male-oriented field," Hilary says. "I feel teaching makes me more visible, and henceforth a good role model for women who choose to pursue careers in this field."

39. Freelance Software Engineer

description: Freelance software engineers design and develop computer programs. These could be applications programs for a large, complex software program or personal and business productivity applications. Sometimes, you could be writing one small component of a huge program that requires the input of many programmers. Other times, you are completely on your own.

Freelance software engineers have the advantage of determining their own hours. Work might be conducted at a company office or out of your home.

As a freelancer, you are likely to find yourself in a consulting position, teaching clients the most effective use of their own technology.

salary: Freelance programmers can command $35 to $45 per hour. That salary level will vary, depending on the size of the job, your experience, and the size of the company. With a specialty in networks or a knowledge of the intricate nuances of the Internet, that figure could rise to more than $100 per hour.

prospects: Qualified programmers have many opportunities for employment. If you are good at operating systems, networks, or user interfaces, and have experience in state-of-the-art programming languages, your chances of getting contracts are quite high. Most companies contract with freelancers to keep down their benefits costs.

qualifications: The main qualification that's required is experience developing software. A four-year degree in computer science will help you gain some of that experience. The rest comes from writing programs of varying sizes and complexities and from customizing existing programs. Because you are your own business, it is wise to acquire a basic understanding of how a business is run.

characteristics: One of the most important qualities of a freelance programmer is confidence in his or her skills. It's also important to know when to say no. A desirable trait is a willingness to work flexible hours and to bend with the needs of others' deadlines. Moving from company to company, you're always the new kid on the block and need to have the ability to fit yourself into the existing environment.

Pete Porzuchek *is a freelance programmer based in Washington state.*

How did you get the job?

"I got thoroughly disgusted with being employed as an engineer at a large airline manufacturer," Pete Porzuchek says. "It drove me crazy to not be in charge of my own destiny and to do things I didn't want to do." Initially, Pete decided to go it on his own and got his first contracts through temporary employment agencies. Many companies solicit freelance programmers through agents who keep their resumes on file. "One of my first jobs took me across the country on a three-month assignment," Pete says. "I got to live in New York City without having to move there permanently."

Pete met his primary client through word of mouth after he moved back to Seattle. The client was interested in information about marketing an applications program he had written. Greatly impressed with Pete's programming, the client hired him to work on an applications program, and has contracted with Pete many times over the past several years.

Pete frequently is asked by whichever client he is working for to become a permanent employee, but so far he has held out in favor of freelancing. "People are always asking me to work for them, but I just can't see me doing the 9 to 5 thing. I'm a lot more productive on my own time," he says.

What do you do all day?

Whether it's in the client's office or in the relaxed atmosphere of his own home, work to Pete constitutes the following: designing software, talking to customers, getting specifications, testing a program, making changes, fixing the bugs, designing, developing, testing, fixing more bugs, redesigning, redeveloping, testing, and fixing other bugs until the program does exactly what the customer wants it to do.

Pete prefers to work on an hourly basis, as opposed to getting paid a flat fee for a project. With all of the testing, redesigning, and customers changing their minds midstream, programs can take a lot longer than anticipated. Small companies, on a tighter budget, prefer a contained cost, which sometimes means sacrificing a few features of the program. Big companies need the product to be perfect, and may hire more people to get a product out the door. They are often more concerned about being on time than they are about being within budget.

Pete often finds himself working with many programmers where he's writing one tiny component of a large software package. "It's hard to always work on a little piece of a big puzzle; it's more fun to work on a total, yet smaller, puzzle," he says.

"The biggest problem for me is finding the next job. As a job nears completion, I call my old computer buddies to see what's shaking," Pete says. "Not much security, you know." The other problem Pete faces is keeping up with rapidly changing technology. "As a freelancer, it's incumbent upon me to keep up with technology." Pete then adds, "No one pays for me to attend classes or supplies me with books."

Where do you see this job leading you?

Pete is very happy with the situation he has created for himself, and would like to continue doing what he's doing. "My career provides me with the income that I need and the freedom that makes me comfortable," Pete says. "You can't beat that."

> ONCE YOUV'E DECIDED ON A CAREER, TEMPORARY EMPLOYMENT AGENCIES OFTENTIMES CAN PLACE YOU IN YOUR CHOSEN FIELD. MANY PEOPLE FIND FULL-TIME JOBS BY TAKING THIS ROUTE.

40. Freenet Director

description: Freenets are community-supported organizations that provide free Internet access to people who otherwise could not afford it. Freenets put computers in public places such as libraries and teach citizens how to get on-line. Individuals can then set up Internet accounts at no cost through the freenet, which enables them to exchange e-mail and spend time on the Internet.

Freenets also run on-line forums that contain information on community events, local government, public transportation, and other items of local interest. Anyone with Internet access can tap into the local forum.

Since freenets rely largely on grants and support from local government and business groups, a director spends a lot of time raising money. Directors oversee the community training programs and maintain the on-line forums. They are frequent speakers at civic group functions, where they educate the public about their mission and explain why it's important that the information age not leave behind low-income communities.

salary: As with most jobs in the nonprofit sector, it's the work, not the salary, that is the incentive. Pay ranges from $22,000 to the mid-$30,000s, depending on the size of the city and how well established the freenet is.

prospects: Though the number of freenets is growing, paid positions are limited. Typically, freenets have one full-time director and a staff of volunteers.

qualifications: Freenet directors come from a wide range of backgrounds. It helps to have experience working for a nonprofit organization, but it's by no means a requirement. Basic computer skills are needed, as are talents for public speaking and for fund-raising.

characteristics: You have to be a true believer in the need to bring technology to the have-nots. Unless you're dedicated to the cause, the long hours and the lack of financial compensation may be difficult to accept.

Kevin Pharp *is a coordinator of the Ozarks Regional Information On-line Network in Springfield, Missouri.*

How did you get the job?

Kevin Pharp earned a bachelor's degree in radio and television from the State University of New York and a master's in communications from Southwest Missouri State. After he graduated, Kevin found work in television and movie production and as an on-air personality for a music and talk radio station. "If it's mass media, I've worked in it," he says.

After losing his job selling advertising at a local newspaper in Springfield, Missouri, Kevin decided he was ready to shift gears. "I got laid off from something I didn't enjoy, and it seemed like the right time to reevaluate where I was going," he says. "I decided that in 10 years I wanted to be able to look back and feel like I had made a difference." He then made the decision to pursue a job in public service. Kevin launched a nationwide job search using the

> **FOR MORE INFORMATION ON FREENETS, CONTACT THE NATIONAL PUBLIC TELECOMPUTING NETWORK. (SEE RESOURCES, PAGE 212.)**

Ozarks Regional Information On-line Network, or ORION, which provides free Internet access to residents of Missouri. After checking out the job market, he would sometimes move to an on-line chat room, where he made friends from around the country. One day he got a message from an on-line pal telling him about a job opening, which just happened to be right in Springfield, at none other than ORION. "It was perfect," he says. "Community Internet access was something I really believed in, and here was a chance to promote it."

His broad media and technology background made him an ideal candidate. "I had the right experience, but the thing that sold them over was my enthusiasm for what they were trying to do," Kevin says. Needless to say, he got the job.

What do you do all day?

When Kevin walks into the office at 8:30 A.M., the phones are already ringing. Callers might be people who have just bought computers and want to know how to use ORION or veteran ORION users who have discovered bugs in the on-line forum.

He adds new information to the on-line community forum, which includes topics such as local history, public announcements, and local government services. He then might head to visit local groups such as the Kiwanis Club to speak about ORION. His motives behind public speaking, which takes up

a good deal of his time, are threefold: to dispense information about the services, to let community groups know they can post information on the forum, and to drum up financial support. "People are always calling and saying, 'Can you speak to our group?' and I never say no," he says.

After lunch, Kevin usually spends the afternoon writing grant proposals and working on a new Internet training program. In the evenings, he often attends dinners, which give him another opportunity to talk about ORION.

Where do you see this job leading you?

Kevin wants to continue to build ORION. "It's hard to imagine doing anything other than this," Kevin says. "Introducing people to the Internet and showing them a whole new world is really rewarding. I've found the right place for myself."

41. Genetic Research Technician

description: Genetic research remains one of the hottest topics in medical technology as it strives to move scientists closer to finding cures for Alzheimer's disease, breast cancer, and even AIDS. Research involving DNA has rushed to the forefront, leading to new practices such as gene therapy. Progress is being made continually by teams of genetic researchers, at the heart of which are research technicians.

In order to conduct this research, an exorbitant amount of data must be gathered through experimentation. It is the job of the research technician to conduct these experiments. As a genetic research technician, you would probably work within a team of four or five other technicians who are led by a principal investigator. Most, if not all, of your work will be conducted in a laboratory setting. Your tasks will vary from something as mundane as creating a petri dish to something as intricate as cloning a strand of DNA.

While the majority of your work will center around conducting experiments, you will also spend a great deal of time collecting and analyzing data.

salary: A research technician with a bachelor's degree working in an entry-level job can expect to make a salary in the low to mid-$20,000s. With a master's degree, starting salaries are more likely to be in the range of the high $20,000s to $30,000.

prospects: Jobs in genetic research are becoming more abundant, as both the private and public sector continue to make headway in the field. Universities are a good place to find entry-level positions, and can provide you with the experience needed for jobs with government or industry labs.

qualifications: In order to be hired as a genetic research technician, you need to have a bachelor's degree in biology or in a related field of study. Some experience, which can be gained through either an internship or college lab work, is also usually required.

characteristics: Genetic technical researchers are usually intelligent and inquisitive people. They are often goal oriented, motivated, and care a great deal about their work. They must have the self-discipline to carry out experiments on their own, but at the same time they should be able to work well with others when compiling information with their research team.

Leslie Iyers *is a genetic researcher at the National Institutes of Health in Washington, D.C.*

How did you get the job?

Leslie Iyers can't remember a time when she wasn't interested in biology. It was always her favorite subject in high school, but it wasn't until her sophomore year in college that she realized that she was specifically interested in genetics. During Leslie's junior year, she began looking for a summer job. She found one in the lab of her university's medical school, where genetic research was being conducted. Leslie was hired to perform routine tasks. After she got to know her way around the lab, however, Leslie became more involved and was able to run experiments that were to be used as part of a larger genetic study known as the Human Genome Project. After graduation, Leslie was hired to work in the lab full-time. This job led to her being hired by the National Center for Human Genome Research to work on the same study at the National Institutes of Health in Washington, D.C.

PERHAPS THE BEST PLACE TO FIND OUT ABOUT JOB OPPORTUNITIES IN THE AREA OF GENETIC RESEARCH IS THROUGH YOUR UNIVERSITY. YOU COULD FIND OUT ABOUT JOB OPENINGS AT OTHER UNIVERSITIES BY SEARCHING THEIR JOB BULLETINS ON THE INTERNET. THE WORLD WIDE WEB CAN ALSO CONNECT YOU WITH A NUMBER OF OTHER ENTITIES THAT GIVE JOB LISTINGS FOR OPENINGS IN THIS FIELD. FOR EXAMPLE, THE NATIONAL CENTER FOR GENOME RESOURCES HAS A LISTING OF EMPLOYMENT OPPORTUNITIES, WHICH CAN BE ACCESSED FROM THEIR WEB SITE (HTTP://WWW.NCGR.ORG).

What do you do all day?

At the National Institutes of Health, Leslie spends her work week in the research lab, where she can be found either conducting experiments or compiling data. In order to help the Human Genome Project meet its goal of sequencing the entire human genome by the year 2005, Leslie's research team is working to construct a high resolution map detailing human chromosome 7.

Leslie spends the majority of her time conducting experiments that aid in the construction of this map. This involves cloning DNA to identify short sequences, as well as separating DNA through a method known as polyerase chain reaction. This method involves running DNA across agarose gels, which allows scientists to separate DNA by size and mark a particular strand for further observation.

While Leslie says she enjoys being able to compile data, her favorite part of the job is actually conducting the experiments.

Where do you see this job leading you?

From this position, Leslie could work her way up to become a principal investigator of a study if she decides to further her education by getting her doctorate. However, working as a principal investigator would not afford her with as much hands-on lab activity. For this reason, Leslie says, she would like to continue working as a genetic research technician, where she hopes to become involved in increasingly more challenging research. The area of gene research is growing so rapidly that if Leslie were ever to tire of being a research technician, she could use her background to launch a career in a related area such as gene therapy.

42. Graphical User Interface Designer

description: A graphical user interface (GUI) designer is the person who creates the little pictures on the computer screen, such as menus and icons.

In many cases, the GUI can make or break a software program, especially those that are consumer-oriented. If it is cumbersome and difficult to navigate, people aren't going to want to mess with the program, regardless of how brilliant it may be.

Creating interfaces requires both software programming knowledge and graphical design skills. You have to take specifications from software engineers and turn them into something that is both utilitarian and user-friendly.

salary: A beginning designer can expect to start at around $28,000 a year. With five years of experience, your salary can increase to $40,000 or more, depending on the size of the company and your level of expertise.

prospects: As the number of software programs on the market has increased in recent years, so has the demand for people to design their interfaces. Still, this has traditionally been an undervalued part of software development, with companies often choosing to let their software engineers create interfaces rather than hiring GUI design experts. This is changing, though. Software companies are putting more emphasis on ease of use, and increasingly this means bringing in GUI designers to oversee the process.

qualifications: GUI designers often have educational backgrounds in psychology so that they understand how people physically interact with computers, such as the convenience of button and key placements. Many designers also have graphic design experience. While this job often involves computer programming, companies often provide training. Since designers write the words that appear on the computer screen and in the help portions of the program, writing skills are also important.

Some companies, particularly large software firms, hire those right out of college, while smaller companies with limited resources for training tend to hire people who have some software design experience.

characteristics: Since GUI designers create the "face" of the software, creativity is valued. You have got to be able to take program requirements and commands and turn them into an intuitive design that users will embrace.

Lee Cookson *is a graphical user interface designer and programmer at a software company in Moorsetown, New Jersey.*

How did you get the job?

Lee Cookson, a computer science major at Trenton State College in New Jersey, was looking for a computer-related job the summer before his senior year. He heard about a software company that was looking for someone with UNIX programming skills. "I had the exact experience they were looking for," Lee says. "That's what got me in the door."

He did design work full-time during the summer, and during his senior year he worked a couple of days a week. Lee found the work to be exciting. "You're creating the picture that a person sitting at a computer works with every day," he says. "There's a lot more to this than drawing pictures on a computer screen. And that's what makes it

so interesting." As graduation approached, the question wasn't whether the company would keep Lee on, but whether the project he was working on would continue. "They were happy with me, but it all rested on the project lasting long enough to support me," he says. There was, it turned out, enough work to keep Lee going. The company created a group that specializes in interface design, and made Lee a permanent employee.

What do you do all day?

Because of his technical background, Lee handles a lot of the underlying programming that controls the GUI. After arriving at work at 8 A.M. and checking his e-mail, Lee usually launches right into programming. That could involve working on the framework of the interface or working with interactions of

different windows. He also develops software tools that make it easier for other GUI designers to create the icons and windows that show up on the screen.

Lee spends a lot of time in meetings with other interface designers, discussing layout, the various functions the interface can incorporate, and how it should look. "They might want to know whether they can have

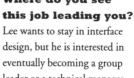

FOR MORE INFORMATION ON GRAPHICAL USER INTERFACE DESIGN, CONTACT EITHER THE ASSOCIATION FOR COMPUTING MACHINERY OR THE HUMAN FACTORS AND ERGONOMICS SOCIETY. (SEE RESOURCES, PAGE 212.)

the program calculate these values while the user is still typing," he says. "I'll look at it and say, 'Well, we can do it, but...' and explain what it will take to make it work."

Lee is also involved in testing the GUIs. "The interface is such a large part of the project as a whole, it has to stand up to a lot of testing," he says. When the people testing it find a bug or a problem, they alert Lee, who figures out what has gone wrong.

When he isn't on deadline, Lee usually heads home around 5 P.M. "But when there's a delivery due and we're behind," he says, "we stay until it's finished."

Where do you see this job leading you?

Lee wants to stay in interface design, but he is interested in eventually becoming a group leader or a technical manager.

43. High-Tech Headhunter

description: Headhunters recruit job candidates to fill technical positions at large companies. In their searches for candidates, they use databases, attend trade fairs, read articles in computer journals, and make cold calls. They are adept at weeding through stacks of resumes to find the person with just the right skill set and personality for the job. That means lots of face-to-face meetings with both job candidates and the company for whom the headhunter is recruiting.

This is a very competitive business. The demand for employees with specialized technical skills far outnumbers the people who have those skills. You will be competing with other headhunters for a relatively small pool of job candidates, and if you make too many unsuccessful placements, you might not have a job for long.

Headhunters say it's the competition that makes this job exciting. No two days are alike, and you will be working with different people every day. And although the hours are long, high salaries make up for it.

salary: A new recruit right out of college might start in the high $20,000 range. Experienced headhunters can earn $100,000 a year, and top recruiters can exceed $300,000. In addition to salary, compensation often includes two to three bonuses a year based on work performance and number of placements. Private firms that specialize in high-tech recruiting pay significantly more than do companies with recruiting departments.

prospects: Companies increasingly need employees with specialized skills, and rather than trying to find candidates themselves, they are more often farming the job out to professionals. Many firms hire headhunters with no experience and then train them, so this is a relatively easy field to break into. Depending on where you live, you may have to be willing to relocate. Most firms are based in large cities, and that's where the best opportunities are.

qualifications: You need a bachelor's degree, but it doesn't matter what field it's in. It helps to be familiar with technology and different high-tech jobs, but it's not a must; many firms hire recruiters straight out of college and train them for six months in both headhunting and the high-tech industry.

characteristics: A quiet, introverted person won't last a day in this job. You also have got to like making cold calls to strangers and convincing them to send you their resume. You also have to be a good listener who can distinguish reality from what a job candidate thinks you want to hear.

Amy Resnik *is a high-tech recruiter in New York City.*

How did you get the job?

Amy Resnik studied business administration in college and later worked for several actuarial firms, handling employee benefit record keeping and savings plans. "The job was very, very mathematically inclined. People who moved up became actuaries," she says. "It was just not me." A friend suggested she join his high-tech recruiting firm, which was in the start-up stage. Amy signed on, mostly just to prove she could do it. "I was the first female recruiter there, and their attitude was that men were better than women," she says. "I wanted to show them that I was just as good."

There was a major learning curve involved. "I knew nothing about computers," she says.

"My strength is being able to deal effectively with people; my weakness is not being a computer genius." It took a year before she felt comfortable with the job, and two years before she got good at it. Now, she is a partner with the firm and one of its top recruiters.

What do you do all day?

When Amy gets in to work, she starts calling people whose names and numbers she has compiled the night before. "Early in the morning is the best time of the day to call people, so you have to make the most of it," she says. If the people she talks to are interested in the job openings, she will arrange for them to come in for a face-to-face interview.

After a morning of cold calls, Amy works on rewriting resumes for job candidates the company wants to place and

> START BY DETERMINING WHICH RECRUITING FIRMS YOU'RE INTERESTED IN WORKING FOR, AND CHECK OUT THEIR WEB SITES FOR JOB LISTINGS. PRESENT YOURSELF AS AN OUTGOING AND EXTROVERTED PERSON, BECAUSE THIS IS A VERY COMPETITIVE FIELD.

then reports back to companies on the progress she is making on filling certain jobs. She often meets with job candidates over lunch or dinner, so she can size them up and decide if they match what her client is looking for.

Amy also spends a lot of time meeting with clients. "I try to get out of the office as much as possible," she says. "It's good PR to make regular appearances." Her company is putting increased emphasis on systems administration placements, and it's Amy's job to build a stronger presence. To do that, she meets with finance and banking companies around New York to tell them what her firm has to offer.

Where do you see this job leading you?

Becoming a partner in the firm was a major achievement. Amy wants to continue as a recruiter and help increase her staff so that the firm remains competitive. "There are a lot of recruiting firms springing up," she says. "We're the leader, but we've got to work hard to stay that way."

44. High-Tech Industry Analyst

description: Analysts forecast what customers are going to want, who they're going to buy it from, and how much they're going to spend. They report trends, follow current events, and comment on them to news reporters. If a respected analyst makes a disparaging remark about a company's performance, the company's stock might take a nose dive.

Similarly, a company that receives a favorable report by an analyst might see its stock double in value. Some analysts work independently, while others are employed by large research firms. Independent analysts might have a group of clients that pays for industry assessments and consulting services. Analysts at big firms do market research on companies and trends, and write reports that are shared with clients and the media. A number of analysts write columns and essays about the industry for high-tech publications.

Because analysts are expected to predict sales upturns and downturns, they must have a broad understanding of the markets, the players, and their strategies. If an analyst makes too many bad calls, the phone stops ringing. No one wants to pay for bad advice.

salary: An independent analyst can make anywhere from $200 to several thousand dollars a day. Often, analysts are paid for just a few days of work a month. Some receive retainers to provide full-time consulting services. Junior analysts working at research firms can expect to start at about $34,000 annually, while experienced analysts can earn over $100,000 a year.

prospects: The booming high-tech industry has created a strong demand for industry analysis. Most chief executives wouldn't dream of making a decision regarding the direction of their company without consulting market reports.

qualifications: Anyone can become an industry analyst; it requires no particular schooling or certification. Most analysts, however, spend at least a few years working in the high-tech industry, either in the technical end or in marketing. But such strong demand has led many large firms to hire more recent college graduates.

characteristics: You can't be afraid of risks, because every time you issue a report or comment to a journalist, you're taking one. You'll be making a lot of presentations and dealing with the media, so you've got to be able to think on your feet.

Sam Albert *is an industry analyst in Scarsdale, New York.*

How did you get the job?

Sam Albert always wanted to be a radio announcer, but instead majored in math at the American University in Washington, D.C. "My mother and father said, 'You can be a doctor or a lawyer, or you can be a bum.'" He didn't become either a doctor or a lawyer, but he did end up with a job that received his parents' blessing: selling computers for IBM to retailers like Tiffany's.

He eventually was put in charge of all sales consultants at IBM's headquarters. After 30 years with the company, Albert was offered a buyout package. He decided to try to leverage his experience working inside one of the leading high-tech companies in the world by becoming an independent analyst. "I used my contacts in the industry to become a commentator on the industry," he says.

Sam set up shop in his home, launched Sam Albert Associates, and set out looking for clients. "I knew I could pontificate about the industry, but I wasn't sure anyone would pay me for it," he says.

It turns out finding paying clients wasn't a problem. He quickly developed a list of customers and became a popular source for industry reporters as an expert on Big Blue.

> MANY DATA RESEARCH FIRMS HIRE RESEARCHERS OR INTERNS. THESE POSITIONS CAN PROVE TO BE GOOD STARTING POINTS FOR GAINING EXPERIENCE IN THE FIELD.

What do you do all day?

Much of Sam's day is spent meeting with clients, which include a range of high-tech businesses, to discuss how their business stacks up against the industry. "They want to know where they fit in, what everyone else is doing, and what they should be doing," he says.

His days are also sprinkled with calls from reporters who want his opinion on a new product or on a news development. If IBM has a major announcement, Sam dials into the company's telephone conference for analysts. During the conference, IBM officials explain what the announcement—be it a new alliance or a round of layoffs—means to the company. He then spends the rest of the day answering calls from reporters who want his take on things.

One reason he gets press calls is his ability to translate jargon into something meaningful.

"Reporters call me because they feel that I'm able to put things into laymen's terms," he says.

Sam spends some time attending trade shows around the country to keep up to date on the latest trends.

He also recently took a step toward fulfilling his dream of becoming a radio announcer. Sam is providing listeners with computer tips on a radio station in New York.

Although he loves working as an independent analyst, the job is not without pressures. "The downside is not knowing where your next source of revenue is going to come from," he says. "You can never be sure."

Where do you see this job leading you?

Sam wants to continue to build his business, and he's also hoping to syndicate his radio program. "My goal," he says, "is to become the Walter Cronkite of computerdom."

45. High-Tech Sales and Marketing Consultant

description: A consultant's job involves advising major computer and software makers and resellers on the best way to boost sales, enter a new market, or introduce a new product.

A consultant might help a business hire a sales force or develop pricing grids. If a company that makes computer monitors wants to break into the retail market, a consultant would introduce the manufacturer to retailers and create a strategy for getting the product into stores.

To come up with a plan of attack, consultants conduct in-depth market surveys, set up focus group meetings, and produce detailed reports that include data on geographic breakdowns, demographics, and industry trends.

Consultants are responsible for making the pitch to potential clients, and spend a lot of time making presentations to sometimes skeptical corporate executives.

Consultants often work on five or six projects simultaneously, which creates hectic days, long hours, and a lot of juggling.

salary: A talented M.B.A. can earn $80,000 to $120,000 a year, and experienced consultants can earn significantly more. Consulting jobs usually require at least five years of business experience with a knowledge of sales, marketing, and research.

prospects: Consulting is a competitive industry, and it has become even more so, thanks to a wave of layoffs in corporate marketing and finance departments. A lot of those people have started their own businesses, which has intensified the competition for corporate clients.

qualifications: While there are entry-level jobs available for those with bachelor's degrees, M.B.A.s will have an easier time finding consulting positions. You need to be computer savvy and know how to use graphics programs to create reports and presentations. Presentation skills are extremely important because it's up to you to convince a corporation's top people to accept your marketing strategy.

characteristics: You have to be assertive but patient. Because you are often working with clients who think they know more about the industry than you do, if you are making the recommendations it can become a battle of wills, something that should be avoided if you are trying to make a sale.

Merridee Matson *is the vice president at a high-tech sales and marketing consulting firm in Dallas.*

How did you get the job?

"After graduating from college, I went into teaching, but I only lasted two years because I didn't like the salary," Merridee says. The aerospace industry caught her eye, and she went back to school to earn a master's degree in aeronautics.

Merridee got her first real business training as an editor for *Aviation Space Magazine.* "I was right there in the middle of things, and I got to see how a business works from all sides," she says. From there, Merridee jumped into the computer business. She worked for a couple of major electronics companies, where she gained a wide range of experience overseeing corporate accounts and handling sales and marketing.

Then she decided it was time for a change. "I wanted a different lifestyle, one that enhanced my career as opposed to enhancing everybody else's career," Merridee says. "I didn't

> JOIN THE AMERICAN MANAGEMENT ASSOCIATION, WHICH OFFERS A NUMBER OF TRAINING WORKSHOPS AND CLASSES.
> (SEE RESOURCES, PAGE 212).

want to manage anyone but myself."

That decision led her to become an industry consultant, and she joined a fast-growing firm in Dallas.

What do you do all day?

"One hundred percent of our work is through referrals, so I'm constantly on the phone talking to people," she says. "I'm selling every day."

When she finds a potential client, she meets with them to get an understanding of what the company wants to do and how it can best accomplish it. "You have to take a look at their entire business and assess what's going on there very quickly," Merridee explains.

Right now, Merridee is consulting for a company in the computer industry that wants to break into telecommunications. "They don't know anything about it, so we're going there to study their whole operation," she says. "They want to know everything from what the market's like, to who does distribution, to how they're positioned to make the move."

In order to advise clients, Merridee has to stay on top of changes in the computer industry. That can include anything from overseeing surveys of computer store shoppers, to doing market studies on how a particular segment of consumers might react to a new product.

She is frequently called on by the computer trade press to offer her take on industry trends and the performance of products and companies.

Project schedules are unpre-

dictable, and so are the hours. Last week Merridee worked on three marketing proposals, finished up a company newsletter, and put together a yearlong strategy to help a client break into retail.

In such a competitive business, even long-term clients are never guaranteed. Merridee's company recently watched as a company they had worked with for 18 months put a project up for a competitive bid. "They chose us again, but it's a reminder that anything can happen."

Where do you see this job leading you?

"I view this as one of my final jobs, because I want to go off and do other things for myself," Merridee says. Many consultants end up joining their clients' companies. "If you're on your own, you can't be sure of your salary or benefits," she says. "A lot of people prefer to settle in with a major company."

46. High-Tech Trade Association Director

description: Trade associations organize seminars and conferences and help companies network and break into foreign markets. There are hundreds of trade associations representing various high-tech industries.

A trade association director is that organization's version of a chief executive officer. The job involves recruiting new members, as well as working with existing members to match them with potential business partners and to educate them about trends in the industry.

Directors oversee industry and membership surveys, which members use to make strategic decisions.

Directors are also responsible for managing the association's budget, which is usually funded by member dues.

In addition, directors follow legislative issues facing the industry and see that their companies' interests are being represented by lobbyists on Capitol Hill.

salary: A director of a small association would probably start out in the $25,000 range. At medium-size associations, directors can earn $50,000 to $80,000 a year, while directors of the largest associations can earn up to $175,000.

prospects: As the high-tech industry grows, so do the number of trade associations representing its members. A large number of trade groups have sprung up in the past few years to work with emerging high-tech industries. Breaking into this field can be easier than getting into some tech-related fields because a technical background is not usually necessary.

qualifications: A bachelor's degree is usually required, but because people with wide-ranging backgrounds come to work for trade associations, your major isn't all that important. Although you don't need technical skills, it is helpful to have an understanding of the high-tech industry, as well as politics and public policy.

characteristics: This is a very social job, so you have to enjoy working with people and feel comfortable speaking in public. You will be meeting with members, speaking at conferences, recruiting companies, and attending countless fund-raisers and banquets.

Joyce Plotkin *is executive director of the Massachusetts Software Council, based in Boston.*

How did you get the job?

Joyce Plotkin earned a degree in radio and television from Ohio University. She worked for a year in a television station newsroom before joining Blue Cross/Blue Shield in Massachusetts, where she handled community relations for the chief executive officer.

Joyce's first job at a trade association was as a staff member of the New England Council, which represents New England businesses on economic issues. After five years, she took a year off to work on a special project for then–Governor Michael Dukakis. While working on the project, which involved reporting on what companies were doing in terms of innovation, she met a couple of people involved with the Massachusetts Software Council. "They were looking for someone to start and run the organization," she says. "I had worked at a trade association, so I had a feel for it. I knew I was the right person for the job."

Joyce wasn't worried about her lack of technical expertise. "That didn't worry me, because I knew I could catch up with the issues," she says. "But every new job is a risk, and this was a risk in that I'd never run an organization before. I knew if I could do a good job, it would open up lots of opportunities."

What do you do all day?

Most days begin with a breakfast meeting, either involving the software council or one of the numerous civic organizations Joyce is involved in. She then usually makes some phone calls to recruit speakers for an upcoming event, holds a staff meeting to discuss the next few weeks' agenda, and answers some messages from other software associations from around the country. Then she holes up in her office to do a final read on the council's latest research project.

After lunch, Joyce often skips out to visit a company that has just joined the software council. "I don't call on all of them, but I do pay personal visits to some of the larger ones," she says. "It's a good investment of my time to introduce myself and meet their contact people." When she returns, voice mail messages await her with questions from a couple of newspaper reporters.

A typical evening might end with a reception thrown by the high-tech division of a local bank. "This is where I meet people and reinforce contact with our members," she says.

> THERE ARE TRADE ASSOCIATIONS FOR SEEMINGLY EVERY HIGH-TECH INDUSTRY. TRADE ASSOCIATION OFFICIALS RECOMMEND DECIDING WHICH FIELD YOU'RE INTERESTED IN AND THEN ASKING A COMPANY DOING THAT TYPE OF WORK WHAT TRADE ASSOCIATIONS EXIST AND HOW TO REACH THEM.

As the single parent of a nine-year-old son, Joyce involves her child in evening events when she can. He has met both the governor of Massachusetts and Senator Ted Kennedy.

Where do you see this job leading you?

Joyce plans to stay where she is. "We're helping software companies meet investors, learn to market their products, and begin to grow," she says. "That's a very satisfying way to spend the day."

Some trade association directors move on to bigger associations or higher-level jobs within the association. Others have gone on to work in government.

47. High-Tech Trade Show Organizer

description: Organizing a trade show for the computer industry is sort of like putting on a high-tech version of the Olympics. Selling exhibit space and handling promotions and registration are just part of what goes on behind the scenes. Organizers are also in charge of scheduling workshops that address topics pertinent to the industry and finding gurus on those subjects to be speakers. There is also convention space and hotel rooms to book and receptions to plan.

When the event begins, you've got to deal with everything from setting up booths, to working with contractors, security people, and exhibitors. The hours can be long and inflexible, especially right before, during, and after the show. But rewards come from helping businesses find new trade partners, educating company officials on issues facing the industry, and promoting U.S. products to new markets abroad.

Some high-tech trade groups have a full-time staff that oversees trade shows. Others contract companies that specialize in planning trade shows.

salary: An entry-level position such as a staff assistant starts out in the low $20,000 range. Experienced organizers who oversee key parts of a show earn $40,000 to $50,000, and organizers of major industry shows earn well over $100,000 a year.

prospects: The emergence of new computer industries in the past five years has resulted in a major rise in the number of industry trade shows. Many industries are also increasing the number of shows they hold and expanding them to other countries in an effort to boost international market share. The end result is an increasing demand for people to plan and execute trade shows.

qualifications: A college degree is generally required, though the area of study isn't usually important. It helps to have a couple of years experience in sales, marketing, or event planning, but many organizations are willing to train otherwise promising job candidates.

characteristics: Because you'll be acting as an ambassador of a trade group, you need to be comfortable conversing with company officials and guest speakers. You also have to be able to remain cool under pressure.

Margaret Cassilly *is director of international programs for a trade association in Arlington, Virginia.*

How did you get the job?

Margaret Cassilly started as a meeting planner at the Electronic Industries Association. When she heard about an opening in trade show planning, she applied. Her experience planning day-long conferences had given her the experience needed to organize weeklong trade shows, and she got the job.

Although she works for a consumer electronics trade group, she admits that she is not techno-savvy. "I'm a pretty embarrassing example of technology usage. I own a television and a juicer," she says.

It is Margaret's language abilities that have helped her excel. She has used her skills—she speaks German, French, and Italian fluently, and is studying Spanish—to carve her own niche. "I felt customer service in the international arena was nonexistent, so I started taking that on," she says. She focused on helping foreign delegations get visas, establishing international phone banks at conferences, and adding translators to help them communicate with exhibitors and participate in seminars.

> **FOR MORE INFORMATION ON TRADE SHOW ORGANIZATION, CONTACT THE INTERNATIONAL ASSOCIATION OF EXPOSITION MANAGEMENT. (SEE RESOURCES, PAGE 212).**

Her attention to international delegates paid off. Margaret now oversees the international aspects of five annual trade shows, including recruiting international buyers to attend the shows and helping arrange their visits. She just completed her second trade show in Mexico City and has helped coordinate the United States pavilion at a trade show in Germany. This year, she will work at trade shows in Las Vegas and Orlando and will travel to London to promote her trade group's shows to international attendees.

What do you do all day?

"It takes a good 18 months to plan a show without losing your hair," she says. "We've got dates secured through the year 2005, and we're already working on shows that will take place in two to three years."

A recent day started out with two calls to exhibitors in Germany, one call to France, and another to Laredo, Texas, where Margaret's freight from a Mexico City show is stuck at customs. After a 10 A.M. budget meeting with her staff, Margaret finished a letter to manufacturers and retailers about the Mexico show. Then she paid some invoices.

Next, she responded to a request from a publication in Argentina that wants to run ads in exchange for a booth at an upcoming show in Las Vegas. She also touched base with organizers from other trade groups. "We share how-to information with each other all the time," she says.

When a show approaches, it is all-consuming. Margaret arrives in town early to work out last-minute details and troubleshoot. "One minute I'll be carting around crates and making photocopies, and the next minute I'm schmoozing with the board at a reception for international companies." Nothing compares to the feeling she gets right before the show opens. "When it's completely quiet, and the lights are on the booths, and all the products are set up, it's like Christmas morning," she says.

During the show, Margaret frequently touches base with foreign delegations to make sure everything is going well. "Some delegations hit the ground running, while there are others you need to meet and bow and shake their hands, and walk them through everything step by step."

When it's all over, she heads back to Arlington, where she starts planning the next trade show.

Where do you see this job leading you?

Margaret plans to continue organizing trade shows. "I love working behind the scenes and accomplishing things in the international arena," she says. And she likes the fact that her work is making a difference. "What's important to me is helping small and medium-size American companies have more access to the global economy."

48. Independent Engineering Consultant

description: A lot of companies need an engineer with specialized skills from time to time to help them with a particular aspect of their business. But that doesn't mean they want to put that person on the payroll full-time. Enter the independent engineering consultant.

An independent engineer works on an as-needed basis, and is paid either on an hourly or a contract basis. An engineer with expertise in electrical design might spend a few days or a few months working with a manufacturer to revamp its production process. Some companies bring in engineering consultants to find changes they can make to cut costs.

Working on your own gives you the freedom to pick and choose your projects and decide what hours to keep, as opposed to a full-time engineer, who is expected to take on whatever assignment is parceled out.

But you also have to find those projects, and that involves skills in promoting yourself. You also forgo company benefits, and are responsible for your own health insurance, office space, and overhead.

salary: Independent consultants generally earn more than their salaried counterparts. Most engineers working on their own expect to make $50,000 to $100,000 a year in their first or second year of business. Pay varies widely, depending on how much work the consultant takes on and their level of expertise. Companies are willing to pay top dollar for specialized skills.

prospects: The use of contract labor is a fast-growing practice, with companies opting to bring in experts when needed rather than hire them full-time. That has made this a very promising field with a lot of opportunities for talented engineers with the right skills.

qualifications: Companies that hire contractors are looking for expertise they can't get from their staff engineers. So to work independently, you will need to have specialized skills that set you apart. You will also need a strong track record—typically, at least five years of experience working for a reputable company.

characteristics: You have to be able to sell yourself and your skills. And, because there's never a guaranteed paycheck, you'll have to be willing to live with instability in both your income and your work schedule.

Eric Gilbert *is an engineering consultant in San Diego, California.*

How did you get the job?

When Eric Gilbert graduated from California Polytechnic State University in San Luis Obispo, California, he decided it was time to see a little of the world. "I had worked really hard all through college, and I wanted to take a little time off," he says. Eric bought a one-way ticket to Japan and spent the next three months traveling through Japan, Hong Kong, and Thailand. Along the way, he taught English part-time and stayed with families he met through friends.

When he got back, he took an engineering job with a company that makes electronics for the semiconductor industry in San Diego. He did production support work and designed equipment used for manufacturing. It wasn't a dream job. "There weren't a lot of challenges, and I didn't feel I was making any headway," he says.

After a year and a half, Eric moved on to another electronics equipment company where he designed power supply products and took them into production. "There was a lot of work and no recognition," he says. "I was doing it because I really liked the work itself, but after a while, I stopped liking any of it." After five years, he decided he didn't want to spend his life working for a company that didn't treat its employees very well.

Eric had always had entrepreneurial leanings—in college he and a friend had a business selling power supply equipment to other students—and he began contemplating breaking out on his own. "I was really thinking about starting my own business, but I was having a hard time finding a business I could do on my own."

As he was debating what to do, he got a call from some friends he had met in Japan. They were starting a business selling replacement parts to the semiconductor manufacturing industry, and they needed a U.S. representative. "Here was an opportunity to step out on my own with a source of steady income while I developed a business as a consultant," he says.

Eric quit his job to take this new one. "It was a huge step, but having the part-time income made it possible to make the transition."

What do you do all day?

In addition to working for the Japanese company—which requires three trips to Japan a year—Eric is working for several companies as an engineering consultant specializing in power supply equipment.

He has an office at home, but he spends a lot of time with his clients. Eric studies their manufacturing processes, works with their equipment, and talks to manufacturing employees about their work. Then he goes home, analyzes the procedures, and decides what could be done differently.

Eric also devotes time to following up on work leads. "Other consultants have told me to plan on working hard at building a client list for at least three years," he says.

Where do you see this job leading you?

Eric likes working for himself and wants to keep growing his business. "I don't see the Japan work as being there forever; it's more of a launching board for other opportunities," he says. In addition to engineering consulting, he is exploring high-tech exports.

> MANY CONSULTANTS ESTABLISH STRONG RELATIONSHIPS WITH THEIR CLIENTS AND THEN TRY TO TAKE THEIR BUSINESS WITH THEM WHEN THEY SET OUT ON THEIR OWN. BEFORE QUITTING YOUR COMPANY JOB, YOU MAY WANT TO CONSIDER HEALTH INSURANCE AND TAX ISSUES— BURDENS YOU WILL BEAR ALONE AS AN INDEPENDENT CONSULTANT.

49. Independent Software Tools Developer

description: Most software writers who work for a company pound out line after line of code that ultimately becomes a software application or a tool that helps other developers write programs. For an independent developer, the goal is the same, but the process is very different.

While a corporate software developer works on an assigned project, an independent developer is more of an inventor. Independent developers dream up a program or a software tool, spend months developing it, and then pitch the idea to a company. If the software company bites, the developer completes the program, turns it over to the company, and earns royalties based on sales.

But it's rarely that simple. More often than not, a developer devotes months to a project only to watch as every company he or she approaches gives a thumbs-down. The end result is that the project gets shelved, and it's back to the old drawing board.

For independent developers, though, the advantages outweigh the downside. You can live where you want, pursue the ideas that interest you, and have more control over a project than most programmers. And you get to see the project through from start to finish.

salary: Pay is unpredictable because it's based on royalties. If you license a product to a company for 15 percent of sales, you might make $100,000. But going six to nine months without any royalties is also common. Many independent developers supplement their income by doing hourly contract programming.

prospects: High-tech companies are increasingly turning to outside developers to cut the costs that come with in-house projects. That's creating more opportunities for independent developers.

qualifications: Because you are working for yourself—at least during the early product development stage—it is novel ideas and the ability to follow through on them that count. Most people in this field have spent years working as software developers for companies before going solo. Veterans caution that it's a hard industry to break into without solid programming experience and a knowledge of the segment you're developing for.

characteristics: You have to be self-disciplined and self-motivated. There's no guaranteed paycheck, so you must be willing to assume a certain level of risk.

Bob England *is an independent software tools developer in Elliott, Iowa.*

How did you get the job?

After earning bachelor's and master's degrees in trumpet performance from the University of Iowa and playing with orchestras in eastern Iowa, Bob England decided that music was better as a hobby than as a profession.

While in grad school, he became interested in computers. "I taught myself how to program and decided I wanted to get a programming job," he says.

He did—becoming an applications developer at a small software company in Omaha, Nebraska. After two years, Bob went to work at another software company where he created software tools to help programmers develop graphical user interfaces.

"That company was bought out, so I left and went into a joint venture with another company to market products," Bob says.

Along the way, he realized he didn't need a partner to develop and market the tools. Five years ago, Bob struck out on his own.

The hardest part of the transition was getting used to not having a guaranteed income. "It really helps to have an understanding spouse," he says.

The arrangement has paid off. Bob walks three blocks from his house to his office in the 400-person town of Elliott. "I'm living and working where I want to," he says. "We have maybe one crime a year, and it takes me two minutes to get to work. When I get to the office I get on the information superhighway and work with the latest technologies."

And working on his own suits Bob. "I find it easier to work with someone over the telephone and modem than I did working in the same building."

What do you do all day?

Bob spends his time either developing software tools for a client, or thinking up what his next idea will be.

> TO SELL YOURSELF AND YOUR IDEAS TO A COMPANY, TALK WITH THE PERSON LEADING THE COMPANY'S SOFTWARE DEVELOPMENT, AND SEE WHAT THEIR NEEDS ARE, AND HOW YOU MIGHT BE ABLE TO CONTRIBUTE.

Companies want to see more than his ideas, though, so Bob has to develop them before he can pitch them. "Unless you have something complete to present, they're not going to believe you," he says.

Even as he's working, he knows the odds that a company will license his product are against him.

A year ago, he brought 10 ideas to a software company, and they said that wasn't the direction they wanted to take. "I'd invested hundreds, if not thousands, of hours on these ideas," he says. "I have a big cabinet full of products that will never go anywhere because

there's no demand."

If he's working on a licensed product, he might spend the day communicating by phone and e-mail with the company's developers, product testers, and marketing people.

When he's working on developing a new idea, he'll spend his time exploring different possibilities to see where they lead.

In between, he has time to serve as the mayor of Elliott. "I can work when I want to and make time for the things that are important to me."

Where do you see this job leading you?

Bob would like to enlarge his company by hiring a few programmers. Others in this field have gone on to work for their clients on a permanent basis. But that's not for Bob. "It would be hard to go back to a company now that I'm used to doing whatever I want," he says.

50. Interactive Advertising Creative Director

description: With the advent of cyberspace came the birth of a new medium in advertising. Traditionally, advertising firms have focused on broadcast and print media as a way to deliver messages to the public, but recently more and more firms have turned their attention toward new media such as the Internet.

Many firms are now seeking people who are knowledgeable in both advertising and in formulating Web sites. Although the focus of jobs in interactive advertising remains on advertising, the nature of the Internet is intrinsically different from more conventional media. For example, once an ad is printed or broadcast, there is no changing it. However, a Web site is forever evolving in order to keep up with its surroundings and to hold the interest of the consumer. Working in interactive advertising requires both the ability to come up with innovative ideas in an environment where no standards have been set, and an interest and knowledge of this new technology. While there are various jobs in interactive advertising in the areas of production and design, someone in a management role, such as the creative director, is most likely to be involved in all aspects of this new field.

salary: The salary for the job of a creative director of interactive advertising will most likely depend on the size of the advertising firm, and could range from $45,000 to $100,000 a year.

prospects: In 1995, it was estimated that 20 to 30 million computer users frequented the Internet, and with the World Wide Web's approximated annual growth rate of 341,000 percent, growth in this industry doesn't seem to be slowing down. The job market should reflect this.

qualifications: Although working in interactive advertising requires a knowledge of computers, it is not necessary that you have a degree in computer science. In fact, a bachelor's degree that is comprised of liberal arts course work, coupled with experience in HTML programming, would be preferable.

characteristics: People working in this field are generally the type who loathe to accept conventional wisdom; their creative side just won't allow it. On the whole, they have an interest in technology and are excited about the new opportunities it offers.

Jake Prescott *is the creative director of interactive advertising for an advertising firm in New York City.*

How did you get the job?

Jake Prescott received his bachelor's degree in art and literature and then went on to work in a variety of jobs, ranging from an associate producer at a cable television network to a cab driver in New York City, before he finally came across a job on which he could begin to launch his career. Working as the marketing communications manager at an electronic publishing systems company, Jake was able to develop a knowledge of technology, as well as build on his skills as a writer. From here, he went on to work as a marketing consultant, more or less freelancing his skills. He received work from various advertising agencies, publishing houses, and a photo agency. Eventually, he received an offer to work with a major advertising firm in New York City as the creative technology director, a position in which he was a pioneer.

"I was hired to do this job, which was somewhat defined, but not completely. It had to do with making technology work in the creative process," Jake recalls. "The whole notion of 'creative' and 'technology' is

> FOR SOMEONE WANTING TO BREAK INTO THIS BUSINESS, THE INTERNET MAY BE YOUR BEST RESOURCE. YOU COULD START BY CONDUCTING A SEARCH OF ADVERTISING COMPANIES USING THE SEARCH ENGINE YAHOO AT HTTP://WWW.YAHOO.COM. ONCE YOU HAVE FOUND AN AGENCY IN WHICH YOU ARE INTERESTED, YOU CAN USE ITS E-MAIL ADDRESS TO INQUIRE ABOUT EMPLOYMENT OPPORTUNITIES.

almost an oxymoron, because technology is very disciplined, and creative is kind of chaotic by nature, but I had done a lot of thinking about these issues. I am a creative person by nature, and I've been intensely involved with both the using and selling of technology."

As the creative technology director, Jake worked closely with both the creative department and the management information systems departments at the agency to determine what type of technology should be purchased by the company and used within the creative department. "By and large, I was riding a wave which was bringing PCs and networks into a creative environment," Jake says.

After four years, the wave Jake was riding seemed to crest with the commercial growth on the Internet and the advertising agency's acquisition of a prominent client. This is when Jake's duties began to focus more on the Internet as a medium for advertising, and he was promoted to his current position of creative director of interactive advertising.

What do you do all day?

Working in such a new area of technology, Jake says his job is constantly evolving. He describes his job as for the most part creative.

"In planning any product in any medium, it's a creative process. It's defining who the audience you're reaching is and

designing communications that are going to reach that audience for an effective result. So there's a lot of analytical work to it. It is very definitely done with a team."

Beyond this, Jake says a lot of the creativity comes in with the development of ideas for Web pages. Initially, this had involved replicating television and print media advertisements onto the Internet, but there has been a shift of late that involves using original ideas for events on the World Wide Web that will be sponsored by an advertising client. Because Jake works in a managerial role, his job also involves making sure that projects are completed on schedule and within budget, as well as interacting with clients to make sure that they are pleased with the work being done.

Where do you see this job leading you?

Jake said he plans to keep on riding the wave to see where it takes him. "It's been quite a ride," he says. "I can tell you that I'm doing what I always did, which is sort of make it up as you go."

51. Internet Access Provider

description: An Internet access provider acts as a bridge between the customer's computer and cyberspace. Providers charge a monthly fee to connect users to the Internet and furnish them with special software to link their computers to the provider's system. The customer's computer dials into the system, and is catapulted onto the information superhighway. In addition to linking users to the Internet, some providers sell services such as news and forums for people to discuss hobbies.

Providers have to maintain their computer networks 24 hours a day, and many are on call around the clock.

Because the technology changes so fast, Internet providers see themselves as cyberpioneers. But if being on the cutting edge is exciting, it is also unpredictable. Most metropolitan areas have more than one access provider, and in many cities that has led to price wars. And with giants like Microsoft offering Internet service, competition is becoming even stiffer.

salary: An owner or partner can earn anywhere from nothing to more than $100,000 a year, depending on the size and state of the business. The owners of smaller providers usually run everything themselves. Larger companies sometimes employ systems administrators to oversee the computers. Administrators' salaries range from $25,000 to $80,000, depending on experience.

prospects: Starting an Internet access firm is relatively simple, and many businesses are only two- or three-person shops. It takes computer savvy and $10,000 to $100,000, depending on the size of the operation. With more people going on-line every day, the market is exploding.

qualifications: This is a business where no one cares what you majored in, or if you have a degree at all. What counts is computer skills, such as programming, piecing computer systems together, and troubleshooting.

characteristics: In addition to being a techie, you'll need to be able to work well with customers. Patience is very important, as is the ability to remain calm when the system crashes and irate customers are calling to scream at you because they can't get onto the Internet.

Bruce Waldack *owns an Internet access and on-line services company in Alexandria, Virginia.*

How did you get the job?

Bruce Waldock's entrepreneurial spirit surfaced at a young age when he organized a group of neighborhood kids to mow lawns. "They wanted to mow, but they didn't want to deal with the business end," he says. "I did the marketing, sold the jobs, and collected the money, and they did the mowing. We split the profits 50-50."

His college career was cut short when, as a sophomore at Washington University in St. Louis, Missouri, he invested his tuition money in the stock market and lost it all. For Bruce, the loss was an opportunity to get into the job market. "There are some people who go to college just to please their parents, and they don't learn a thing," he says. "I didn't want to do that. I was ready to move on." He took a job as a salesperson at a computer chain store in Alexandria,

Virginia. Within a year he was running the place as operations manager, and eventually he was overseeing all the stores.

After a few years, Bruce had had enough. "I realized I was doing all of the work, and my boss was relaxing at the lake and making all the money," he says. "I decided to go out on my own." He started a consulting firm that specialized in helping businesses move to desktop publishing, which was just beginning to take hold. He sold that business when he saw a new business opportunity: the Internet. His company, which now has 26 employees, sells Internet access and other on-line services.

What do you do all day?

Bruce spends a lot of his time overseeing the computer system that links customers to the Internet. "I'm the firefighter who's constantly putting out problems," he says. "If a technician makes a change that affects

a customer in New York, I have to find the best way to get everything back up and running."

He also works with businesses to figure out the best way to get them on-line. He recently helped get a tire factory in the Brazilian jungle onto the Internet.

> **MOST MIDSIZE TOWNS HAVE AT LEAST ONE LOCAL INTERNET ACCESS PROVIDER. CONSIDER TAKING AN ENTRY-LEVEL POSITION, SUCH AS ANSWERING CALLS OR PROVIDING TECHNICAL SUPPORT. YOU WILL LEARN WHAT IT TAKES TO RUN AN INTERNET SERVICE AND MAY MEET SOMEONE WHO ALSO WANTS TO START ONE.**

In addition to the day-to-day chores of keeping the services up and running, Bruce focuses on long-range planning. "In this industry, you can have a way of doing something, and two weeks later that's dead and it's something new," he says. "I have to always be looking forward and anticipating the next trend."

Marketing the company is another big responsibility. Right now Bruce is working with a team to create 30-second advertisements that will run on CNN and MTV.

Where do you see this job leading you?

"I'm always looking for the next big thing," Bruce says. If another opportunity came along, he would consider selling the Internet business. He also hasn't ruled out taking the business public before selling out.

52. Internet and World Wide Web Page Designer

description: A lot of businesses are thinking about putting an electric storefront on the portion of the Internet known as the World Wide Web. Problem is, they don't know where to start. Enter the Internet Web page designer.

A Web page designer helps businesses ranging from florists to yacht-makers design a "shingle," or "home page," on the Web. As a Web page designer, you'll help decide how the site should look and what information it should provide, and how that information should be organized. You'll then help write text, scan photos, build graphics, and create the underlying software code to run the program.

In addition to creating the site, some Web page designers maintain the site on the Internet for a monthly fee.

While Web page designers might prefer to spend their time creating cool, cutting-edge sites, most, especially those working for tiny start-ups, are also responsible for finding new clients. That can mean doing mailings, making cold calls, and doing a lot of demos for skeptical business owners. Convincing the uninitiated to spend their advertising dollars in cyberspace isn't easy.

salary: A Web page designer at a small Internet marketing firm could start at $30,000 a year. Many designers work independently or with a partner, and profits can range anywhere from a few thousand dollars to $100,000, depending on the clients.

prospects: The explosion of companies jumping on the Internet is creating a huge market for consultants. Most Web design houses are very small, and hire few salaried employees. But this is a relatively easy business to start on your own. Many in this business start by designing Web sites on their own, part time.

qualifications: Web page design requires creativity and graphic design talent, as well as the technical skills to write software code and maintain the computer system that stores the information. Most Web sites contain a lot of text, so good writing skills are also important.

characteristics: In this field, being patient is more than a virtue, it's the only way to stay sane. Many businesses are still very dubious about the Internet's potential, and you've got to convince them of the advantages of getting wired. With some clients you'll face a steep learning curve. If they've never been on the Internet before, you're going to have to take them there.

Sara Riley *is a partner at an Internet consulting firm in Coconut Grove, Florida.*

How did you get the job?

After graduating from law school at the Widener University School of Law, Sara Riley took a job as an attorney at a firm in Miami. "I loved the law firm," she says, "but it wasn't what I wanted to do for the rest of my life."

Sara and her husband, Chris, a lawyer and a computer aficionado, began thinking about starting their own business specializing in Internet services. "We realized that the opportunity to be on the forefront of something like this comes along very rarely," she says. "And we thought we had the combination of skills to make a go at it."

In March, Sara and Chris quit their jobs (although Chris still does part-time computer consulting) and they invested about $30,000 in computer equipment. They set up shop in their home and began looking for clients to put on the Internet.

Working from home was a big adjustment. "You can't leave your work at the office. If the phone rings at 8 A.M. or 8 P.M., no matter what I'm doing, I'm at work," she says. There are advantages: "If you want to go in-line skating at 2 in the afternoon, you can." Such moments are rare, though. "I spend my free time making calls, looking for business," she says.

So far, Sara and Chris have designed Web sites for such customers as a stand-up comic, real estate agents, a soccer mail-order catalog, and a couple of resorts. "We do have some paying customers," Sara says, "but it's not enough to retire on."

What do you do all day?

A good part of Sara's time is spent showing businesses how a Web site could boost their sales.

Since she works from her home, Sara prefers to visit potential customers. "I take my color laptop computer to them and demonstrate what a Web site is all about."

It's often a tough sell. "Businesses are very cautious when it comes to making a move like this," she says. "And a lot of times they don't understand the medium."

Sara and Chris work together to design Web sites for new customers. Sara oversees the overall design, including writing the text, deciding what art to use, and, if needed, hiring a graphic designer. Chris does the software programming and manages the computer system.

Once the site is up and running, they maintain it on their computer system and update the information every few weeks.

Where do you see this job leading you?

Sara and Chris want to grow their business. Eventually, they would like to team up with an

> JOBS FOR INTERNET CONSULTANTS AND WEB DESIGNERS ARE OFTEN ADVERTISED IN THE NEWSPAPER. IN LARGER CITIES, CONTACT COMPANIES DIRECTLY AND INTRODUCE YOURSELF. EVEN IF THERE'S NO IMMEDIATE WORK, PROJECTS OFTEN ARISE, AND HOPEFULLY SO WILL YOUR NAME.

advertising agency to provide Web design services to the agency's customers. Being acquired by an agency is also a possibility. "Companies like us are going to end up having to affiliate with or be absorbed by advertising agencies," Sara says.

53. Internet Curriculum Specialist

description: Training teachers how to use the Internet in the classroom is becoming a full-time job. Many state governments and education departments are creating positions to help teachers make the most of the Internet and other high-tech resources. Although it is becoming increasingly important for students to be computer literate, if teachers aren't comfortable with technology, they can't educate their students.

Curriculum specialists help schools arrange Internet access, and work with administrators and teachers to develop classroom lessons that mix traditional and high-tech learning methods.

Organizing workshops and conferences for teachers is a big part of this job. Specialists also reach teachers by setting up on-line forums. Training lessons can be posted in the forums, and teachers can participate by posting questions as well as ideas.

In addition to training, Internet specialists also come up with projects in which schools can take part. At one school, students are exchanging e-mail with people bicycling through South America. At another, students are having discussions over the Internet with state representatives about issues that affect kids.

Introducing teachers and students to the world of the Internet can be very fulfilling. But funding tends to be touch-and-go, with these positions often completely dependent on state funding and grants. If the budget gets cut, so does the position.

salary: Pay depends on who is funding the position. Jobs funded by the state usually pay in the $30,000 to $40,000 range, depending on experience and responsibility.

prospects: Teaching kids how to use technology has become a priority for schools and state government. But this is still a very new field that is just beginning to take shape. The opportunities are increasing, but so is competition for the positions.

qualifications: A master's degree in education or liberal arts is preferred. Teaching experience is important, as is expertise in the Internet and computer networking. It also helps to be familiar with nonprofit organizations and grant writing, since you may end up applying for grants to continue funding your own job.

characteristics: You will be acting as a sort of high-tech evangelist, so you need to believe strongly in the importance of computer literacy. This job involves working with people who have never been around computers and may be scared to start learning, so patience and understanding are key.

Mick Souder *is an Internet curriculum specialist in St. Paul, Minnesota.*

How did you get the job?

Mick Souder was teaching math and science to junior high students on a Zuni reservation in New Mexico when he had his first encounter with a computer. He took a couple of computer programming classes and became involved in helping the school incorporate computers into its science programs. He was soon recruited to teach programming classes part-time at a community college.

Mick eventually returned to the Midwest and was hired by a college in St. Paul, Minnesota, to help develop a distance learning program. "The idea was to help women who couldn't get to campus earn degrees," he says. "We wanted to come up with a way they could learn at home." The program was a mixed success. "We built a network and made a lot of progress," he says. "But eventually our group got burned out."

> **LEARN WHAT'S AVAILABLE ON THE INTERNET IN THE AREA OF EDUCATION, AND VOLUNTEER FOR A NON-PROFIT GROUP TO GET EXPERIENCE WRITING GRANTS. SCHOOL DISTRICTS OFTEN POST OPENINGS FOR THESE JOBS.**

Mick was ready for a change, and one day he spotted an ad in the paper for a job that seemed written for him. The position, which was funded in part by the state and through grants, involved training teachers to use the Internet and developing school curriculum centered around technology. "Computer literacy and information literacy were things I had spent a lot of time thinking about. It seems like a lot of people are getting left behind, but I didn't know how to change that," he says. "Teachers seemed like a good place to start."

His combination of teaching skills and computer background made him the right man for the job. "It was a good match," he says. "It's hard to imagine a job I'd be better suited for."

What do you do all day?

Mick checks his e-mail when he wakes up at 6 A.M. to make sure there are no emergency messages from teachers or school administrators. When he gets into the office at 7:45 A.M. he checks it again, and spends about a half hour responding to various queries. Next, he logs onto the on-line help line, where he finds messages posted from teachers and superintendents from around the state. There is a question from a teacher about a new software program. Another wants to know more about an upcoming conference. He responds, and then moves on to configuring an Internet software program he is preparing to send to schools.

Mick spends a lot of time planning and conducting workshops about using the Internet in the classroom. He also works with teachers to develop cur-

riculums that enhance existing learning tools. If students are studying Africa, they can use the Internet to make contact with students there.

He is also invited to speak about Internet issues at various state and education organizations at luncheons, and at staff meetings. He most recently spoke to the county library system, which wanted general advice on connecting to and using the Internet. Mick also fields questions about issues such as pornography on the Internet, and what projects help students learn the most about technology.

Where do you see this job leading you?

"I have to think about what I'm going to do when the money runs out," Mick says. He loves working with educators, but there are no guarantees the job will continue to get state funding. If and when his position is eliminated, Mick will consider becoming a private Internet consultant.

54. Internet Electronic Storefront Operator

description: Everything from florists to travel agencies to T-shirt shops is popping up on the Information Superhighway, and many computer users are choosing to do their buying electronically. Internet users enter the stores, most of which are sites on the World Wide Web, by typing in the electronic address.

Opening a "virtual" business on the Internet is relatively easy and inexpensive—typically less than $15,000—compared with opening a real store. And although very few people have gotten rich selling products over the Internet, electronic commerce is catching on, and analysts predict that the number of cyberspace shoppers will increase sharply in the next year or two.

There's still enough uncertainty, however, to make launching a business over the Internet a risky venture. Even though millions of people use the Internet, the fact that there is no main directory makes it hard to spread the word about your store.

Still, Net surfers and industry analysts alike predict an explosion in Internet use, and it's a safe bet that where there are consumers, there is money to be made.

salary: A number of virtual stores claim to be doing hundreds of dollars a day in sales via the Net. But the majority of Internet storefronts have yet to become profitable.

prospects: More than 16 million people are estimated to be using the Internet. But while anyone can open a store on the Internet, few people will succeed in turning it into a full-time job. Experts recommend keeping your job for at least a year after launching an Internet business. If at that point you feel confident enough, you can quit your day job.

qualifications: Technical expertise, including some programming skills, is very helpful. While most Internet store owners pay an Internet access provider a monthly fee to maintain the store on the Net, you'll want to do design work on the site itself. You'll be constantly adding new information, updating old information, and improving graphics and sound, which requires basic HTML programming skills.

characteristics: Investing in a business that has yet to prove itself is risky, so you'll have to be willing to chance losing some money in the process. You also have to be flexible. Technology changes fast, and so do Net surfers' tastes, and you will have to adjust to that.

Charles Cox *owns a virtual mall in Decatur, Indiana, that offers books, toys, and jewelry.*

How did you get the job?

Charles Cox owns a heating and air-conditioning company, and has been self-employed for 13 years. He began contemplating the Internet after reading a magazine article about its growth. "You don't have to be a rocket scientist to figure out there is a whole lot of potential here," he says. He found a software programmer who shared his excitement about the Internet, and they began designing the mall.

He decided to offer things that people like to buy but don't necessarily make a trip to a shopping center to find. He and his programmer developed the mall and found an Internet access provider to put it on-line.

Charles estimates it cost about $10,000 to get the mall off the ground.

One of the major advantages of a virtual store versus a physical one is stock. "I didn't have to buy anything up front," Charles says. "The majority of products I can order when I get the order, and it goes out the same day." That means he didn't have to invest thousands of dollars in merchandise he can't be sure he'll sell. Arranging that setup wasn't easy. "It took a while to find warehouses that were willing to deal with sending an individual item," he says. "That took some negotiating."

What do you do all day?

Charles, who is taking a leave from his business as he gets the mall off the ground, is devoting much of his time to marketing.

> IMMERSE YOURSELF IN INTERNET TRADE MAGAZINES, WHICH ARE EXCELLENT RESOURCES FOR INFORMATION ON TRENDS AND WORLD WIDE WEB TECHNOLOGY ISSUES.

Getting word out on the mall, which opened very recently, is key. His efforts have included faxing announcements to 150 newspapers and magazines across the country, and speaking personally with dozens of reporters and editors.

In the short time it has been on-line, response has been good—the mall has received several orders for toys and jewelry.

When he's not marketing the site, Charles focuses on expanding his mall. A store that sells compact discs and CD-ROMs will be his next addition.

"The fun part about this is running a business and never having to leave your home," he says. "And this is a work in progress. As technology gets better, the store will keep changing."

Where do you see this job leading you?

Charles plans to continue building the mall and getting word out on its existence. "I think this is the future Sears, Roebuck," he says. "Ten years from now we expect to be a major player."

55. Investor Relations Specialist

FOR A HIGH-TECH COMPANY

description: Most high-tech companies that are publicly traded have investor relations departments. The investor relations team handles financial information, answers shareholders' questions, and works with financial analysts who cover the company. The stockmarket can be a roller-coaster ride for tech companies because any hiccup in the industry can send stocks shooting up or tumbling down.

Investor relations is responsible for releasing quarterly earnings reports. When the numbers are lower than expected, they arrange phone conferences so company officials can explain to industry analysts what happened. Public speaking is a big part of this job. Investor relations specialists field questions from analysts and reporters about their company's performance. Because any answer can have a major impact on the stock's value, the ability to choose your words carefully is extremely important.

Writing and publishing the annual report that goes out to all shareholders and arranging the company's annual shareholder's meeting are also a part of this job.

salary: For someone just out of school, pay usually starts in the upper $20,000 range. With a few years of experience, it increases to the mid-$30,000s. At the senior level, pay ranges from $50,000 to $60,000 a year.

prospects: A record number of high-tech companies have gone public in the last two years, and that has created a lot of new jobs in this area. Companies are realizing the important role investor relations plays in the movement of their stock and in their relations with investors. Still, even large companies usually have fewer than 10 people in investor relations. So even though there are more jobs, this remains a competitive field.

qualifications: People come to investor relations with a wide variety of backgrounds, ranging from business and marketing to computer science and journalism. Companies often prefer to hire someone who has had experience working with the public. A good understanding of how financial markets work and knowledge of the company's industry is helpful.

characteristics: People who excel in this field are not easily intimidated. They are good at thinking on their feet and are articulate. Because this job calls for setting up meetings and conferences, organizational skills are also important.

James Wharton *is director of investor relations at a computer manufacturer in North Sioux City, South Dakota.*

How did you get the job?

James Wharton got his degree in journalism and spent years in radio, both as a reporter and news director. He left journalism to run for mayor of Sioux City, Iowa. As mayor, he got to know the chief executive of a major computer maker in the area which supported various civic causes. When his term ended, James decided to inquire about work at the company. "I asked him flat out if there were any opportunities for me," he says. "He said, 'We're going to go public in two months. What would you think of being our investor relations department?'" James, who had always had an interest in the stock market and was a longtime investor, jumped at the chance.

James is the first to say he isn't a financial expert. "I frankly don't understand some of it," he says. But his ability to work well with shareholders and his firsthand knowledge of investing made him the right person for the job. "For me, a job involving the public and the stock market is the best of both worlds," he says.

> LEARN EVERYTHING YOU CAN ABOUT HOW PUBLIC COMPANIES OPERATE. THE WALL STREET JOURNAL IS AN EXCELLENT BUSINESS PRIMER, AND THERE ARE MANY GOOD REFERENCE BOOKS ABOUT HOW CORPORATIONS OPERATE. BE WILLING TO TAKE AN ENTRY-LEVEL JOB IN MARKETING OR PUBLIC RELATIONS IF YOU DON'T HAVE EXPERIENCE IN INVESTOR RELATIONS.

What do you do all day?

The first thing James does when he arrives at work at 7:30 A.M. is tap into an electronic service that pulls up notes from analysts and brokers around the world. If an analyst is down on the stock, he braces himself for a rocky day. Next he logs onto the Dow Jones news service to see if there are any stories about his company or its competitors. "Then you just try to ride out the day, knowing anything can happen."

When the stock market opens at 8:30 A.M., James keeps an eye on his company's and other high-tech companies' stock. "Anytime one company goes down, everyone else usually gets dragged down with it, at least temporarily," he says. "Most calls come from people who own 100 or 500 shares, and they panic when there's any fluctuation," he says. "We reassure them."

When the stock moves up and the calls taper off, James turns to organizing three upcoming analysts conferences in New York and San Francisco. Each conference involves a 25-minute presentation by the company officials and a 10-minute question-and-answer period. James, who logs about 60,000 travel miles a year, will accompany officials on the trips. Because public companies are governed by very strict Securities Exchange Commission regulations, he has to make sure that nothing comes out in the Q&A session that shouldn't. "If they say something you hadn't intended them to say, you've got to be ready to put out a press release to make it public record," he says.

James is also organizing visits to the company by the 15 financial analysts who cover it. That involves making hotel and dinner reservations and planning their daytime agendas.

At the end of the day, he touches base with accounting to check on when the company's quarterly earnings figures will be available for release. When they are, he will write the report that goes out to shareholders, analysts, and the press.

Where do you see this job leading you?

James thinks he might eventually like to move up the marketing ladder, which is often the track that many in investor relations take. "That's usually the common goal," he says. "But if I end up staying right here, that would be fine with me. This is fun, and that's what's important."

56. ISO 9000 Quality Auditor

description: ISO 9000 certification is sort of a *Good Housekeeping* seal of approval for industrial products. Demands from competition, regulators, and customers are convincing a growing number of companies to pursue ISO 9000 registration. Many of those companies are adding auditors to their staffs to oversee the registration process, which can take two years and cost tens of thousands of dollars. Once a company is certified, ISO auditors ensure that procedures are followed.

Basically, ISO 9000s are guidelines for documenting quality of the design, production, inspection, and testing of industrial products. But there's no checklist that tells companies what to do—each must define and put in writing how it achieves quality. An international board awards certification.

Auditors help companies through the process and then keep them on their toes. (Certification is withdrawn if a company grows lax and fails to follow quality procedures.) The job involves traveling to different plants and meeting with managers and employees to discuss how they do their jobs and to watch as they work. If particular procedures are not being followed, it's the auditor's job to bring it to the company's attention.

salary: Most auditors earn in the $35,000 to $45,000 range. Salaries vary greatly, depending on the size of the company and its location.

prospects: Quality certification is a fast-growing field. As global competition increases, more and more companies are pursuing it as a way to break into international markets. Increasingly, companies are hiring full-time staff to oversee the process. But the number of people being hired is still small; a company with 1,000 workers might have an ISO audit staff of five people.

qualifications: A number of colleges have begun offering quality engineering degrees, which employers like to see. But because this is a relatively new field, it's possible to break in without formal training. People have moved into quality certification from working in departments such as technical support, management, and internal auditing.

characteristics: This is a good job for people who like to set their own work schedules and operate independently. You have to have a good eye for detail and must be self-assured enough to take a stand if you discover mistakes being made.

Ben Redler *is a quality auditor for a desktop computer service company in Austin, Texas.*

How did you get the job?

Ben Redler started at the company as a service engineer, which involved repairing desktop computers both in-house and in the field. He made customer satisfaction a priority. "It comes from being a perfectionist," he says. "As I worked on various assignments, I didn't settle for anything less than excellent quality. It's always been a passion of mine." Whenever there was a choice of assignments, Ben migrated to the jobs that involved working closely with customers.

When the company began training employees on quality procedures, Ben was tapped to

FOR MORE INFORMATION ON ISO 9000, CONTACT THE AMERICAN SOCIETY FOR QUALITY CONTROL. (SEE RESOURCES, PAGE 212).

attend classes. "They looked around and said, 'We're going to send the person most dedicated to quality, and that's you,'" he says.

He went through extensive training, and when the company began going through the certification process, Ben was asked to oversee it as an ISO auditor.

What do you do all day?

Ben oversees internal audits all over the country, which means he's on the road a lot. When it's time for an audit, he calls or e-mails the plant to arrange a preaudit conference and ask for a guide to show him and his fellow auditors around.

He reviews process documentation before he gets into town so he's got an understanding of the work being done and the quality requirements. When he arrives, he meets with all the managers. Then he meets with workers and shadows them to see whether they are following the procedures outlined in the company's quality policy.

If workers aren't following the guidelines correctly, Ben reports it in the company database. The plant must then develop a plan to make sure they conform to the standards, which Ben reviews. That doesn't always win him friends.

"There is a certain stigma to being an auditor, and that can be a downer," he says. But the fact that he believes strongly in what he's doing is the reward. "I have always valued quality, and this is one way to make sure the whole company values it too."

Where do you see this job leading you?

Ben loves his job and plans to stay there. A number of internal quality auditors go on to work as consultants. Ben has given that idea some thought. "It would be nice," he says, "to work at your own discretion and pick and choose the jobs you want."

57. Local Area Network Specialist

description: Since the late 1980s, companies have been shifting from huge mainframe computer systems to local area networks, which are groups of computers and other devices connected together so they can pass information back and forth. Known as LANs, these networks are the nerve centers of many businesses. If the LAN goes down, work grinds to a halt and the company can kiss thousands—or even millions—of dollars goodbye. Because LANs play such a key role in companies, many have created support divisions that focus on keeping the networked machines humming. LAN specialists build networks by weaving together hundreds of computers and servers, printers, and fax machines in a way that lets them talk to each other. LAN specialists also support employees who use the network. That means upgrading software, giving new employees access to the network, and figuring out what went wrong when it all goes down.

salary: Annual salaries for newcomers start in the low- to mid-$20,000 range. Senior technicians with five to eight years of experience usually earn around $40,000 a year. Pay is based on experience, and the size of both the company and the local area network are determining factors.

prospects: With just about every part of a company's business tied to an LAN, companies are doubling and tripling the size of their LAN support teams. Companies report that they can't hire LAN specialists fast enough. Many companies are turning to high-tech recruitment for contract workers to fill the gap. Bottom line: If you have the skills, you should have no trouble finding a good job in LAN management.

qualifications: People come into this field with wide-ranging backgrounds. What counts here is knowledge of computer networking, and that doesn't necessarily require a college degree. Although this job does attract computer science grads, others learn while doing programming and systems support, and move into LANs after developing the right skill set.

characteristics: You have got to thrive in a fast-paced, high-pressure environment. You'll be on your own to figure out what went wrong and how to fix it, so you need to be good at troubleshooting and working independently. Often you won't have the luxury of a coworker off which to bounce ideas. It's just you and a piece of software you have never seen before. And for every minute you spend reviving the network, the company loses thousands of dollars.

Dan Reddy *is an LAN technician at a mutual fund management company in Menomonee Falls, Wisconsin.*

How did you get the job?

After studying computers and office systems at a technical college, Dan Reddy got a job repairing fax machines. Computers were his passion. "I was always toying around with computers, and I thought if somebody paid me to do this, it would be great," he says. That opportunity came through a job opening at a major mutual management company. Dan didn't have the exact skills the job required, but the company didn't mind. "They hire people based on their dedication, their drive, and their work ethic," he says. "They look for that in an interview, and base their decision on it." Then the company invests in training.

Even with training classes and help from other technicians, the job has involved a learning curve for Dan. "It's still a struggle," he says. "But I'm picking it up quickly. And I'm taking advantage of the training opportunities."

What do you do all day?

Dan arrives at 7 A.M. and immediately swings into action. His agenda typically includes adding new software and computers to the LAN and giving new employees access to the network. But his to-do list takes a backseat to the immediate needs

of the company's computer users. And the minute he gets in, someone inevitably has a problem. "It might take a minute, it might take three hours," he says. Traders are particularly demanding. "They live and die on information, and if their file server goes down, somebody's going to pay."

In between putting out fires, Dan continues his scheduled work. Right when he's in the middle of installing new equipment, his beeper sounds, and he's off to help another user. It's often 7:30 P.M. before his day is done. That translates into a lot

of 60-hour workweeks.

For Dan, the enjoyment he gets from the hands-on LAN work outweighs the long hours and the stress. "In some ways, you feel like a mechanic with a tie, but instead of getting your hands dirty, you're using your brain," he says. "You're not sitting at a desk doing the same thing over and over. You're moving around, jumping up and down, and fixing things. That's a good feeling."

Where do you see this job leading you?

Dan wants to continue to work with LANs, and he would like to get more involved with the technical aspects of the system. That might mean moving from working with end users to administering the hardware and software that form the LAN.

> **LEARN AS MUCH AS YOU CAN, IN SCHOOL OR ON YOUR OWN, ABOUT HOW COMPUTER NETWORKS WORK. MANY COMMUNITY COLLEGES AND TECHNICAL SCHOOLS OFFER CLASSES.**

58. Manufacturing Engineer

description: Manufacturing engineers design the machinery that makes electronic devices such as cellular phones, VCRs, and semiconductors. Manufacturing engineers choose which equipment to use and how to configure it.

Manufacturing engineers meet with vendors, and work closely with them to make sure they build the manufacturing machinery according to specifications. If the company has foreign manufacturing facilities, engineers also oversee the installation of equipment at those sites. For many, the international travel, which typically includes first-class accommodations, is a major selling point.

Once the equipment is built, the engineer oversees its installation and continues to tinker with it to make it more efficient. Not all projects involve starting from scratch. In some cases, it's a matter of reengineering a process to speed it up or add features to a product.

salary: Manufacturing engineers just out of college can expect to start in the $35,000 to $40,000 range. With 10 years of experience, salary rises to $60,000 to $70,000 a year. Pay is highest in the chip industry, which uses some of the world's most advanced technology.

prospects: There are vast opportunities for manufacturing engineers. The hottest area right now is chip manufacturing. Chip makers are currently building nine manufacturing plants in the United States, each costing $1 billion to $5 billion. Three other chip plants, known as "fabs," have opened recently. Manufacturing engineers will play a key role at each plant, and chip companies are already complaining about a shortage of people qualified to do this job.

qualifications: A bachelor's degree in mechanical, electrical, or chemical engineering or material science is usually a basic requirement. Many companies recruit college seniors, but it helps to have done a summer or semester internship.

characteristics: You need to like troubleshooting and thinking analytically. Because the job usually involves a lot of travel, it certainly helps if you enjoy being on the road and exploring new places and cultures.

Zod Bozorgmehr *is a manufacturing engineer specializing in chip manufacturing at a fabrication plant in Austin, Texas.*

How did you get the job?

Zod Bozorgmehr grew up in Iran, and came to the United States to study. "I grew up playing with Legos, and mechanical engineering was the closest thing to that, so that's what I studied." During his senior year, he interviewed with IBM, and was hired as a manufacturing engineer in New York. The field he ended up in was not one he knew well. "My manager said, 'Do you know optics?' and I told him I had taken a basic optics class in college. He said, 'OK, you're our new photo lithography guru,'" Zod recalls. "That's the equivalent of saying, 'Have you ever driven a car? You're our new engine design guru.'" That meant a steep and painful learning curve. He did eventually become a guru, but three years later the company was going through a major downsizing, and Zod opted to take a buyout.

> ZOD HIGHLY RECOMMENDS DOING AN INTERNSHIP OR A CO-OP PROGRAM (WHICH INVOLVES WORKING AT A COMPANY FOR A SEMESTER AND A SUMMER). MANY LARGE MANUFACTURING COMPANIES HAVE CO-OP PROGRAMS. FOR INFORMATION ON INDIVIDUAL PROGRAMS, CONTACT THE COMPANY'S HUMAN RESOURCES DEPARTMENT.

He sent out a bunch of resumes, and was soon offered a job overseeing the chip manufacturing process for a large manufacturing company. Zod thinks it's his approach to problem solving, as much as any particular skills, that has helped him excel at his job. "I look at problems a lot differently than other people," he says. "If somebody's trying to get a table through a door, but it doesn't fit, I immediately start thinking, 'Can the feet be taken off? Will a different angle work?'"

What do you do all day?

When Zod is in town, he arrives at work at 8:30 A.M. and heads to the manufacturing floor where he checks to make sure the equipment is working. If something has gone wrong, he tries to figure out what happened. He then spends a lot of time on the phone with vendors who are working on new equipment, to check on where it stands.

He spends a couple of weeks a month on out-of-town visits to vendors. "Sometimes the only way to check on how much progress they've made is to be there," he says. He also spends a lot of time at Motorola sites around the world, overseeing the installation of millions of dollars' worth of new chip manufacturing equipment and seeing that it works.

His travels have taken Zod up and down the California coast and around the United States. Internationally, he's been to Singapore, Malaysia, Japan, Hong Kong, and many countries in Europe. "The traveling is the fun part of the job," he says. "When you meet with vendors, they make sure you have a really good time. That means staying at the best hotels and eating at the best restaurants."

Where do you see this job leading you?

Zod is interested in selling the equipment that he is now responsible for buying. "Equipment sales is where the money is," he says. "And since I know the equipment inside out at this point, I think I'd be a good person to sell it."

59. Market Researcher

description: Market researchers are paid to put their thumb on the pulse of a particular industry and predict where it's headed. Most large high-tech companies employ an internal staff of market researchers. Other researchers work for private firms that specialize in providing data on a particular high-tech industry to industry players.

In some ways, being a market researcher is like being an intelligence agent. Market researchers working for a company collect business "intelligence" on their competitors. Private firms line up all companies in the industry, analyze their performance, and forecast where they're headed. That involves interviewing company officials and scrutinizing financial reports. Because companies aren't always up-front about their performance, an ability to find the hidden meaning behind the numbers is important.

Researchers turn their findings into a market report, which is presented to company officials. That usually involves making presentations, which makes public speaking an important part of this job.

salary: High-tech companies pay more than private consulting firms. Companies usually start researchers just out of college in the high $20,000 range. Senior market researchers (seven to ten years of experience) and principals in private firms can earn $50,000 to $100,000 a year.

prospects: Many high-tech companies are putting more emphasis on market research as a way to gauge the direction of the industry. Large companies offer the most opportunities, because they tend to have full market research staffs and provide training for those just out of college. Private firms tend to look for people with some experience because they can't afford to spend time on training.

qualifications: Market researchers are a diverse group. Some come into this field with a degree in business, while others have studied economics, engineering, or communications. The common denominators are an aptitude for math and an affinity for public speaking.

characteristics: You have to be comfortable asking questions that companies may not want to answer and digging until you get what you need to paint an accurate picture of the industry. You will be making a lot of presentations and working closely with company officials if you work for a corporation, and with clients if you work for a private research firm. This isn't a job for introverts.

Dean McCaron *is a market researcher at a Scottsdale, Arizona, firm that specializes in the semiconductor industry.*

How did you get the job?

Dean McCaron was studying business at the University of Arizona when he was hired by a market research company to do software programming. The company specialized in semiconductors, and Dean learned about the industry on the job. "I was hired to do systems support, but I ended up getting sucked into the analyst side because of my knowledge about the products," he says. "It was a case of extreme need. They really needed someone, and couldn't get anyone from outside. So I learned research on the job." When he left the company seven years later, it was as vice president of technology.

Dean left to work for a newly created trade publication that specialized in the semiconductor industry. But not long after he joined the magazine, it was put up for sale and eventually folded. He and a coworker decided to pool their severance pay and launch their own semiconductor market research firm. "In some ways it was a survival decision," he says. "No other opportunities were presenting themselves." Although he could have joined a company's market research staff, he really wanted to continue to do independent research.

Starting a firm was a risk, but both Dean and his partner had assurances from enough old clients to guarantee some business in the beginning. The firm is now two years old.

What do you do all day?

Dean is usually juggling a number of projects for different companies. He starts the day talking with a client company by phone to update them on a project studying methods of product delivery.

Then he works on an upcoming presentation to another company about its position in the semiconductor market and the industry outlook. After that, Dean analyzes spreadsheets on his computer, and studies earnings reports to update the market share forecasts. He also talks with officials from different semiconductor companies to get their take on the market.

In the afternoon, he works on various projects for other companies and takes a call from a company that doesn't like the way it has come off in one of his market reports. "There is always a company that has an ax to grind about the way their products are portrayed," he says. "That's where diplomacy skills come in."

Throughout the day, Dean reads financial wire service reports to keep up with industry news. He also spends as much time as he can poring over semiconductor trade publications to keep up with trends.

Although he arrives at the office by 9 A.M., he is often busy until 10 P.M. "The hours can get really extreme. But it seems like there's always a deadline."

Where do you see this job leading you?

Dean is dedicated to building his research firm. Many researchers at private firms go on to join corporate research staffs. And corporate market researchers sometimes move into other departments, such as marketing and product development.

> **IF YOU KNOW WHICH INDUSTRY YOU WOULD LIKE TO WORK IN, CONTACT A TRADE ASSOCIATION FOR A LIST OF THE INDUSTRY'S LEADING COMPANIES AND THE MARKET RESEARCH FIRMS WHO FOLLOW IT.**

60. Marketing Artist/Advertising Artist

FOR A NEWSPAPER

description: A marketing artist at a newspaper is responsible for building new advertising spreads and altering existing ones. Marketing artists work on all sections of the newspaper, including on the special sections and any supplemental magazines. National supplements, such as *Parade,* often run regional advertisements. For larger newspapers, all ads are filed in the company's database and are traced by number, thus allowing marketing artists to pull up any ad for pertinent information. A sales representative on staff discusses the advertising client's information with the artist, who then incorporates the relevant information into the spread. At times, the artist is given license to create the actual design of the ad.

salary: Full-time entry-level marketing artists can make from $21,000 to $23,000 per year. Experienced artists can make up to $35,000. Many companies, newspapers included, use the Hay System to establish their pay range. Each worker receives a rating for job knowledge, accountability, and problem solving. These are plugged into a complex grid to determine wages and annual increases.

prospects: Graphic design is an ever growing field. As technology advances, so does the need for artists who can skillfully and creatively work with what's currently available.

qualifications: At a minimum, marketing artists need an associate's degree in graphic design. Their prospects are better with a bachelor of fine arts or a four-year degree in graphic design, with training in computer graphics and layout design. To work for a newspaper, you also need skills in typography.

characteristics: Marketing artists need to be artistic, have a good eye for style, be patient, and work well under the pressure of unrealistic deadlines. They also must also be good at interpreting vague, muddled information and producing exactly what customers wish they had thought of.

Kristin Cornell *is a marketing artist/advertising artist for a large daily newspaper in Ft. Lauderdale, Florida.*

How did you get the job?

Kristin Cornell holds a B.S. in fine arts with a concentration in graphic design from SUNY–New Paltz, where she worked on the school paper doing layout and design.

Kristin initially heard of the position with the *Sun Sentinel* newspaper from a personal contact. She was granted an interview and offered a full-time temporary position. "I entered temp work with no prior work experience, and was learning from the very beginning," says Kristin. "I was eager to please, and willingly took the suggestions of my superiors."

At this newspaper, as is the case with many, temps are hired to fill in during crunch times, which seem to happen before major holidays. There was no guarantee of permanent employment when she accepted the job, but she knew the possibility existed. Kristin and two others temped for one and a half years. When a full-time position came open, she was originally passed over because she lacked the bilingual skills the job required. "I took a leave of absence, and returned after two months, hell-bent on landing full-time employment," states Kristin.

What do you do all day?

Upon arrival, Kristin pulls out all the ads she has to do that day. "Prioritizing my work flow is the key to crisis management," she says. Invariably she gets approached by sales representatives from the newspaper wanting her to alter her previous day's labor. "Minor changes may get done immediately," says Kristin, "but major alterations get added to the day's pile and prioritized along with the rest of the workload for that day."

Sales reps from within the newspaper are the conduit between the advertisers and Kristin. "Some clients know exactly what they want their ad to look like," says Kristin, "yet others look to me for advice, layout ideas, style, and even suggestions on copy." With a plethora of electronic artwork and equipment at her disposal, Kristin begins designing and building ads, pasting up, scanning, and sending her work on

> COLLEGE PUBLICATIONS, SUCH AS NEWSPAPERS AND YEARBOOKS, CAN OFFER A GREAT DEAL OF PRACTICAL EXPERIENCE NOT ONLY WRITING AND PRODUCING THE PUBLICATION, BUT WITH BUDGETING, SCHEDULING, AND NEGOTIATING AS WELL.

for approval and printing.

The *Sun Sentinel* has the most advanced cutting-edge technology of any newspaper in the country. "I feel fortunate to be able to experiment with such high-quality color and graphic capabilities," says Kristin. She adds, "I see how quality, user-friendly equipment and software programs allow one to more quickly produce an aesthetically pleasing publication."

Where do you see this job leading you?

Kristin would like to move to the promotions department of this company, where they design longer-running national campaigns. There sponsors promote very visible clients, such as football teams or sports equipment companies. "This kind of high-profile advertising provides more depth with one topic or theme. There's a lot more opportunity and resources for creative artistry," Kristin says.

If she leaves the newspaper, Kristin would like to design ads for a magazine. "One can be a lot more creative with a full-color glossy magazine," she says. "The eye-catching visuals bring out the content of the ad, which then draws people into the copy."

Kristin could work for an advertising agency, where she would have more of an opportunity to enhance her 3-D graphics skills. A less conventional route could lead her into illustrating posters and books, designing T-shirts, or owning her own graphics business.

61. Marketing Specialist

FOR A HIGH-TECH COMPANY

description: The marketing department picks up where the development team leaves off. It's marketing's job to sell the company's product to customers and the trade press. That can involve everything from creating an advertising campaign to overseeing distribution channels, generating sales leads, and promoting products at trade shows.

Marketing specialists work closely with engineers during the development stage so that they are familiar with a product's features and improvements. In addition, the marketing department is charged with setting up contracts with resellers and retailers, and working with them to get the products on store shelves.

It can be exciting to take a product that no one has heard of and help it grow into a multimillion-dollar

seller. But if it bombs—even if the product is the reason—marketing takes the rap.

salary: Entry-level positions start at $20,000 to $32,000 a year. With five years of experience or more, you can earn $40,000 to $80,000.

prospects: High-tech companies always have a need for marketing talent. But because many tech start-ups—which are good places to get experience—fold after only creating a product or two, marketing specialists tend to move around. If you are willing to jump around, there are a lot of opportunities.

qualifications: A bachelor's degree, usually in business or engineering, is required. Some marketers start as sales representatives, which is an excellent background for marketing. General knowledge of computers and familiarity with the company's niche are very helpful. Some companies, especially small ones, hire marketing specialists straight out of college for entry-level positions.

characteristics: You will need to be a good public speaker, because making presentations to resellers, retailers, potential customers, and the trade press is an important part of this job.

Cheri Hildebrand *is marketing director for a software company in Tucson, Arizona.*

How did you get the job?

Cheri Hildebrand grew up in Ogallala, Nebraska, and studied speech communications and business at the University of Nebraska. After graduating, she visited a sister in Tucson, interviewed for jobs, and accepted an offer from Tandy Corp.'s education division as a sales representative. "It was kind of a gutsy move," she says. "I took the job, went home and packed my stuff, and within two weeks I was in Tucson reporting to work."

Sales came naturally for Cheri, who sold computers and networking solutions to the southern Arizona school system, colleges, and local and state governments. She had learned a little about computers while working as a teller and new accounts rep for a bank during college, but she picked up most of it on the job. Within a year and a half, Cheri was named district manager, and for the next three and a half years she oversaw sales in four states.

Ready for a new challenge, Cheri went to another software development company as a product marketer, which involved a lot of travel. "I was on the road all the time, and I had no personal life, no social life," she says. "I decided I needed a change." She moved into product management, and after two and a half years was offered a marketing director position at a start-up company that was too good to pass up.

"I wanted to be right in the middle of things, which is why I picked a small company where I could see things happen," she says.

Cheri says her experience as a sales rep and as a product marketer and manager was the perfect stepping-stone to her current job.

What do you do all day?

A typical day for Cheri might include editing a direct-mail campaign, giving final approval for a new series of trade magazine advertisements, and discussing product distribution with vendors. Cheri also oversees the content the company posts on its Internet Web site.

If product engineers are wrapping up a beta version of a new product, Cheri meets with them to discuss the differences between this product and its predecessor and to test it herself. Based on what she learns from talking with developers and testing the product, she and her staff of five write product literature and news releases and create ad promos.

Cheri travels to trade shows and other meetings once or twice a month for three to five days at a time. She makes product presentations and takes questions from potential clients and vendors. "If you don't know the technology and you're not up-to-speed on the product, people will know," she says. "That's why working so closely with engineering really pays off."

Where do you see this job leading you?

"If I'm going to go any further in this career, I'll need a master's degree," Cheri says. In that spirit, Cheri has begun an M.B.A. program at the University of Arizona. After finishing her degree, she would like to be director of marketing for a larger firm or go on to open her own marketing firm.

> DO AS MANY COLLEGE INTERNSHIPS AS YOU CAN, EVEN IF THEY'RE UNPAID. SALES EXPERIENCE OF ANY KIND— EVEN RETAIL— IS AN EXCELLENT BACKGROUND FOR MARKETING AND LOOKS GOOD ON A RESUME. WRITING, SPELLING, AND EDITING SKILLS ARE ALSO IMPORTANT.

62. Mechanical Engineer

FOR A SMALL LASER COMPANY

description: Mechanical engineers design hardware and software, lay out systems, analyze specs and weight load, design pneumatic systems, and work with lasers and other high-tech tools currently at their disposal—in short, all the mechanical and physical properties of a product or a system. Graham Coffee, a mechanical engineer for a small laser company, says, "A mechanical engineer could be designing anything from airplanes to zippers."

salary: Starting salary for mechanical engineering positions is $25,000 to $35,000 annually. With experience, that salary can rise to $45,000 to $75,000 annually.

prospects: This is a tough market. At entry-level, your chances are better at a bigger company—you are less expensive, and the big companies can train you. Smaller companies are usually more interested in people with a few years' experience.

"The high-tech industries are where the money is now," says Graham. "Communications and electronic equipment is the growth industry of the '90s."

qualifications: A four-year mechanical engineering degree is required for mechanical engineering positions. Companies look for a competency in CAD (computer aided design) and programming—the more computer experience you have the better.

characteristics: Graham says that intuition and common sense are crucial to being a successful mechanical engineer. "You need to be able to identify, among a myriad of options, the practical, reasonable solution to your client's problem."

Graham Coffee *is a mechanical engineer for a small laser company.*

How did you get the job?

After graduating from college as a mechanical engineer, Graham Coffee worked in the oil industry as a subcontractor for NASA—designing payloads for the space shuttle. He went to the South Pacific for four years to work on testing instrumentation range for the Department of Defense. "The job was tough, but worth it. Working overseas increases both your skill base and your employability," says Graham. "You become much more resourceful when you don't have all the comforts of home." He subcontracted for NASA for a few more years when he returned to the States.

Graham met the owner of Control Micro Systems, Inc. through a NASA contact. When he found out that Control Micro Systems designs systems for laser label equipment and products, he took note. Graham had had a limited exposure to laser technology with NASA and the Department of Defense, so the thought of working on industrial laser applications piqued his interest. "Lasers have always fascinated me. What else can cut through steel, reshape a cornea, and do light shows on the ceiling?" Graham exclaims. "You can be pretty creative with that kind of technology." After five years with Control Micro Systems, he's still experimenting with new laser methods and applications, testing the effects of lasers on metals, plastics, and any combination thereof.

What do you do all day?

Graham spends his time designing on CAD (computer aided design) systems, procuring material, ordering parts, interfacing with people in the machine shop (who in his case are subcontractors), evaluating proposals and price quotes from customers, and performing managerial responsibilities. "I like to spend time working in the shop. It's important to keep in touch with the products of the company, and to manage by example," says Graham. "Workers trust you more when you work among them."

Of his management style Graham says, "Understanding the human condition and being well organized are the keys to good management." He feels he has a knack for juggling sched-

> IF YOU'RE INTERESTED IN DESIGN, AVAIL YOURSELF OF YOUR COLLEGE'S COMPUTER FACILITIES AND LEARN AS MANY COMPUTER AIDED DESIGN SYSTEMS AND DRAWING SOFTWARE APPLICATIONS AS POSSIBLE.

ules, people's needs, and workload. "In a small, 20-person company like this, where everyone does everything, managers have to keep sight of the bigger picture." He makes himself available to his staff, and is ready for any crisis. Graham adds with a smile, "Management is when interruptions are interrupted by interruptions."

Where do you see this job leading you?

Graham sees this job taking him to retirement. "I'm happy with the size of the company, and enjoy the autonomy and responsibilities I have," he says. "My superiors take my input seriously, and my workers respect my judgment. What more could a guy ask for?"

Graham sits back and reflects on how the industry has changed. "With the steady influx of new computer and laser capabilities, I'm in continual on-the-job training." He feels computers have made mechanical engineering a much more creative process. "Drawings can be tweaked, redesigned, and rotated, all with the push of a few keys," he says. "With such immediate feedback from changing variables, we are expected and able to produce more at a higher quality."

63. Medical Field Service Engineer

description: The introduction of new technologies have created a wealth of jobs in the technological/medical area. Doctors now regularly use MRIs and CAT scans in their practices, but they can't be expected to maintain and service such high-tech equipment. They must depend on medical field service engineers to keep the equipment in working order. Because these medical field service engineers generally service equipment at various locations, they don't normally work out of an office. Instead, these technicians circulate among different facilities, conducting general maintenance on a regular basis.

salary: Medical field service engineers just starting out can expect to make somewhere from $25,000 to $30,000 a year. The salary can get as high as $50,000 to $60,000 for someone with five to seven years of experience in the field, but it won't go much higher unless a shift to a management position is made.

prospects: The uncertainty created by the possibility of health care reform has caused many hospitals to stop spending money on equipment. Furthermore, federal cutbacks have caused the amount of reimbursement hospitals receive from Medicare and Medicaid for procedures using MRIs to shrink from about $1,500 to $700. In response to this, companies designing and making the equipment have also cut back.

qualifications: Getting a bachelor's degree in electrical engineering would make you a very desirable candidate in a job market that is becoming increasingly competitive. Experience in the medical field could also be helpful. Finding a part-time job working in medical records or volunteering at a hospital is a good way to familiarize yourself with the medical working environment.

characteristics: To work as a field service engineer, you must be proficient at maintaining both the equipment and a professional relationship with your customers. You also need to be motivated and organized, because your day really isn't structured. You must determine your own schedule of maintenance for the accounts that you acquire.

Jay Fowler *is a medical field service engineer.*

How did you get the job?

During his high school years, Jay Fowler was always interested in computers and technology, so after graduation it seemed like a natural progression for him to attend the Albuquerque Technical Vocational Institute. While he was working toward his associate's degree, Jay also worked part-time as a network technician on patient information systems at one of the hospitals in Albuquerque. He knew that he wanted to incorporate his interest in technology into his career path, but his work at the hospital allowed him to develop an interest in the medical field as well, and he began looking for ways to combine his interests. Jay soon came across the perfect mix when he met some of the field service engineers working with equipment at the hospital where he was employed.

After he received his associate's degree, Jay moved very quickly into a job as a medical service engineer at General Elec-

SOMEONE LOOKING FOR WORK AS A MEDICAL FIELD SERVICE ENGINEER CAN FIND OUT ABOUT JOB OPPORTUNITIES BY LOOKING AT A **MEDICAL IMAGING JOURNAL**, WHICH CAN BE FOUND IN THE PERIODICAL SECTION OF ANY LIBRARY. THIS JOURNAL HAS A CLASSIFIED AD SECTION THAT ADVERTISES OPENINGS IN THE FIELD.

tric in Albuquerque. He worked there four years before he moved to Colorado to take some time off.

After he had gotten all of the skis and snowflakes out of his system, Jay began searching for employment. He used the services of a headhunter who found him a job as a medical field service engineer with

InnoSERV Technologies, Inc., the largest independent service company of medical equipment.

What do you do all day?

Because of the nature of the job, Jay says, there is no typical day for a medical field service engineer. Rather than driving to an office to sit at a desk, Jay just turns on his pager when it's time for work. He is on call 16 hours a day, and must be available to respond to any sites that may have problems with their systems.

Normally when Jay is called in, it is because a medical technician conducting an MRI or CAT scan has experienced problems—such as a computer or operating controls freezing up while a patient is on the table. Jay's job is to find out what the problem is, rectify it, and get the system up and running again as quickly as possible.

"Sometimes it can be real stressful if you have a doctor screaming at you and a patient lying on the table with an aneurysm," Jay says, adding

that MRIs are not typically given to trauma patients.

There is no way to predict how many calls will come in on any given day. "It really varies. It comes in cycles. Sometimes there's a call every hour, and sometimes there won't be any calls in one day," Jay says.

But even during the slow times, there is still work to be done. At least four times a month Jay spends about four to six evening hours conducting planned maintenance on the machines that he services. These maintenance sessions are time consuming, but necessary for heading off possible problems with the equipment.

Where do you see this job leading you?

Jay is currently looking at making a career change. He would like to go to law school, and then combine his knowledge of the medical and technology fields with a legal practice.

64. Medical Research Technician

description: Medical research technicians can be involved in a wide variety of tasks. The degree of independence a lab tech has is determined by the principal investigator (PI) and the policy at that lab. In some labs, you are given an assignment and directed as to the techniques and technologies necessary to implement it. In other labs you are given a project, and with close collaboration with your PI, you handle the investigation. "The more freedom you have with a project, the more likely you are to be given credit for that project's published article," explains Catherine Alexander, who is a lab technician level II. Lab responsibilities could include cell and tissue culture, blood handling, setting up databases, ordering materials, and fixing broken equipment.

salary: Starting salary is $17,000 to $20,000 per year, and can increase to $40,000 to $45,000, at level III. Academic institutions pay less than private research foundations.

prospects: Most lab research funding is drawn from National Institutes of Health, the American Cancer Society, the American Arthritis Association, and the March of Dimes. Your job security is contingent on how well your PI brings in grant money. With lab experience one could work at a privately owned company such as Bristol Meyers, Immunex, Cell Pro, or Targeted Genetics.

qualifications: Lab techs usually have a bachelor's degree in one of the sciences and two to three years' experience in biochemistry, molecular biology, chemistry, or life science. "Most labs have specific techniques, and prefer to train you their way," Catherine says. "I've experienced some overzealous hand-holding along the way." She feels work-study, or volunteering in a lab, really provides you valuable experience and exposure.

characteristics: As a lab tech, you need to be able to carry out independent research, maintain a well-documented notebook, and communicate clearly with other lab members. "Most important," Catherine adds, "is you need to humbly take guidance and instruction from those above you." Lab tech is a good entry-level position for a professional career in science and research.

Catherine Alexander *is a research technician II in a molecular immunology lab at Virginia Mason Research Center in Seattle, Washington.*

How did you get the job?

Catherine Alexander walked in the back door of this career. She needed lab experience for a possible Ph.D. candidacy, and was willing to do any kind of lab work. Three lab jobs came up. Two were volunteer positions with mentors at a university. The third paid $7 an hour. Catherine was 36 years old. "I was a single parent of a teenager, and paying for my own education," says Catherine. "It's no surprise that I took the paying job." Had she been able to take a volunteer position, she would now be working in cell development or plant biology.

A college degree was the basic requirement. Her bachelor's in fine arts and credits toward a molecular biology degree seemed to suit the principal investigator. Not paying much attention to her resume,

the PI gave her leave to work on her second B.A. She took a molecular biology technology lab course to add to her skill base.

Catherine feels she was selected because of her interest, skills, and enthusiasm. "Because I was older, I offered maturity and real life experiences to the lab environment, and that was appreciated," Catherine adds.

What do you do all day?

Catherine has a 40-hour week that is flexible. Some night work and weekends are required. She generally has several experiments running simultaneously. Each can require several days of close observation and regular checking. The day is spent attending each of these experiments. "Invariably, someone's procrastination becomes my crisis," she adds. Sometimes the job takes until 9 P.M.

Technology runs a research lab. "The techniques I do routinely were science fiction 15 years ago," says Catherine. She

goes on to explain. "For instance, PCR—polymerize chain reaction—is a technique where you take a single copy of a gene and replicate it to millions of copies in a test tube. This is used for cloning, quantitation, and manipulation." Catherine plays with and manipulates DNA, running experiments with gelelectrophoresis—a cloning technique—and Southern blot, which is a way to identify genes on fragments of DNA.

Catherine routinely replicates and clones chimpanzee antibody genes for study. "Jane Goodall—eat your heart out!" she grins.

Where do you see this job leading you?

Catherine would like to move up to Lab Tech level III. In her lab, this requires first being the author of a published research paper. She has received credit on two other research papers as "et al."

The step beyond Lab Tech III is the PI, which requires a

> GRANT WRITING IS AN IMPORTANT ASPECT OF MANY JOBS. SUBMITTING WRITING SAMPLES CAN GIVE A PROSPECTIVE EMPLOYER AN IDEA OF YOUR ABILITY TO WRITE AN EFFECTIVE GRANT PROPOSAL.

Ph. D., proven grant writing ability, and being published. "A PI needs a competitive strength that goes a mile deep," says Catherine. "As a 46-year-old woman, I'm not looking to climb the academic ladder." She likes her work; she feels she is contributing to science. Plus, they offer her a great benefits package.

"Working in a high-tech field supports my dance habit which, although fun and exhilarating, is not a particularly lucrative endeavor," Catherine says in closing.

65. Multimedia Producer

description: A multimedia producer's role is similar to a movie producer's. The job involves taking a vague concept or plot and molding contributions from dozens of people into a computer program with moving pictures and sound. That involves a lot of brainstorming and a lot of coaching.

Producers make assignments and oversee the progress of writers, graphic artists, animators, programmers, video editors, and game testers. The producer reins the staff in when they're over budget, and inspires them when they're out of ideas for a particular sequence.

Depending on the skills and the size of their team, producers also do programming and artwork. Once the creative work is done, producers turn their attention to the production process, which involves testing for "bugs" and usability. Just because the game runs beautifully on a top-of-the-line Macintosh doesn't guarantee it will work on the average personal computer that most people have in their homes. If that's the case, it's time for reengineering.

salary: Pay starts in the mid-$30,000 range. Like in the movie industry, hot producers who freelance can demand (and receive) salaries in the $100,000 range.

Pay varies widely, depending on whether you work for a five-person multimedia start-up or full-time for a major corporation.

prospects: The number of multimedia companies and CD-ROMs is multiplying quickly and shows no signs of slowing. Talented producers are in great demand, especially at start-up companies. There are risks, of course, in joining a start-up. Many fail before putting out a single CD-ROM title.

qualifications: Ask 10 multimedia producers what kind of skills are needed, and you'll get 10 different answers. This field attracts people with an amazing range of backgrounds. Some spent their childhoods playing video games, others studied computer science. Still others are artists and musicians who like the idea of combining art and technology. The common denominator seems to be a love of computers—although heavy computer skills aren't required—and a creative bent.

characteristics: You need to be a leader who can carry out a vision. Everyone involved in the project will be looking to you for direction, and you need to be able to take charge. You have also got to be a motivator. Good morale is very important when you're embarking on a project like this, and your attitude determines your group's outlook.

Marty Coleman *is a multimedia producer at a multimedia development house in Tulsa, Oklahoma.*

How did you get the job?

For many years, Marty Coleman's goal was to support himself as an artist. He exhibited his paintings and photography in a number of art shows, and taught college-level art classes part-time to supplement his income. But what he really needed to support himself was a full-time teaching job. "I actually tried to get a full-time position for seven years," he says. "Finally I decided it was time to move in a different direction."

He decided to teach himself computers. A friend let Marty use his Macintosh, and his father-in-law let him fiddle around on his IBM-compatible personal computer. "I got comfortable with them, but my skills were very minimal," he says. He liked it enough to decide to focus on computer art. Because he was living in San Jose, California, otherwise known as Silicon Valley, there seemed to be a lot of opportunities. "I wanted to work in the entertainment or game area, so I started applying for jobs," he says. Instead of job offers, though, he got tips on what software programs he needed to learn before he could be hired. "They said, 'We like your artwork, but you need to know X.' I didn't know a single one of those programs." But he learned them. Every time a company suggested a program, he would buy or borrow it and teach himself how to use it.

After more than a year of trying, his efforts paid off. A Tulsa, Oklahoma, multimedia company put an ad in the San Jose newspaper seeking a computer graphic artist. Marty applied, got an interview, and got the job. "It was an entry-level position, but that was fine with me," he says. He and his wife and kids moved to Tulsa, which was a refreshing change from smoggy downtown San Jose. Within a year and a half, Marty had moved from production assistant to producer.

"I feel really blessed to have this job," he says. "While I'm good at handling rejection, I wanted a success. It took a long time, but it finally happened."

What do you do all day?

Marty's company develops educational CD-ROMs for children that feature Ozzie, a world-traveling otter. Lately Marty has been spending his time reworking a recently completed CD-ROM, a project he inherited when he became producer. The reworking was spurred by a magazine review. "It said the animation wasn't as good as it could have been," he says. "We went into a real revamping mode because we agreed it could be better."

Marty is also completing another CD-ROM project, which involves working with a programmer to put on the finishing touches. "The design process is like a funnel, and the producer and the programmer are at the bottom." After the writers and the animators and the graphic artists sign off, Marty and the programmer are left to tweak and fine-tune.

Except when a deadline is approaching, Marty usually works an 8 A.M. to 5:30 P.M. day. That gives him time to spend with his family.

After the current products are wrapped up, he and his team will brainstorm about their next project.

Where do you see this job leading you?

Marty plans to continue to develop his skills as a producer and to work to turn out attention-getting educational CD-ROMs.

66. NASA Life Sciences Team Member

description: How would plants and animals fare during a three-month journey in space? To find out, a NASA research team is building a suite of habitat boxes to house rats, mice, fish, plants, insects, cells, and tissue cultures sent into orbit.

The team—which has sent plants and animals up on short-term space shuttle missions—hopes to make the first long-term launch in 1999. Building habitats where living things can survive for such a stretch requires the expertise of researchers, mechanical engineers, electrical engineers, and scientists.

Team members must develop temperature controls and feeding systems, as well as ways to record data during the journey, which will shed light on how a lack of gravity affects living organisms.

Engineers use computers to design model "homes," and then build prototypes based on their designs. Hundreds of tests will be carried out before the final hardware is sent into space. As a NASA researcher, you experience the thrill of taking part in what are potentially groundbreaking studies. But with federal funding for NASA shrinking, there's also the constant danger that after years of work, your project will be killed before the results are even in.

salary: Project members with limited experience will start at about $30,000 a year, and salaries for experienced engineers and scientists range from $50,000 to $80,000 a year. Salary is based on experience and expertise.

prospects: With NASA's shrinking budget, jobs have become very competitive. Still, new and existing projects frequently need talented people, and it is possible to get hired right out of college if you have strong credentials, including good grades and relevant work experience.

qualifications: To be hired for a research project, you'll need at least a bachelor's degree in computer, mechanical, or electrical engineering. Experience in project analysis, conceptual design, and computer programming also helps.

characteristics: You have to be an analytical thinker with a mind that works like a flow chart. That means you need to understand how doing one thing will affect the next steps in the process.

Kelly McKeown *is project manager of the team that develops hardware for life sciences research at NASA's Ames Research Center.*

How did you get the job?

Kelly McKeown graduated with a degree in computer science from Virginia Polytechnic Institute, and moved to California to look for a job. She applied for a job at NASA's Ames Research Center in Mountain View, California, and, to her surprise, was hired as a computer graphics software developer.

After seven years she decided to move to the hardware end. Joining life sciences, she began doing low-level design work, then schedule analysis and development, and eventually became a group leader. Kelly eventually became manager of the entire project.

"It wasn't a conscious effort," she says. "I just kind of fell into project management, and it turned out to be the exactly right thing for me. It makes use of my organizational and coordination skills."

Kelly believes she got the job because she has a rare combination of talents. "You have to be

> NASA OFFERS A NUMBER OF STUDENT INTERNSHIPS, BOTH DURING THE SCHOOL YEAR AND IN SUMMER. AND EVEN IF YOU CAN'T DO AN INTERNSHIP WITH NASA, GET ENGINEERING OR LAB EXPERIENCE WHEREVER YOU CAN. INFORMATIONAL INTERVIEWS ARE HELPFUL WAYS TO GET TIPS ON WHERE JOBS ARE AVAILABLE AND WHAT KIND OF BACKGROUND IS REQUIRED.

technically capable, politically astute, and able to work with people," she says. "It's hard to find people with all that in one package."

What do you do all day?

Although she loves her job, it has its price. For three years, Kelly worked seven days a week, putting in about 80 hours a week. Now it's down to 60 hours a week. "The downside is I have no life," she says. "I just work, and I'm going gray very rapidly."

The work schedule of her engineers and scientists isn't much lighter. Most average 45 to 65 hours a week.

She spends a lot of time exchanging e-mail with her team members and reporting on progress to her managers. Kelly is constantly evaluating the status of various parts of the project.

Kelly is also called upon to make key hardware judgments. "It might be deciding the best approach to get a piece of hardware developed or how to get back on schedule if we're off," she says. In addition, she oversees budgeting, long-range planning, and hiring.

Kelly is also responsible for representing her department when senators and congressional representatives pass through.

"We get a lot of VIPs coming through, and if we're going to be funded, we need to give them a good idea of what we do here," she says.

Losing funding is a constant worry. "There's always the risk of seeing your funding reduced or canceled all together," she says. "So when people want to see our work, I'm always ready to show them."

Where do you see this job leading you?

Kelly wants to stay in project management, preferably in life sciences. Although she would like to advance, she hopes to stay close to research and technology rather than move into administrative work. "That's not interesting to me," she says. "What we're doing is really neat, and I'd like to stay in life sciences to see it through."

67. Natural Gas Vehicle Industry Consultant

description: As Dodge, Chrysler, and other passenger car companies join the mass transit and service industries in developing vehicles that use natural gas as an alternative fuel, the need to set standards and regulate the distribution of natural gas becomes more imperative. For example, it is taken for granted when you pull into a gas station to fill up your car with gasoline that the dispenser's nozzle will fit into your car's tank. However, for many operators of natural gas vehicles, the size of the nozzle used to dispense natural gas could vary from station to station until the industry agrees on a standard.

In an effort to set standards in this new territory, research and trade associations within the industry have enlisted numerous engineers both as permanent employees on their staff and as consultants.

Engineers working with or for these associations need to be knowledgeable of the commodity and the equipment in order to guide those forming legislation to make appropriate decisions involving every aspect of the industry—from emissions to dispensing mechanisms. Consultants must work directly with utility companies, as well as with government lobbyists. And, as the scope expands past the United States, consultants will travel to Europe, Latin America, and Southeast Asia to aid in the development of standards.

salary: Entry-level salaries in this field won't usually start at below $30,000, and they will grow as you gain experience. A middle-level manager with about five to ten years of experience can bring in a salary in the range of $60,000.

prospects: The number of jobs in the area of natural gas engine design is growing as more companies develop vehicles that use natural gas as an alternative fuel.

qualifications: A bachelor's degree in some type of engineering, preferably mechanical, is a requirement for anyone seeking this type of work. In order to set yourself ahead of others who may be vying for the same jobs, it is important to gain experience. This can be done by participating in student competitions or by becoming involved in an internship.

characteristics: People in this field typically will be ambitious and tenacious. They are also very analytical and love to solve problems. They are not characteristically sociable, and tend to put their work above social engagements.

Sean Turner *is a natural gas vehicle industry consultant.*

How did you get the job?

While in high school, Sean Turner loved racing cars. Living in Phoenix, Arizona, gave him the perfect opportunity to race sand dragsters. But after high school graduation, Sean wanted to take his love for race cars beyond the sandy terrain of Arizona, and so he began his studies in mechanical engineering.

Driven by his love for engines and his newfound knowledge of their inner workings, Sean entered a national competition for students that required him to construct an engine using natural gas. He attended a conference on natural gas as a part of his research on this project and, while there, he asked one of the speakers specific questions surrounding the project. Sean kept in contact with this man after the conference, calling him occasionally with another question regarding his project. The relationship Sean cultivated actually led to his first job as an associate at a newly created engineering firm.

GETTING INVOLVED IN YOUR COLLEGE'S STUDENT ENGINEERING GROUP WILL ALLOW YOU TO BECOME INVOLVED WITH THE LOCAL PROFESSIONAL ENGINEERS, WHICH IS A GOOD WAY TO FIND OUT ABOUT INTERNSHIPS AND JOB OPENINGS. THE SOCIETY OF AUTOMOTIVE ENGINEERS IN WARRENDALE, PENNSYLVANIA, DISTRIBUTES A MONTHLY NEWSLETTER THAT ADVERTISES EMPLOYMENT OPPORTUNITIES. (SEE RESOURCES, PAGE 213).

At this firm, Sean worked as a consultant for the natural gas industry. Much of his work required that Sean act as a consultant for the Natural Gas Vehicle Coalition, and, after he had worked in this capacity for four years, the coalition offered Sean a full-time job as its director of technology.

What do you do all day?

Sean says one of the aspects he likes most about his job is that no two days are alike. On any given day Sean may find himself testifying on the Senate floor, traveling to New Mexico to work with a utility company that has run into problems with local officials over concerns about the handling of natural gas, or traveling to Europe to discuss the development of natural gas vehicles with the makers of BMW.

For the most part, Sean says, his job revolves around the development of standards. He describes this as a dynamic process, and says that it keeps him busy because he may be working with the development of seven different standards at all times. Most recently, he worked with an ad-hoc committee that proposed a test procedure to measure the quantity of natural gas coming out of a dispenser. The solution to that test will now become a part of the regulatory information disseminated by the National Institute of Standards in Technology. This information is used to instruct field officials in measuring natural gas dispensers.

Sean's job also requires him to keep abreast of trends in the industry. He will then be able to advise lobbyists contracted by the coalition as to which areas need funding for research and development.

Where do you see this job leading you?

Sean would like to be able to transfer the experience he has gained in this job to an international post, perhaps in Europe or Africa. "I'd like to be able to take what we've already learned here to the rest of the world."

68. New Media Publisher

description: Changes in technology have transformed numerous industries, and book publishing is no exception. Within the past two to three years, most publishing houses have gone so far as to create a division for the publication of new media. It is the job of people working in these areas to create products that will ensure the publishing house will not be caught behind the times during this technological wave.

Many of the projects created in these departments represent an extension of the publishing house's work. For example, Web pages allow these companies to advertise upcoming books. In other instances, new media such as CD-ROMs can allow the publishing companies to offer consumers almanacs or encyclopedias that will never go out of date because they can be upgraded on-line. These electronic products also offer visual and audio advantages for how-to books.

salary: Someone working as a publisher or executive producer of interactive media might make an annual salary close to $150,000. However, this field is so new that no standard has been set, and salaries vary greatly from company to company.

prospects: With all the changes in the area of new media publishing, the market for these types of jobs changes as well. Last year there was a high demand for people who were familiar with CD-ROMs. Although that demand is still present, there is now an added need for people familiar with the Internet and creating Web pages.

qualifications: The qualifications for a person entering this multifaceted field will vary depending on the area of focus. It takes numerous employees to produce these products, so the options are vast, ranging from editors to designers to programmers. Someone getting into the editorial side will want to have a liberal arts degree, as well as editing experience. However, someone interested in the programming aspect may have his or her bachelor's degree in computer science and be familiar with writing code. From whatever angle you enter the field, experience with the technology is a requirement.

characteristics: People working in new media must be creative, but they also must be flexible enough to alter their creative impulses to match different types of new media. It is rare that someone working in new media publishing will tackle a project alone, so people in this field must also be able to work in a group setting.

Carol Cohen *is a new media publisher for a major publishing house in New York City.*

How did you get the job?

In her position as the publisher of HarperCollins' reference division, Carol Cohen kept close tabs on the advances being made in the area of new media. It was her interest in this technology that led to her idea of publishing Harper's *Dictionary of American Sign Language* on CD-ROM. "The signs are really very visual. It just made sense to do that on CD-ROM so with each sign, you can actually see them being created, and you learn how to do them," Carol says.

The initiative Carol took in this new field did not go unnoticed at HarperCollins, and when the company decided to open a division for adult-trade new media in 1994, they didn't have to look too far to find its vice president and publisher.

During the first year, the division—under Carol's supervision—published four CD-ROMs. This year, the division has continued to grow along with the increasing changes in technology. The division has published eight CD-ROMs, and has developed its own Web site on the Internet.

What do you do all day?

A large majority of Carol's job is keeping up with the industry. She does this by reading numerous newsletters and trade journals, and attending conferences where advances in new media are the topic of discussion. Although it is exciting to learn what is going on, Carol says that in a field where changes are coming about daily, keeping up can become a big chore.

But keeping up with the products that her own company is producing is also a great task.

Carol spends a lot of time with the planning and budgeting of new products, as well as attending various meetings to monitor their progress.

Amid all this activity, Carol must concentrate on coming up with ideas for new products. She says there is no set way to do this. Many of her ideas come out of the regular editorial

PERHAPS THE BEST WAY FOR SOMEONE TO FIND JOBS IN THE NEW MEDIA PUBLISHING FIELD IS TO SEARCH THE JOB LISTINGS ON THE INTERNET. THERE ARE USUALLY LISTINGS FOR THESE TYPES OF POSITIONS ON THE WORLD WIDE WEB JOBTRACK SITE, WHICH CAN BE REACHED AT HTTP://WWW. JOBTRAK.COM.

board meetings, and others may come out of a personal conversation Carol has with someone outside of work; some come from developers and agents, while still others just come to her when she's doing something as mundane as reading the newspaper.

But, Carol says, coming up with new ideas—no matter how it is done—and seeing those ideas developed into a new project is by far the best part of her job.

Where do you see this job leading you?

Carol says this job has brought her exactly where she wants to be in this career, and she doesn't foresee that she will make any career changes now.

"I'm very happy where I am. I think the job is going to continue to grow because the field is growing. I think I'm going to stay where I am."

69. News Products Instructor

description: Gone are the days when broadcast news reporters were required to spend hours fast-forwarding and rewinding videotape in order to line up their sound bites. The introduction of new technology allows reporters and editors to transfer the shots they take on video to a computer disk so they can edit their stories digitally, greatly reducing the amount of time it takes to edit tape while increasing production values.

Many editors currently working in the field are used to editing tape, not computer disks, and training an entire staff to do their job in an entirely different way is a timely venture. That is why it is necessary for the companies selling this new technology to provide training to the stations and networks that are willing to make the shift. This is usually done by news products instructors who travel from newsroom to newsroom teaching editors, reporters, and photographers how to use the new technology being installed at their station.

salary: For someone starting out in this field with a bachelor's degree, an entry-level position will probably pay around $30,000 to $35,000 a year. After four years of experience, a news products instructor could make around $40,000 to $45,000 a year. An instructor with more than five years of experience could make somewhere around $50,000 to $80,000 a year.

prospects: While the concept for this type of editing technology has been around for several years, the products themselves have only been on the market for about two years. As a growing number of television stations move toward using advanced technology, and as the technology continues to evolve, there will continue to be a need for people to train those using the products.

qualifications: People moving into this field must either be familiar with this technology or have the ability to pick up new things quickly. Equally important is knowledge of what goes on in a newsroom. Typically, someone in this position will have worked in the broadcast journalism field either as a reporter or editor or in some area of production.

characteristics: Aside from being able to learn the technology, news products instructors must be able to have the patience to teach someone else to produce footage with it. For the most part, these instructors have a genuine interest in the broadcast news industry and are excited about the changes technology is bringing about.

Scott Sobel *is a news products instructor.*

How did you get the job?

In the '60s, when Scott Sobel was in high school, he realized that society, with its swelling desire for immediacy, was putting a stronger emphasis on technology—specifically television. Once he reached college, Scott's desire to become a part of this wave led him to get his bachelor's degree in broadcast journalism and political science.

Now a 20-year veteran of the broadcast industry, Scott has begun to focus more on the technology behind the news as a news products instructor for AVID Technologies. When Scott first heard about the company's news products, he couldn't help but realize the potential this cutting-edge technology had for the industry as a whole. He knew that he had to be a part of it.

"Because of the speed, efficiency, and adaptiveness, these products are going to open up all sorts of informational frontiers for the news business,

> SOMEONE WANTING TO GET INTO THIS FIELD SHOULD DEFINITELY START BY GETTING EXPERIENCE USING AVID OR A SIMILAR TYPE OF TECHNOLOGY. THIS EQUIPMENT CAN USUALLY BE FOUND ON COLLEGE CAMPUSES IN THE FILMMAKING OR BROADCAST JOURNALISM DEPARTMENTS.

which I was associated with for so long. It's exciting to be able to be part of a real jump in knowledge and technology that will enable viewers to know so much more about their world and so much faster."

Scott's 20 years of work experience in the news industry, coupled with some time teaching college journalism courses, made him a prime candidate for a news products instructor position at AVID Technologies.

What do you do all day?

When Scott is in the office, he spends his time preparing for future classes, working with technical writers on various product manuals, and making suggestions to developers about new features for the products or improvements of old features. But Scott says he most enjoys the time spent out of the office, where he works with editors, reporters, and photographers, teaching them how to use the equipment that is revolutionizing the broadcast industry.

His trips can last anywhere from one day to two weeks, depending on how large a staff he is working with and how many products have been purchased by the news facility in which he is teaching. The size of a staff can be as small as one or as large as 80.

Scott says he will usually start out his trips by talking to the managers of the station or network in order to determine

who he needs to teach and what he needs to teach them. Then he gives his students an overview of the technology before he gets them into a classroom where they can start learning. One of the challenges is that his students come from varied backgrounds, which is almost always reflected in their diverse levels of knowledge.

"Power of observation is essential, so you can gear and change your teaching techniques on the subject matter to the experience level of the students," Scott says.

Where do you see this job leading you?

Scott views his future opportunities to be as broad as the potential changes in the technology. Consequently, he doesn't know exactly what the future will bring for him, but he is sure that the future is with AVID.

70. Petroleum Research Engineer

description: Once crude oil is removed from the ground, it can be transformed into anything from gasoline to a motor oil lubricant or a pesticide. Modifying the oil is a complex task that requires the substance be taken through specific processing steps, which are usually determined by a research engineer. It is the job of these engineers to design the refining process of crude oil in order to produce the desired final product. Close attention is paid to the volatility, the oxidation stability, and the viscosity of the oil during the testing process.

Rather than using enormous batches of oil, which could become costly, these engineers conduct their research on the computer, using various programs that will simulate processing changes. This enables them to estimate what variables will be required for the different products made from crude.

But the job of a petroleum products engineer doesn't end once the formulation for a specific product has been determined. Research engineers are also needed to supply technical support to customers. In this capacity, research engineers will often write numerous technical reports describing the properties of a particular product in great depth, as well as conducting follow-up testing on products that are suspected to be contaminated or defective.

salary: A research engineer will usually start out making somewhere around $37,000 to $45,000 a year. Typically, these engineers will receive a raise of about three percent every year. Larger raises come about as proficiency in the field increases.

prospects: The job market in the oil industry is tight right now. As the profit potential in the U.S. petroleum market continues to diminish, large companies who previously invested in sizable research and development departments are discontinuing this practice.

qualifications: Anyone getting into this field must at least hold a bachelor's degree in chemistry or chemical engineering. It is also helpful to have previous experience in the industry, which can be gained through an internship or summer job.

characteristics: On the whole, research engineers aren't expected to show up at their offices in a coat and tie. This casual dress code is a reflection of the people in the field. Although there are times when work can pile up, this job is generally not stressful and the people doing the work enjoy it.

E. Dennis *is a petroleum research engineer.*

How did you get the job?

As a freshman majoring in chemical engineering at Princeton University, E. Dennis thought more than once about choosing a different discipline on which to focus.

"A lot of times I really felt like quitting. It's just really tough. It was time-consuming, there were a lot of classes, a lot of labs, and there are a lot of easier majors out there that I thought I might be just as interested in."

But now that he has graduated and secured a job at a major oil refining company as a research engineer, E. says he is glad that he stuck with it.

At the conclusion of his laborious freshman year, E. was placed in an internship at the company where he is currently employed through Inroads Inc., a minority business placement program. For the first two summers, E. worked on the processing side of operations at the company, where he researched refinery operations. The summer after his junior year, E. began interning in the product research and development department, where the results of crude oil processing are further manipulated into consumer products. E. says he became partial to this department because it allowed him to work more closely with the customer in developing products.

During E.'s senior year at Princeton, the company offered him a job working as a research engineer, and he started work immediately after graduation.

> PERHAPS THE BEST RESOURCE FOR SOMEONE SEEKING WORK IN THE FIELD OF PETROLEUM RESEARCH IS THE AMERICAN INSTITUTE OF CHEMICAL ENGINEERS (AICHE). THIS ORGANIZATION OFFERS NUMEROUS SERVICES TO ITS MEMBERS, INCLUDING AN EMPLOYMENT SERVICES DEPARTMENT AND A MONTHLY PUBLICATION THAT CONTAINS JOB LISTINGS. STUDENT MEMBERSHIPS COST AROUND $19 A YEAR, AND ANY COLLEGE CHEMICAL ENGINEERING DEPARTMENT SHOULD HAVE MEMBERSHIP APPLICATIONS. (FOR MORE INFORMATION ON HOW TO CONTACT AICHE, SEE RESOURCES, PAGE 212.)

What do you do all day?

E.'s time in the office is generally divided between designing new petroleum blends and troubleshooting with old ones. The difference between the two is that the design work can usually be planned, whereas the troubleshooting comes in as the phone rings.

E. will usually start the day working on a long-term project, such as one that requires finding the variables needed to create a passenger car motor oil that will meet the stringent standards of new environmental laws. Or he might try to determine a way for oil in a diesel engine to produce less soot in the engine. These types of projects require numerous hours in front of the computer or in the lab before E. finds the set of conditions that creates the right blend.

But E. most likely won't spend the whole day working on one project. His work may be interrupted by a phone call from a client who is experiencing a problem with a particular product. In such a case, E. will usually request that the client send in samples of the product, which he will test before writing a detailed report for the customer.

Because all of these projects are too extensive to wrap up in one day, E. generally finds himself adding new projects to his list as he finishes up old ones.

Where do you see this job leading you?

E. would like to go back to school to get his M.B.A. so that he can eventually combine his knowledge of the technology and engineering fields with business by working in an area such as technical sales.

71. Physicist

description: Put simply, physicists use technical skills to answer questions. The questions might come from the government, research institutions, or high-tech sectors like the semiconductor industry. Physicists deal with the physical properties of matter, which means figuring out how to develop new materials or how to use existing materials in new, innovative ways. That can involve everything from creating newer and faster semiconductor materials, to designing longer-lasting, lighter-weight batteries for pollution-free cars, or even developing nuclear energy.

Physicists often work in teams with electronic engineers. Once a physicist proves something can be done, engineers take over to figure out how it can be done better, faster, and 1,000 times in a row.

Between 30 and 40 percent of physicists work for the government, another 30 to 40 percent work for private industry, and the rest work in academia. One difference between recent grads and physicists who have been in the field a while is that while recent grads think they can learn it all, veterans realize that that's impossible. That's why most physicists specialize in a particular area. But regardless of your specialty, there is one constant: The job always involves problem solving.

"Why" and "what if" are questions you will always be striving to answer.

salary: If you can find a job, you can expect to be well paid. At the Ph.D. level, positions with the government and private companies start at $55,000 to $65,000 a year. With 10 to 15 years of experience, salaries can climb to $80,000 to $90,000. Academia pays far less. A professor might start at $35,000 or $40,000 annually.

prospects: Your prospects depend on your area of expertise and the sector. Cutbacks in defense spending and in government research budgets have tightened the market for government jobs. But opportunities are increasing in areas such as the semiconductor industry.

qualifications: You will need a minimum of a master's degree in physics, and in many cases a Ph.D. Despite the image of physicists as loners who prefer science experiments to people, this job involves a lot of communication. Physicists typically work in teams, sharing information and collaborating to find answers, so you have to work well with others. Because the job involves writing a lot of proposals and reports, good writing skills are important.

characteristics: Most physicists spent their childhoods wondering how things work. That insatiable curiosity is what motivates physicists to find answers.

Rick Spielman *is a physicist at a Department of Energy laboratory in Albuquerque, New Mexico.*

How did you get the job?

"As a kid, I was always taking apart toys and trying to rebuild them," Rick Spielman says. "I was always putting a screwdriver into something." When he entered the University of California at Davis, there was no question he would be a physics major. He went on to earn a Ph.D. in applied physics.

When he completed the degree, Rick was ready to leave California. "When you stay, the people you know always treat you like a grad student," he says. But leaving was a big step. "Leaving the university is like leaving the womb," he says. A colleague suggested he apply at a government research lab in Albuquerque. He did, and he got the job. "Having an applied science background got me in the door, because [the lab] had a reputation for being engineering-driven," he says. Plus,

"They needed to hire a bunch of people, and I was there during a hiring window. Luck counts as much as skill sometimes."

Rick spent the first several years moving from project to project and learning everything he could from senior physicists along the way. He eventually moved into a project management position, and today he has 20 people working for him.

What do you do all day?

Rick spends about a quarter of his day in meetings. A typical day might include a budget meeting, a meeting with his team of physicists to discuss ideas, and a meeting to assess which physicists have the right skills to be part of a new project.

Meetings that involve team problem solving are his favorite. "People spend a lot of time waving their hands around and talking things out. We may spend a whole day like that," he says. "It might look like we're not getting any work done, but the sum of all the ideas is always better than any individual idea. You look up and realize there are a lot of pieces that can be combined. And from that, we come up with a technical response."

He spends about an hour dealing with technical memos from government labs all over the country. Sometimes he answers questions about how to solve a particular problem; sometimes he asks them.

Rick also checks calculations and works his own calculations for his group's project.

Where do you see this job leading you?

Rick is debating whether to move into full-time project management or to continue to do technical work, which he loves. "There are two career paths, technical and management," he says. "I really love finding technical solutions to things. I don't know if I want to give that up."

72. Product Evaluator

FOR A SOFTWARE DISTRIBUTION COMPANY

description: Software distributors are the companies that get CD-ROMs onto store shelves. Product evaluators decide which software titles their distribution company will offer.

Evaluators look at thousands of new products every year. A lot of their time is spent testing software programs to see whether they live up to the developer's hype. More often than not, evaluators wade through a lot of mediocre stuff. But despite the inevitable duds, getting the first peek at new software and being responsible for getting it to consumers is exciting. Keeping abreast of industry trends is important, since there is a lot of competition. To stay plugged in, evaluators attend trade shows around the country to scout for new products.

When evaluators see a program that has promise but needs work, they sometimes work directly with the software developer to make changes. To excel at this job you need to have a knack for picking hits. That's where a combination of marketing savvy and intuition comes in.

salary: Large software distributors, most of which are located in Silicon Valley, offer the highest salaries. Smaller, regional distributors pay less, but they also offer more opportunities to newcomers. At a large company, you can expect to start at about $35,000. Smaller firms begin in the high $20,000 range. With five years of experience, that can increase to $40,000 to $45,000 a year.

prospects: An explosion of multimedia titles, and the fact that chains like K-Mart and Wal-Mart now carry software has been a boon to distributors, and, in turn, to evaluators. Distributors realize that unless they pick and choose the right products, they won't last long. As a result, many are expanding their evaluating departments and rewarding them for snagging hits.

qualifications: A background in marketing and an understanding of the computer industry are two things distributors like to see. Technical skills also help, because you'll be testing a lot of products.

characteristics: There is no way to study for this job. Instinct is a big part of choosing a winning product, and you need to be able to trust yours. Patience is also a virtue in this job, since you'll be guiding a lot of software developers with no experience in distribution.

Don Kenny *is director of product evaluation at a leading software distributor in Santa Ana, California.*

How did you get the job?

Don Kenny was working in a civilian job for the Navy when he ran into a friend who was reselling computer software. This was in the late 1970s, when Apple computers were king, and IBM personal computers had yet to take off. Don, a long-time Apple user, advised his friend to pay attention to IBM. Don's friend introduced him to his boss, who was debating how to approach IBM systems. "I told him he'd better pay attention, because IBM was going to be bigger than Apple," Don says. The company hired Don to decide which IBM PC products to carry. "I didn't have a degree in computer science, so I was judging things from a consumer standpoint. I had a feel for what would appeal to other computer users."

His prediction that IBM would one day rule the roost came true. Today, IBM-com-patible machines make up more than 85 percent of the market, making Don's department a very important one. Don now oversees the whole evaluation process, from picking products to negotiating contracts. He oversees a staff of eight people.

Does he ever get tired of evaluating software? "For a computer nut like myself," he says, "there is nothing better than getting showered with software every day."

> **PRODUCT EVALUATORS OFTEN START IN OTHER AREAS, SUCH AS SALES OR MARKETING, AT SOFTWARE DISTRIBUTION COMPANIES BEFORE MOVING INTO THESE POSITIONS.**

What do you do all day?

Don looks at about 300 software titles a month. But he actually tests less than a third of them. "Over 200 of them get rejected before we even break the plastic on the box," he says.

Those that do make it past that point get a test run. If he likes what he sees, he considers the box design, the price, and the market potential to decide whether it's worth carrying. When the answer is yes, he meets with the developer and cuts a deal. Don has yet to bet on a bomb. "It's easy for me to look at something and tell whether or not it's going to sell," he says.

Even developers who get the thumbs-down can get some time with Don. "A lot of these people developed the software in their garage, and they have no idea what to do next," he says. "I give them feedback on what they might do differently, and advise them on their chances of ever getting it into a store."

Don also spends time talking to retailers about what is selling well and what customers are asking for. Don attends several trade shows a year where he sniffs around for promising products. When he spies something good, he swings into action. "The goal is to get an exclusive deal," he says. "When you've got a leading-edge product that you know is going to be a good seller, you sign them as quickly as you can."

Where do you see this job leading you?

"I really like what I'm doing right now," Don says. "For a computer aficionado, this is a dream job."

73. Product Manager

description: Product managers oversee every step of the process, from determining the development schedule of a product to monitoring production to helping close sales. They help decide how to position their product against the competition and how to price it.

Product managers for large software companies help with the package design and advertising campaigns. They make sure software disks are packaged properly, that orders are being placed, and that products are being shipped. At a smaller company, the product manager is closely involved with every step of the development process. If a salesperson is closing a big deal, it is not unusual for the product manager to go along and provide a technical demonstration.

A good deal of time is spent traveling to customers' sites to finalize deals and oversee installation of the product. Product managers also do a lot of presentations, which often involve explaining how the product works to a roomful of skeptical people. Negotiating skills are important, because angry customers are a fact of life. If they don't think the product does what you promised, it's up to you to assuage them.

This job involves a lot of accountability. If your product isn't meeting expectations, you are the one who has to explain to company officials why that's so.

salary: Pay depends on the size of the company, the region of the country, and yearly sales figures. It can range from $35,000 at a small company to as high as $100,000 at a large corporation.

prospects: Most high-tech companies appoint managers to oversee each product offering, but this is usually considered an upper-management job, so you need several years' experience and a lot of talent to land this kind of position.

qualifications: Education is less important than experience in the industry. You need to be well versed in the type of technology that you want to represent. Equally important are public-speaking skills and the ability to think fast on your feet.

characteristics: To use a computer term, you have to be good at "multitasking," or doing a number of different things at once. Everyone on the product development, marketing, and sales team is looking to you for leadership, so you have to be good at taking charge. You will be spending a lot of time on the road, so it helps if you like to travel.

John Zwerlein *is a product manager at a software company in Milwaukee, Wisconsin.*

How did you get the job?

"I didn't take the usual route to becoming a product manager," John Zwerlein says. John learned how to use computer-aided design, or CAD, software while working for the government designing ships. His expertise made him a prime candidate when an acquaintance started a company specializing in CAD software on a very bare-bones budget. "He asked me if I wanted to take a risk and join him," John recalls. "Against the wishes of my family, I decided to take it." He took a cut in pay to join the start-up, and prepared himself for long hours.

In the beginning, John did a little bit of everything—working with developers, helping with sales, doing training. "Now that we've grown, everyone is falling into their slots," he says. "Now we have a sales department, a training department, and a marketing department." John oversees all of those areas as they relate to the product he represents. For him,

joining the start-up was the right move. "After five years it's beginning to pay off," he says. "There's a very bright light at the end of the tunnel."

What do you do all day?

When John arrives at the office at 7 A.M., his voice mail light is already flashing. "There are usually two or three calls waiting for me from customers on the East Coast," he says. "I handle them right away." Many times they are calling with a question about specifications that they want the software to include. John meets with developers to discuss how to incorporate the customers' requests and to discuss the testing schedule for upcoming releases.

John is also popular with the tech-support team. "They're continually coming into my office and asking me questions," he says. "They've got a person who needs help waiting on the phone, and I give them suggestions on how to fix the problem."

A part of his day that John would just as soon avoid occurs when he receives a call from a

customer who is upset because his customized software won't include all of the features he had wanted. "We sometimes get into very heated conversations," John says. "It starts with a marketing person who tells the customer they can add a feature and it will still be done in a certain time. Then there are delays, and it's not ready." Sometimes the customer wants to back out of the deal altogether. That's where those people skills come in. "I have to convince them that we'll get them 80 percent of what they want on time and we'll get them the other 20

> **PRODUCT MANAGERS USUALLY BEGIN AT THE BOTTOM OF THE LADDER. TAKE AN ENTRY-LEVEL POSITION, LEARN EVERYTHING YOU CAN ABOUT THE PRODUCT, AND FOCUS ON GETTING EXPERIENCE IN AREAS LIKE MARKETING AND DEVELOPMENT.**

percent shortly after." Reasoning with the customer usually works. But success requires staying calm.

John spends 10 days a month traveling to meet with customers and potential buyers. In five years, his job has taken him to Venezuela, Argentina, Germany, and all but four of the United States. In an effort to spend more time with his family, John now avoids traveling on weekends. During his visits, he often gives product demonstrations to a roomful of people. It's at those times he's grateful he participated on his high school debate team. "When they ask you questions, you cannot be hesitant for a minute or they'll eat you alive," he says. "If you are, they write you off immediately."

Where do you see this job leading you?

John wants to continue to help the company grow, which should triple in size this year. "We've come a long way, and I want to be around to see us reach the next level," he says.

74. Product Planner

description: A product planner helps a company develop its product lines by listening to customers, attending trade shows, and forecasting the direction of the market. Product planners take that information and work with product developers to create a strategy.

Planners spend a lot of their time working with customers to learn how they use the company's products and how they see their needs changing. Planners also meet regularly with field representatives and salespeople who work directly with the customers and get feedback on products that planners need.

One of the best parts of this job is acting as the voice of the customers and seeing that their needs are incorporated into new products. But influencing what the finished product looks like can have a downside. When you make a wrong turn and release a product that isn't what the customers had in mind, it can be both disappointing and financially costly to your company.

salary: Product planners with five or more years of sales or marketing experience usually earn in the $40,000 to $45,000 range. If you're just entering the field, you might start anywhere from $28,000 to $35,000 a year, depending on your experience.

prospects: Technology companies are paying much closer attention to their customers' needs, rather than the old model of developing products and expecting customers to go along with them. This approach has made product planners a key part of the development process, and many companies are putting increased emphasis in this area, making this a field with a very healthy job outlook.

qualifications: Computer science graduates are increasingly entering this field, but a technical degree is not usually required. Companies rarely hire product planners who don't have work experience in an area that involves working with customers, such as sales or other fieldwork. To help a company plan its product lines, you need to have a feel for customers and their world, and it's hard to convince someone to hire you if you've never dealt with consumers.

characteristics: Product planners work with a wide range of people, including customers, salespeople, and developers, so they have to be able to shift languages and work well with different personalities. This isn't a sit-in-the-office kind of job. You've got to enjoy getting out and meeting with people. And perhaps most importantly, you've got to be a good listener.

Robin Ringo *is a product planner for a corporation that makes computer printers and copy machines in El Segundo, California.*

How did you get the job?

As an administrative assistant in Fort Worth, Robin Ringo used Xerox electronic typewriters that were the precursor to word processors. She became the in-house Xerox expert, and eventually Xerox hired her to do technical support.

She spent several years doing national tech support, where she helped customers when they had problems with their systems. She then moved to California to work in a Xerox sales office where she became an analyst at customer sites. That involved working with customers to figure out what kind of problems they were having and helping them devise new systems to meet their needs.

The job required Robin to report to the senior staff about the difficulties customers were encountering. After one impassioned speech in which she told them they weren't delivering the kinds of products that customers wanted, she got a call. "It was from someone who had heard me pleading, and he said,

'I've got an offer that you can't refuse,'" she recalls. "They wanted me to help them deliver the products that customers needed." She accepted the job and became a product planner. During her presentation, she had pointed out that a competitor was 18 months ahead of what her development team was doing, and urged the staff to do something about it. "Since I knew exactly what customers were looking for, it made sense to pull me into the process," she says. "It was a big step for me, and it turned out to be the right one."

What do you do all day?

Robin's days vary according to what phase a particular product is in. She travels a lot, including a recent trip to Seattle to oversee the installation of a new product. "I wanted to be there to make sure it was working and see what they thought about it," she says.

If a product is in the development stage, she will work with customers and engineers to gather requirements for the

product and follow through as it is designed to see that it incorporates certain features. When a new product is released, Robin meets frequently with salespeople to pick their brains about how customers are responding to it. And she also fields calls from salespeople who are on the verge of a big sale and need to make sure they can configure the system in a particular way. "They call me saying, 'Can we do this? Please tell me we can do this,'" she says. "And we

> IF YOU'RE INTERESTED IN THE PRODUCTS THAT A PARTICULAR COMPANY SELLS, CONSIDER TAKING A JOB WITH THE COMPANY IN ANOTHER AREA— ANY JOB CAN BE A STEPPING STONE TO THE POSITION YOU ULTIMATELY DESIRE. USE IT TO LEARN ABOUT THE COMPANY, ITS PRODUCTS, AND ITS CULTURE.

figure out how to do it the way the customer wants it."

She and her fellow product planners also spend time looking ahead at where the market is going and discussing which direction the company needs to be heading in order to stay ahead of the curve.

When she can, Robin skips out of the office and works at home. "I can get more work done sitting two hours at my dining room table with no phone than half a day at the office," she says. "Sometimes I really love the peace and quiet."

Where do you see this job leading you?

"I absolutely want to stay in technology, because it fascinates me," she says. Although her job involves working with customers, she misses the days when her whole job revolved around them. "I miss not being around customers as much," she says. If she ever changes jobs, finding one that involves working closely with customers will be a priority.

75. Production Manager

FOR A DIGITAL STOCK PHOTOGRAPHY COMPANY

description: As desktop publishing becomes more advanced, the equipment that is used also progresses. One accessory of desktop publishing is clip art, which consists of numerous illustrations saved onto one disk. Now, pre-scanned photographs are also available on disk. This is known as digital stock photography, and it is used mainly by graphic artist professionals. Photographic images are transposed onto a computer disk by a high-resolution scanner. The images are then touched up with a digital airbrush. Once the images are spotless, they are packaged with others on a CD-ROM, and a computer program is developed that allows a graphic artist to pull up an image using a key word. This entire process involves numerous people and would become very disorganized if it weren't for production managers who direct the activity and ensure that deadlines are met.

salary: In an entry-level job, such as a production assistant, you could expect to make a salary in the low-$20,000s. As a production manager, your salary will be in the range of $30,000 to $40,000 a year. With experience in a management role, your salary could become as large as $60,000.

prospects: The job market in digital stock photography is growing, much like the field itself. However, starting out as a production manager is rare. It may be helpful to gain experience first as a production assistant in a similar field such as publishing or graphic art, if you don't immediately land a job in digital stock photography.

qualifications: In order to secure this type of job, you will definitely need a bachelor's degree. It would be wise to direct your studies toward disciplines that will give you experience in both graphic design and business management. Strong computer skills are also a must in this field. You should be familiar with applications used in desktop publishing such as QuarkXpress, Adobe Photoshop, Adobe Illustrator, and Macromedia FreeHand.

characteristics: People in this type of position must be extremely organized, be able to juggle multiple tasks simultaneously, and flourish in a chaotic environment. They must have a healthy respect for deadlines, but also be flexible enough to calmly and effectively deal with a situation where a deadline is missed.

Karl Haberl *is a production manager for a digital stock photography company in Seattle, Washington.*

How did you get the job?

When Karl Haberl was attending business classes at the University of Washington, he held down various jobs through which he gained experience in both computers and photography. During the summers of his freshman and sophomore years, Karl worked for a commercial photographer. Throughout his junior year he worked for a start-up software company, and his senior year was spent working in the customer service department of a computer manufacturing company. Karl graduated with a business degree that carried a concentration in marketing and business management, and he immediately began sending out resumes. One of the companies he sent a resume to was a photographic

service bureau company. The company did not hire Karl; however, they did pass his resume along to a digital stock photography company. Luckily, this company was looking for someone who had experience in photography, computers, and business. Karl got the job.

What do you do all day?

Because Karl's job is to shepherd a project from start to finish, he spends the majority of his time making sure that everything is happening according to

THERE ARE A NUMBER OF SOURCES YOU CAN USE TO FIND A JOB IN THIS FIELD, RANGING FROM THE WANT ADS IN YOUR LOCAL NEWSPAPER TO THE INTERNET, BUT PERHAPS ONE OF THE MOST USEFUL SOURCES WOULD BE AN INDUSTRY MAGAZINE SUCH AS COMMUNICATION ARTS, HOW, OR PUBLISH!. ANY OF THESE MAGAZINES CAN GIVE YOU INSIGHT INTO WHAT COMPANIES IN THE INDUSTRY ARE UP TO, SO YOU WILL GET A BETTER IDEA OF WHERE TO TARGET YOUR SEARCH.

schedule. However, he is never working on just one project at a time, so this job proves more complicated than it might at first sound. Karl says his job can be broken down into different categories, such as troubleshooting with computers, negotiating with vendors, and scheduling with freelancers, printers, or production artists. The largest part of his job centers around managing people. This requires him to act as a perpetual reminder to those with pending deadlines. Although it is Karl's

duty to manage those involved in the creative process, he says it is very important never to meddle with the process himself. "I consider myself more of a project manager and a scheduler, planner, and troubleshooter. A project manager is best when they are able to manage the creative process. When they try to get involved with it themselves, they are more likely to slow things down rather than help the process."

Where do you see this job leading you?

Karl says this job could lead him to a job as a production manager either in a design firm or in the book publishing arena.

76. Sales Engineer

description: A sales engineer acts as a liaison between a company's engineers and its sales and marketing staff. It's the sales engineer's job to learn the ins and outs of a product from the engineers and then work with the marketing department to translate the technical jargon in a way that will help sell the product. Because engineers are typically not good at selling things and salespeople are usually not astute in engineering, the sales engineer enters the picture as the interpreter.

Sales engineers also work with the sales force to educate them about particular applications and features of the product. When salespeople have questions out in the field, they call the sales engineer, who provides the answers.

salary: Pay is based on experience and the size of the company for which you are working. A newcomer can expect to start at about $35,000 a year, and experienced sales engineers can earn more than $75,000 annually. Some companies also offer bonus programs which give sales engineers quarterly or yearly commissions based on the sales staff's performance.

prospects: Technology is becoming more and more complex, but the people who are advertising and selling it often do not have technical backgrounds. Companies are realizing that if their sales and marketing teams aren't on top of the technology, they can't sell it. As a result, companies are adding sales engineering positions, and this field's future is bright.

qualifications: A degree in computer science, electrical engineering, or telecommunications is usually required. It also helps to have experience in the field, preferably in sales or technical support.

characteristics: You will need to be both a left-brained and a right-brained person to do this job. You have to be able to understand highly technical terminology and equipment and then turn around and explain it in English to people with fairly limited technical backgrounds.

Vernon Suesse *is a sales engineer at a telecommunications company in Chandler, Arizona.*

How did you get the job?

Vernon Suesse studied electronic engineering and computer science at Cleveland State University, and after graduating took a job with a telecommunications company, doing programming. "I didn't know anything about the telephone industry going in, but I got more and more into telecommunications, and I really liked it," he says. Vernon eventually moved to another telecommunications company in Cleveland, doing similar work. One day he spotted a classified ad for a telecommunications company across the country. "When I saw it was in beautiful Denver, Colorado, I knew I wanted the job," he recalls. Hired over the phone, he packed his car and moved to Denver.

He eventually became a service manager. "I found I was being called on to help the salespeople more and more," Vernon says. "They wanted to know 'Will it do this?' 'Can it

> YOU CAN ENTER THIS JOB FROM EITHER THE SALES OR THE ENGINEERING SIDE, BUT YOU NEED SOME SOLID EXPERIENCE IN ONE OR THE OTHER. YOU WILL ALSO NEED A GOOD TECHNICAL UNDERSTANDING OF THE PRODUCT AND THE ABILITY TO EXPLAIN IT.

do that?'" With technology becoming much more complicated, the learning curve for salespeople was getting steeper. Vernon's company created a sales engineering department to assist the sales force, and he was recruited to help the sales team close deals. "Probably the best thing I ever did was get out of operations and into the sales end," he says. "I loved going out with a salesperson, sitting down with a prospective client, and coming out with a signed contract."

When his company decided to open a sales engineering department at the headquarters in Arizona, they asked Vernon to oversee it. "They made me an offer to move my family to Phoenix that was too good to refuse," he says. Although it meant giving up the sales calls, the job allowed Vernon to make the most of his skills by working with both engineers and salespeople. "I've worked on both sides, so I was a good person to serve as a bridge between the two," he says.

What do you do all day?

Vernon arrives at work at 8 A.M. and checks his voice mail, e-mail, and daily planner to remind himself of his agenda for the day. He returns calls to salespeople and sales managers from the day before. "I get lots of messages from people saying, 'You said it could do this, but I can't figure it out,'" he says. "I explain it to them, and they go out and do it."

He spends some days with the engineering department, which briefs him on their latest product. Other days he will work with salespeople and marketing specialists to bring them up to speed. Using a whiteboard, he goes over all the aspects of the products and what needs to be conveyed to the customer. "It's not enough to memorize the jargon," he says. "Our customers are technical people and they need in-depth descriptions. My job is to ensure that our sales staff give just that."

Where do you see this job leading you?

The sales engineering department is growing, and Vernon wants to continue to oversee its expansion. "This department is playing an important role in our company's growth, and for me that's exciting."

77. Semiconductor Device Engineer

description: Today, semiconductors can be found in a plethora of electronic products ranging from computers to automobiles to cellular phones. Much like the products they accompany, these electronic bits are very complex. Each chip is made up of millions of individual microscopic transistors, which work together to form a circuit. It is the job of a semiconductor device engineer to ensure that every transistor in each circuit produced is in peak working condition.

These engineers are often called upon to boost the performance of a particular product or to find out what is amiss in a defective one. In order to accomplish either of these tasks, the engineer will most likely look to the manufacturing process of the transistors. Because these transistors are minuscule—about the size of one micron squared—these parts can't be worked on in the same way an auto mechanic would repair a car's transmission. Instead, statistical data regarding the manufacturing process is gathered and analyzed by engineers who determine from their findings what changes in the manufacturing process should be made. Using this data and their understanding of solid-state physics and electronic principles, engineers are able to optimize the performance and yield of the transistors.

salary: Someone with a bachelor's degree in this type of work could start off making a salary upwards of $30,000, whereas someone with a master's could expect to make somewhere in the range of $45,000 to $60,000 in an entry-level position. The salary, including bonuses and incentives, typically increases with the number of years of experience. Someone with 10 years of experience could be making anywhere from $100,000 to $200,000 a year.

prospects: There has been a tremendous amount of growth in the semiconductor field over the last two years, and with an increasing number of products requiring semiconductors for their development, more growth can be expected.

qualifications: At minimum, someone going into this field will need a bachelor's degree in either electrical engineering, physics, or some sort of material science. Further education, such as a master's degree, is valuable and would better your chances of finding a job.

characteristics: People working in this field are generally very intelligent and analytical. These engineers are usually interested in technology, motivated by problem-solving, and love working with computers.

Adam Brand *is senior device physicist for a microchip manufacturer in California.*

How did you get the job?

Growing up, Adam Brand was always interested in computers, but he wasn't able to act on that interest until he got to college.

"When I was still pretty young, computers were just starting to show up, and I was pretty fascinated in how they worked. I figured out that they had a lot of these chips inside, and I wondered how people made them. When I got to school they had answers, and I kept pursuing that."

Adam's quest for answers in the making of computers led him to study electrical engineering, which became his subject of choice for both a bachelor's and a master's degree. While studying to get his degrees, Adam interned at David Sarnoff Research Laboratories, where he was able to work with computers in the area of design, programming, and device physics.

PERHAPS THE <u>SAN JOSE MERCURY NEWS</u> WILL BE THE BEST SOURCE FOR SOMEONE LOOKING FOR A JOB IN THIS FIELD. ALTHOUGH THE PAPER SERVICES THE SAN JOSE, CALIFORNIA, AREA, JOB LISTINGS FROM OTHER AREAS OF THE COUNTRY CAN OFTEN BE FOUND IN ITS CLASSIFIED ADS. DON'T WORRY ABOUT GETTING YOUR HANDS ON THE PAPER IF YOU'RE NOT LIVING ON THE WEST COAST. JUST LOOK ON THE WORLD WIDE WEB AT HTTP://WWW.SJMERCURY.COM/CLASS.

After completing his academic courses, Adam was able to get a job at a major manufacturer of microchips in the Silicon Valley through the placement office at his school.

He started working in a rotation program that required him to work in a variety of different jobs in marketing, design, and device engineering. After about a year in the rotation, he was moved into his current position as senior device physicist.

What do you do all day?

The majority of Adam's day is spent conducting research and attending meetings to discuss his findings. While the research itself centers around the fabrication plants where transistors are created, he doesn't actually go to the plant. Most of his research is conducted on a computer from his desk or laboratory, where Adam studies transistors at a wafer probe station or through an electron microscope.

Because the field of technology moves at such a fast pace, and no one wants to be left behind, Adam says, his company is constantly looking to improve existing products. "We're always finishing up what we were just working on, and starting all over again," he says, adding that this is one of the more exciting aspects of the job. "We are constantly reinventing and the work is always challenging."

Where do you see this job leading you?

While Adam says he pictures himself eventually getting involved with some of the design work at his company, for now he wants to stay right where he is.

78. Software Buyer

FOR A COMPUTER STORE CHAIN

description: From intergalactic war games to spreadsheets and databases, all the software on the shelf of your computer store was chosen by a retail buyer. As a buyer, you decide what the store sells, and it's your job to advertise it, arrange special promotions, and oversee how it's displayed in stores.

Buyers spend a lot of time reviewing software to separate the duds from the stars. They travel to trade shows and visit stores around the country to check up on how products are being merchandised. They also meet with software vendors to negotiate prices and place orders.

Software buyers are among the first to see the hottest new technology. But there's plenty of pressure—if you fill the aisles with stuff no one wants, you'll have some explaining to do. If you fail to meet your numbers at the same time other chains are hitting theirs, your job may be on the line.

salary: An assistant buyer might start at $20,000 a year, with mid-level buyers earning $30,000 to $40,000. Veteran buyers can double that. Salary is based on experience and your track record in sales.

prospects: A high turnover rate and major growth in the consumer software industry mean companies are regularly recruiting new buyers.

qualifications: A college degree in marketing or retail is helpful but by no means required. Computer literacy and an understanding of the software industry are also valued by recruiters. Most people start out as assistant buyers, which involves keeping purchase orders, tracking new releases, and coordinating advertising with vendors.

characteristics: You will need thick skin and good negotiating skills. Since every vendor is convinced their software is the greatest, you have to be able to separate reality from hype. And you must be able to say no.

Gary Sousa *is a senior buyer for computer software at a retail store in Minnesota.*

How did you get the job?

After graduating from college, Gary Sousa took a job working for a department store chain as an assistant buyer in Manhattan. As part of the training program, he was transferred to a store in Nashville, Tennessee, after a couple of years. He spent four years in the trenches as a department manager for housewares, luggage, and appliances.

After paying his dues, Gary was promoted to luggage buyer, and a year later took a job as luggage buyer at a major electronics retailer. "I was there six months when the senior computer buyer found out that computers were my hobby," he says. "Luggage buyers are a dime a dozen, so he made me a computer buyer."

Gary spent the next few years buying computers, software, computer supplies and accessories, and stereo equipment. Then he moved to a software chain as a buyer, and two years ago took his current job as senior buyer.

"Going from luggage to technology was a big switch, and it was all because I happened to have the right hobby," Gary says.

What do you do all day?

Gary spends a lot of his time thinking about what will motivate his customers to shell out $35 for a software program. When he meets with vendors to check out their latest offerings, he gives the program a test run and pays close attention to packaging and pricing. "The question you're always asking yourself is, 'Will it sell?'" When it comes to deciding yes or no,

Gary trusts his instincts. For instance, he knows that no matter how much fun a game is, if the art on the box is lousy, kids won't look twice. If he likes the game enough, he'll suggest packaging changes.

Gary also decides which of the products to push. If he chooses a new interactive encyclopedia CD-ROM, he might promote it in newspaper ads, work with stores to set up eye-catching displays, and work with vendors to offer special discounts.

Gary's usual workday runs from 8 A.M. to 7 P.M., and he usually takes some work home. He's constantly engineering promotions and meeting with vendors, so there's rarely any downtime. In August, September, and October the pace is nonstop as he gears up for the holiday season. His chain opens most of its new stores during the second half of the year. So when other retailers might be taking a breather, Gary is buying software to fill empty stores.

> ONE GOOD WAY TO GET RETAIL EXPERIENCE IN THE FIELD IS BY GETTING A PART-TIME JOB AT A COMPUTER STORE. YOU'LL WORK WITH CUSTOMERS AND LEARN HOW TO MAKE BUYING DECISIONS.

Where do you see this job leading you?

Gary would like to work his way to merchandise manager, which is the person to whom senior buyers report. His ultimate goal is vice president of merchandise, where he would be able to focus on strategies rather than inventory counts.

Gary has many colleagues who have become sales representatives for software vendors. "Sales pay more," he says. "And if you've already been a buyer, you know exactly what they're looking for."

79. Software Developer

FOR A SMALL MANUFACTURING COMPANY

description: A software developer creates programs for in-house use as well as for specific needs of the customer. You could be writing software for construction, aerospace, banking, or any kind of engineering. Since many companies can't use off-the-shelf software, the trend is to hire an in-house programmer to create new programs or to customize existing software. As a software developer for a small production company, you will do a lot of observation and work-flow analysis assessing current working operations. After analyzing which activities can best be done by computer, a developer writes programs accordingly.

salary: Salaries will vary widely, depending on location and the size of the company. Software developers at a small company can start at $25,000 per year, and $30,000 per year is typical for larger companies. That figure can go as high as $80,000 per year or more as you specialize and gain experience.

prospects: As the computer industry grows, so grows the need for software developers, and you could be working in a myriad of places. More and more small companies are discovering the value of an in-house programmer who can write programs to expedite systems within the company and who keeps the company abreast of rapid changes in technology.

qualifications: Most companies look for a four-year engineering or computer science degree. Software developer Jim DeVries says, "You often don't learn in school the things you really need to know. Most computer knowledge is acquired by working with computers." If you can prove you have skills in addition to a degree, the job is often yours.

characteristics: Resourcefulness seems to be key among programmers. Since you are creating a tool, you must think through all the possibilities of what that tool could do, what the most valuable features would be, and how you will make that happen. "As a programmer," Jim says, "you are always on the lookout for tasks that a computer can expedite."

B. James DeVries *is a software developer for a small manufacturing company.*

How did you get the job?

"My computer career started with a small home computer and a college course in FORTRAN [a computer language]," Jim DeVries says. "That's the extent of my formal computer training." As is true with many computer programmers, Jim is self-taught.

He attended Michigan Technological University, and earned a bachelor's degree in mechanical engineering. "I liked the idea of a small company, so that's where I targeted my resume in my senior year." He was hired as a mechanical engineer straight out of school. Jim says, "The next thing I knew, I was packing my bags for Florida."

Jim works for Alpine Engineered Products, Inc., which manufactures connector plates for wooden trusses that are used for home construction. Alpine writes the programs for engineering the trusses, and has a research and development team testing their product both on computer and in the field.

Jim's talents for programming surfaced when, as a mechanical engineer, he began writing programs to make his job easier. "I started sharing my programs with my work buddies," Jim says, "and the company turned their programming needs over to me."

"I was more than an in-house hire," Jim says. "I created my position by performing a job the company hadn't realized it needed."

Jim doesn't just write programs at work. Speaking of one of his home hobbies, Jim says, "I just finished a program cataloging my CDs and cassette tapes that has 10-second sound bites of songs."

What do you do all day?

Jim closely collaborates with the company's engineers, writing programs to fit their needs. He says, "I'm given the global assignments, and narrow them down to something manageable."

His hours are very flexible, and usually run pretty long. "No one's watching me as long as my work gets done," says Jim.

Because he has such vast computer experience, Jim often

> TARGETING SMALL COMPANIES IN YOUR JOB SEARCH IS A GOOD IDEA. SMALLER COMPANIES OFTEN ALLOW EMPLOYEES THE CHANCE TO WORK IN A VARIETY OF AREAS, GIVING RECENT GRADS THE OPPORTUNITY TO EXPLORE DIFFERENT CAREER AVENUES, FROM SOFTWARE DEVELOPMENT TO MARKETING.

finds himself working on customers' hardware, and troubleshooting problems for both customers and engineers in the office. "I'm the last resort—the final word in computers," Jim grins. "This is flattering, and I'm glad to alleviate people's computer frustrations, but it often keeps me from getting my own programming done."

Where do you see this job leading you?

Jim is happy where he is. "I'll soon get to try my hand at management," he says. "We are hiring another programmer who can do my work while I handle the computer crisis intervention I end up doing."

These skills could lead him to freelance programming or producing and marketing his own software. "Some programmers have hit it just right," Jim says with a smile, "and are currently sunbathing on the French Riviera drinking Jolt Cola."

80. Software Engineer

description: Software engineers write lines of code that control the way a software program looks, feels, and runs. The code is written in a computer language, such as COBOL or C, which is transferred into a computer program.

When developing a software program, engineers usually work in teams, with each member creating a different part of the application. If the project is an accounting program, for example, one engineer might write code to handle the billing process, while another would focus on the data-entry section.

Some engineers' work changes depending on the application, while others, particularly those at large corporations, might concentrate on writing a set piece of code for program after program.

Engineers say developing software is a creative process. You get to watch as months worth of code is transformed into a shrink-wrapped product. Deadlines are always lurking, occasionally turning eight-hour days into all-nighters. Intense deadlines, and the sometimes repetitive nature of writing code, can lead to burnout.

salary: Software engineers straight out of college can start at $25,000 a year. Experienced engineers with expertise in a hot area, such as database programming, can earn as much as $90,000.

prospects: It's fairly easy to get a job writing software. This isn't a field that requires years of experience to break into—most companies hire recent grads. And the boom in the home computer market has increased demand for software applications, creating a big market for software engineers.

qualifications: Most companies prefer that you have a bachelor's degree in computer science or management information systems (MIS). But there are many successful programmers who never took a computer course and taught themselves to program. The bottom line: Companies are more interested in your skills than in your major.

characteristics: You have to be a logical thinker and able to sit down and concentrate on one thing for hours at a time. Because you're always working under deadline, the ability to set goals and pace yourself is important. You will spend a lot of time integrating your work with other programmers' code, so you've got to be able to work well as part of a team.

Jon Steinmetz *is a software engineer at a multimedia software publishing company in Minneapolis, Minnesota.*

How did you get the job?

As a computer science major at Augsburg College in Minneapolis, Jon Steinmetz had an internship with the county government doing mainframe computer programming. After graduating, Jon went to work for American Public Radio in Minneapolis. "I was sort of their general purpose computer person," he says. "I did some programming, some network administering, made sure the computers worked, and pretty much kept everything going."

When he was offered a job as an engineer at a software publishing house that makes interactive CD-ROMs, Jon went for it. "It involved working in the hot new area of multimedia, and that was an exciting opportunity."

Jon thinks the fact that he's a Macintosh computer programmer gave him an edge. "They needed a Macintosh programmer, and we're quite a bit more rare," he says. "I had also worked on a lot of projects by myself and done some consulting work on my own, and I think that experience helped get me in the door."

What do you do all day?

Jon's job involves turning books and magazines published by the Mayo Clinic into interactive CD-ROMs. On a typical day, he'll arrive at about 7:15 A.M., check his e-mail, listen to voice mail messages, and pick up where he left off the day before.

That would usually be either writing or testing code. He might spend days writing code that will allow the user to click on a button to bring up pictures or text.

> CHECK OUT THE CLASSIFIEDS OF AREAS SUCH AS SILICON VALLEY, BOSTON, AND AUSTIN, TEXAS, WHERE THERE ARE HUNDREDS OF SMALL START-UPS IN NEED OF PROGRAMMERS. BE WILLING TO MOVE EVEN IF THE CITY IS NOT YOUR FIRST CHOICE.

"In the software development cycle, you don't write the whole program and then run it to see if it'll work," he says. "You complete a small part, and you test it. And it rarely works the first time."

When it doesn't, Jon uses special tools that let him see what's happening inside the code so he can figure out where it's going wrong. When that doesn't work, he'll call on a colleague for help. "Sometimes when you're staring at something long enough, you can't find the problem," he says. "That's when you go find someone else and get a fresh perspective."

Jon also attends weekly meetings where the engineers give status reports on their projects. His day usually ends at about 4:30 P.M., except when there's a deadline to meet. Although he tries to avoid it, he has worked around the clock to finish coding.

Where do you see this job leading you?

"This is it for me right now," Jon says. "I've always wanted to keep doing some form of programming. It's my hobby."

As for his colleagues, many either move up or move out. "You see people either going on to management or getting completely burned out and leaving to open a bait shop or something."

81. Software Industry Analyst

description: Advances in software have everyone paying close attention to what is on the market, but perhaps no one pays closer attention than those who analyze the market. Because the software industry is still young, there is really no one place to look when researching the market, so analysts often conduct research by keeping in close contact with software vendors; this allows them to keep tabs on the movement of products within the market. The information they gather is used to generate reports that are purchased by vendors interested in the market's trends. Software industry analysts are usually the first to find out about up-and-coming software because they are hired by the software vendors to report on the impact market trends will have on new products. These analysts represent a wealth of information to the software vendors, and they are often called upon to give advice concerning product positioning and sales strategies.

salary: Most starting out in this field can expect to make a salary in the low $30,000s. Someone who stays in this type of position for the long term can eventually make somewhere in the range of $60,000 to $75,000 a year. A shift to management would be required to earn more.

prospects: The job market for this type of work is growing as software vendors realize increased profits and become more interested in tracking their investments.

qualifications: Anyone interested in going into this type of work should equip him- or herself with at least a bachelor's degree in economics or some other discipline pertaining to business. Advanced degrees, such as an M.B.A., could be helpful but are not required. Knowledge of technology would also be beneficial to someone vying for a position as a research analyst.

characteristics: Software analysts work hard, but not all of their time is spent behind a computer. They will often meet with vendors to discuss different products and market trends; therefore they must be personable. Analysts must also be bold enough to assert their opinion of market trends diplomatically and without fear of clashing with a vendor or client.

Brian Burba *is a software industry analyst.*

How did you get the job?

Brian Burba graduated from Brown University with a bachelor's degree in mathematical economics, and immediately got a job working for an economic consulting company where he provided support for expert witness testimony in court cases involving patent infringements, anticompetitive issues, and mergers and acquisitions. This gave Brian experience in a variety of industries, and allowed him to discover the industry he found most interesting.

"The cases I liked most were technology oriented, so I decided to focus my work a little bit more. I knew that I wanted to move toward technology, and it made good sense to me for a lot of reasons."

Brian then went to work for a publishing company as part of an internal economics research organization tracking the electronics and technology markets. This job was more focused on technology, but because the company wasn't financially stable, Brian decided to use this opportunity to sharpen his

> **IT'S NOT WHO YOU KNOW, BUT WHO YOU CAN GET TO KNOW. EVEN IF YOU DON'T KNOW ANYONE IN SOFTWARE INDUSTRY ANALYSIS, YOU WOULDN'T BE HARD PRESSED TO MEET SOMEONE IF YOU WERE WILLING TO PUT SOME TIME INTO TRACKING THEM DOWN, JUST BY LOOKING THROUGH A COUPLE OF TRADE MAGAZINES SUCH AS PC WEEK OR DATA COMMUNICATIONS.**

career's focus on technology.

He found out about a job as a software industry analyst for International Data Corporation from his upstairs neighbor, who worked for the company. Although Brian's past experience hadn't given him training that was industry specific, the work had prepared him in a different way for the challenges he encounters as a software analyst.

"I was able to study a market and understand the interaction between competing products and companies. I also learned to communicate effectively through writing and speaking," he says.

What do you do all day?

Writing a market study was one of the first tasks that Brian was required to do when he started working as a software industry analyst at International Data Corporation, and he quickly found out that it wasn't an easy task.

"It was my second day, and my boss went out of town for three weeks on a business trip. My job was to write a market study, and I was staring at 30 blank pages. I knew I had to fill them in a set amount of time, get all the information and pull it all together," Brian recalls. "I had never written anything that long, particularly in a professional situation."

Brian has since become more comfortable with the task that requires him to map out what is important in the market and to provide data to support his stance. In fact, he now considers it to be one of the most interesting facets of his job.

Writing these reports represents only about 60 percent of Brian's total responsibilities. He also spends his time interacting with vendors who want guidance on the best way to position a new product. Usually, after the vendors have told Brian about their new product, he will spend the next couple of days fielding calls from members of the press wanting to know his opinion of the software.

Where do you see this job leading you?

From his position as a software industry analyst, Brian could continue to work as an analyst and move into a more managerial role, but with his knowledge of the industry he could also work for a software vendor.

82. Software Integration Engineer

description: There are thousands of software products on the market today, and there are even more businesses looking for software that will encompass all of their specific needs. For many businesses, it is easy to find a couple of software programs that will perform specific tasks. The only problem is that these software programs don't always work in conjunction with each other or with the business's operating system. To solve this problem, a software engineer could design new software to meet its needs, but it is often more economical to turn the problem over to a software integration engineer.

A software integration engineer writes code that will act as an interface between two software programs that weren't meant to work together, allowing them to communicate with each other. For example, a software integration engineer might be called upon to write code that will allow a data acquisitions software program to read data coming out of a large information system. The software program will output the code in a format that the operators of the system are able to read. Without the integration, the information system operators would be left with a mess of illegible data.

salary: Entry-level positions in this field usually pay somewhere around $30,000 a year. The salary for this position will increase with years of experience, and can pay as high as $60,000 a year.

prospects: The job market is growing for integration software engineers as more and more companies realize the amount of money and time that can be saved by integrating software programs that already exist rather than creating new ones.

qualifications: It is necessary to have a bachelor's degree, preferably in computer science or computer engineering, in order to be eligible for employment as an integration software engineer. It is also important to have experience writing code and working with a variety of computer languages, especially fourth-generation languages such as SQL and C++. This type of experience can be gained through an internship.

characteristics: People who work in this field are usually very dedicated. They usually enjoy losing themselves in their work, and are willing to spend long hours at their job. Most software integration engineers are very analytical and don't accept "it can't be done" as an answer.

David Dominguez *is a software integration engineer.*

How did you get the job?

David Dominguez first developed an interest in computers and technology in the Air Force, where he worked with telephone switching equipment. Upon leaving the Air Force, he decided to cultivate that interest, so he worked to get his associate's degree in technology from a small college in Texas.

With this degree, he was able to find work as a technician for Fisher-Rosemount, a process controls engineering firm in Austin, Texas. As a technician, David spent a lot of time testing discrete and analog equipment. It wasn't until he started back to school that he was able to secure a position as an industry technician, where he was able to write code.

David continued to work in this position until he graduated with his bachelor's degree in computer science, at which time he started working in the company's technical support division. After about two years, he was chosen for his current position within the company.

> THERE ARE MANY OPENINGS FOR INTEGRATION SOFTWARE ENGINEERS LISTED IN TRADE MAGAZINES SUCH AS **CONTROLS ENGINEERING**, BUT THE POSITIONS ADVERTISED THERE ARE NOT OFTEN ENTRY LEVEL. PERHAPS THE BEST PLACE TO LOOK FOR ENTRY-LEVEL POSITIONS IS ON THE INTERNET.

What do you do all day?

On a typical day, David will come into the office sometime between 8 and 9 in the morning, and he probably won't leave the office until around 7 P.M. Depending on what phase of a project he is in, he will spend most of the day either writing a design document that outlines the proposed finished product or writing code for the project.

On each project, David works as part of a team. He is responsible for writing one specific part of each proposal and the corresponding code. About 70 percent of the work on any given project involves writing documentation, but the combination of writing design documentation with writing code gives his job just enough variety to keep him from becoming restless. "By the time it comes time to write the code, you're tired of writing documentation and you're ready for some sort of change."

Most of these projects last up to eight months; however, some can last for as long as two to four years. But for these extensive projects, even two years can be considered a tight deadline. Because David is often working against the clock, his job can be stressful, but it can also be enjoyable.

"What I like most about this job is having the ability to get lost in the problem solving and coding and actually have fun doing this. There are times when I'll be working on my code and someone will walk by and say, 'See you tomorrow, David,' and I'll say, 'OK, bye.' By the next time I look up, it will seem like only five minutes have passed, but I'll look at the clock and it'll be already 10 o'clock."

Where do you see this job leading you?

Rather than continuing to move up the ranks into a management position, David sees himself eventually starting his own company in computer consulting or something similar.

83. Software Project Leader

description: A software project leader oversees the development of software applications. It's the leader's responsibility to keep the project on schedule, monitor the quality of the work and manage the team of programmers. Many project leaders also write software.

While a software programmer's work can sometimes be monotonous, a project leader's job is more varied. One day might be spent interviewing users about what features they want the program to contain. The next day might involve meeting with programmers to assess where their assignments stand. Hours can be long, especially when a deadline is nearing, but project leaders are typically well compensated financially. On the downside, when something goes wrong, the leader, not the programmers, usually takes the blame.

salary: Project leaders usually earn anywhere from $70,000 to $85,000 a year. Pay is based on experience and skills. Project leaders who have expertise in a hot area can command a higher salary.

prospects: This is a competitive field. Because a good project leader is crucial to keeping the team on track and delivering the program on time, it's hard to land a job without a good track record.

qualifications: A minimum of three to five years of programming experience is usually required. Programming skills needed vary, depending on the project.

characteristics: You have to be patient and good with people, because you've got to keep your team motivated and productive. Seeing a software program through from beginning to end takes both an eye for detail and an ability to see the big picture.

Michael Silver *is a project leader for a software company in San Francisco.*

How did you get the job?

After graduating from Northeastern University in Boston, Michael Silver moved to California and took a job placing temporary employees. "I had a degree in business, and it seemed like a businesslike job," he says. "But I hated it."

He left and became a temp himself, doing word processing and data entry. The company he was working for needed an Oracle database programmer, but couldn't afford to hire one. "My boss said, 'If you're interested, we can show you some basic programming skills,'" Michael recalls. "I ended up getting an education in what a software development project is."

Michael eventually left to become a full-time programmer, and jumped from job to job at companies including a yellow pages publisher and a cellular communications company.

"People give me a hard time about moving around so much, and they always ask when I'm going to settle down, but each time I got a different job, I drastically increased my responsibility and my salary."

Michael took his current job, which involves developing software for the shipping industry, because it combined his management skills and technical experience.

What do you do all day?

Another day, another decision. When his programmers reach a juncture, they look to Michael, who makes the calls regarding how the software should look and function. "It might be deciding how to lay out the fields on the screen or how we should program a behind-the-scenes feature," he says.

Some days are spent watching beta testers take the software on a test spin. "We present what we have and get feedback," he says. "If it's negative, we go back and try to do it differently."

Meetings with management also tie up a lot of time. As the link between upper management and the programmers in the trenches, Michael reports on progress and takes recommendations back to his troops.

At the moment, all thoughts are focused on a major deadline that is fast approaching. "We're supposed to start training customers in two weeks, and we're crunching," Michael says. That means Michael's usual 50-hour workweek will increase accordingly. "When you're supposed to have the product in the customers' hands by a certain date, you'll work whatever hours it takes to get it there," he says.

> TAKE EVERY OPPORTUNITY YOU CAN TO GET EXPERIENCE LEADING PEOPLE, EVEN IF IT'S JUST FOR A SMALL PROJECT. YOU CAN GAIN VALUABLE MANAGEMENT EXPERIENCE VOLUNTEERING TO OVERSEE PIECES OF PROJECTS.

Where do you see this job leading you?

"I haven't found my calling yet," Michael says. "I might want to own my own software consulting company, or just open a small business that uses this technology."

Michael has seen other project leaders move on to manage larger teams of programmers or break away and start their own businesses.

177

84. Supplier Quality Engineer

description: Manufacturing companies rely on small suppliers for many of their parts. Supplier quality engineers make sure those parts make the grade. They work closely with suppliers to monitor their manufacturing systems and help them improve their production.

That involves analyzing the faulty parts and meeting with the supplier to pick apart the manufacturing process and figure out where things went wrong. Once the problem is isolated, the engineer works with the supplier to create a plan to make sure it doesn't happen again.

This is a good job for people who don't like to be tied down to a desk. You'll spend a lot of time on the road paying visits to suppliers and walking around their manufacturing floors. Quality engineers help companies save money and increase profits by improving their manufacturing methods.

Suppliers themselves also employ quality engineers, who work in-house to see that quality standards are being maintained.

salary: College graduates just entering this field can expect to start at about $40,000 a year. With five to seven years of experience, salary can increase to $55,000. Quality engineers at large manufacturing companies usually earn more than those employed by suppliers.

prospects: U.S. manufacturers are making quality a top priority. As a result, they are increasing the size of their quality engineering departments and taking their recommendations seriously. Increased global competition has also focused attention on quality. Those factors add up to a very healthy outlook for this field. Industries that offer the best opportunities include automakers and computer chip manufacturers.

qualifications: A technical background is required, although the particular area of expertise isn't as important. People come into this job with degrees in mechanical engineering, material science, and, in some cases, business. Regardless of the industry, you'll need a solid understanding of statistics.

characteristics: You have to be an analytical thinker. You also need to work well with people. In some cases you'll be trying to convince suppliers to completely change their production system. That's when diplomacy comes in. You have to be able to present your proposals in a way that will get the best response.

Charlene Napiewocki *is a supplier quality engineer for an auto maker in Detroit, Michigan.*

How did you get the job?

Charlene Napiewocki studied material science at Michigan State University because it matched her interests. "I love math and physics, but getting a job as a math major isn't easy," she says. "I figured engineering would be easier to get a job that paid well."

She was right. After graduating, she was hired by a major auto maker to test parts from suppliers to make sure they met blueprint specifications. It was good experience, but after a year and a half, Charlene was ready to move on. "I had gotten to the point where there weren't a lot of challenges left," she says. When an opportunity to work directly with suppliers came along, Charlene snagged it. "I had spent enough time testing finished products," she says. "I was ready to get in on the process of making them."

What do you do all day?

When she's in the office, Charlene spends a lot of time on the phone talking with suppliers in her division: medium-duty trucks. Much of her time, though, is spent on the road meeting directly with suppliers in Ohio, northern Kentucky, and Indiana. During her visits

> FOR MORE INFORMATION ON SUPPLIER QUALITY ENGINEERS, CONTACT THE AMERICAN SOCIETY FOR QUALITY CONTROL. (SEE RESOURCES, PAGE 212.)

she watches workers turn out parts in order to verify they're following necessary procedures. If she spots something being done wrong, she makes a note and later discusses with supplier officials how to address it.

There's no place Charlene would rather be than listening to the machines hum and watching the parts whiz by. "I love walking around on the manufacturing floors," she says. "It's exciting to be right in the middle of where it's all happening."

If she and the supplier come up with a plan to resolve a problem, she returns to the floor in a month or so to make sure corrective actions have been taken. Charlene also spends as much time as she can talking with the people doing the work to get their take on the process. "I like talking with the guys right out on the lines producing the parts, because they know so much," she says. "It really helps to pick their brains, because they have a lot of ideas that I might not even think of."

Often Charlene's visits involve more than just fixing glitches. She helps suppliers change their plant layouts to make them more efficient, and brings others up to speed on new manufacturing requirements. This is a job where you really can see the difference. "You remember what it looked like the first day you walked in to the supplier, and you can see the concrete improvements," Charlene says. "That's what a lot of supplier quality engineers find so rewarding."

Where do you see this job leading you?

Charlene completed her M.B.A. a year and a half ago, and she is interested in moving into an area within her company like business planning, where she could put her M.B.A. to use. She has seen colleagues go on to work in purchasing or to become buyers. Some are also hired away to work directly for suppliers.

85. Systems Administrator

description: When computers crash, a systems administrator is the person who gets them up and running again. As the manager of a company's computer system, an administrator installs new equipment, keeps the system humming, and, like an emergency room doctor, performs high-tech CPR to bring it back to life if necessary. At a small company, you might do everything from dragging wires under the floor to installing printers. Large corporations, on the other hand, have dozens of administrators who oversee a particular area—such as a network of 200 computers. Living on the front line can be stressful, and burnout is common. A pager acts as an around-the-clock electronic leash, and when a software virus strikes at 3 A.M., it's up to you to wipe it out.

salary: If you've got a college degree, you can expect to walk in at $45,000 a year. Experienced administrators earn around $70,000, and with specialized skills can top $200,000. Contractors make $45 to $150 an hour.

prospects: As companies move to more advanced—and more complicated—computer systems, the demand for administrators is increasing dramatically. Because a computer glitch can cost millions, many businesses are expanding their systems administration staffs and paying top dollar for top talent. A shortage of administrators has made breaking into this field with little experience possible.

qualifications: There is no college degree designed specifically for systems administration; most move into it from related areas like software programming. Still others arrive from fields as diverse as nursing or music. While a college degree isn't a must, a knack for troubleshooting and problem solving is.

characteristics: You have to think logically and instinctively and thrive under pressure. You have to appreciate a good adrenaline rush.

Curt Vincent *is a systems administrator for a company in Sommerset, New York.*

How did you get the job?

Curt Vincent studied engineering as an undergraduate and earned a master's degree in telecommunications. He worked as a network engineer in the Army for 20 years, where his work involved putting together a computer system during Desert Storm. It was the hands-on element that drew Curt to systems administration when he got out of the military. "Unlike a programmer, who works in a cubicle and never gets to see the finished product, a systems administrator solves problems and gets instant gratification," he says.

At a time when the computer industry is increasingly specialized, systems administrators work with a wide range of cutting-edge technologies. "A lot of computer science majors who wanted to be programmers have ended up here because they've found it to be a lot more fun and a lot more satisfying," he says. Still, this isn't the place Curt imagined he'd end up. "I never told my mother I wanted to be a systems administrator when I grew up," he says. "Like a lot of people in this field, I just stumbled into it."

What do you do all day?

Administrators arrive before anyone else to make sure the system is ready. Part of the day is spent helping computer users with day-to-day problems and monitoring operations. Since you can't make changes to the system while workers are using it, administrators add new software applications and make other adjustments after hours. That, coupled with the fact that software bugs have little respect for business hours, means irregular hours. "It's a lot of weekends, a lot of holidays, and very little vacation," Curt says. But the unpredictable nature of the business is part of its appeal. "You spend your day right in the middle of things, trying to achieve harmony," he says. "And you never know when it's going to explode." Curt is currently responsible for installing a software product on 5,000 computer workstations worldwide. To help ensure a smooth transition, he's meeting with high-level company executives to discuss the software's benefits and with systems administrators to talk about technical considerations.

Where do you see this job leading you?

"I'm here forever," Curt says, explaining that systems administrators have a hard time going back to office work. Many make their way up the ladder, from opening computer boxes to managing far-flung computer networks. Others move into management, where they oversee the people who oversee the computers.

> CONSIDER USING A HEADHUNTER OR A HIGH-TECH RECRUITMENT FIRM TO FIND A POSITION. MOST LARGE CITIES HAVE A NUMBER OF FIRMS THAT CAN TAKE YOUR SKILLS AND MATCH YOU UP WITH A COMPANY.

86. Systems Analyst

description: Systems analysts help companies get the most out of their computer systems. Businesses hire analysts to study their computer setups and make recommendations on how they can use their computers more efficiently. An analyst might suggest that the company purchase new software or upgrade computers.

The report would detail exactly what type of equipment is needed, how much it costs, and how the company might finance it.

The company might follow the advice on its own, or pay the analyst to oversee the installation of new equipment. In many cases, analysts also write software to improve the computer systems' performance. Systems analysts enjoy a great deal of autonomy.

Their recommendations are based on personal observations and interactions with their client. Work is varied. An analyst could spend a couple of months working with a large corporation, and then move on to assist a small start-up.

Trying to convince a business that hasn't changed its computer system in ten years that it ought to invest thousands of dollars to modernize it isn't always easy. A lot of time is spent educating technophobic management about new technology.

salary: Recent college graduates can expect to start at $25,000 a year, with $35,000 to $45,000 as the mid-range. Systems analysts with experience in hot areas can make more than $80,000 a year.

prospects: There is always strong demand for talented analysts. Companies are increasingly turning to technology to improve their business operations and manufacturing processes. Thanks to their emphasis, the need for systems analysts is growing.

qualifications: A college degree in general business or finance and a good working understanding of computers is a good combination. But systems analysts stress that a college degree isn't a must. What is most important is being able to relate your knowledge of computer hardware and software to a company's business needs.

characteristics: In addition to being technically capable, you've got to be articulate and persuasive. It is your job to convince the company's vice president that your plan is the right one for the company.

How did you get the job?

Scott Gilbert put his electrical engineering degree from the University of California at Santa Barbara to work designing spacecraft computers for General Dynamics. When the project was canceled, Scott got another job in engineering. But he was ready for a change.

"I was kind of unhappy with my job," he says. "I didn't necessarily want to give up on engineering, but I did want to try something different." Around that time, he got a call from a friend of a friend of a cousin asking him to apply for a job as a systems analyst at a small start-up in San Antonio.

Never mind that he had never worked as a systems analyst. Or that his experience writing software consisted of some dabbling in college. Or that he knew nothing about the type of computers the start-up specialized in. And even if he did, the very idea of working for a start-up would be scary in itself.

"It sounded really exciting, but I knew it was a little start-up, and start-ups have a very poor track record," Scott says. But he decided it would be a big mistake to pass it up. "I realized I had nothing to lose. I decided if they wanted me, I'd give it a try." They did, and, to the surprise of family and friends, Scott packed his bags and moved to Texas.

He spent the first couple of months alone at the office polishing his software programming skills. "They said, 'Write a program to do so and so, and when you run into a wall, call us.'" It was trial and error, but Scott picked it up, and within six months was meeting with clients, analyzing their systems, and writing software.

What do you do all day?

"My days are flexible to the extent that they can be much longer than eight hours," Scott jokes. On a typical day, he heads straight to his client's business. He spends the morning talking to people who use the computers and trying to get a feel for what's right and what's wrong with the system.

Then he heads back to the office to spend a few hours writing software to help another company better manage its data. Next he orders computers for yet another client, and works on the proposal he'll present to the business he visited that morning.

Scott's job has taken him across Texas, to Germany, and to Mexico, where he met with plant managers to analyze the company's manufacturing, purchasing, and inventory systems.

Where do you see this job leading you?

Scott loves the variety his job provides, and he prefers working for a small company that's free of bureaucracy. He hopes to stay where he is. He has seen colleagues go on to work as internal systems analysts for large companies.

> **WORK IN AS MANY INTERNSHIPS AS POSSIBLE DURING COLLEGE.**

87. Systems Consultant

description: Within a large corporation, the decision to purchase computer systems and software is usually made at the top, even though the offices using the equipment are sometimes located far away from corporate headquarters. Therefore, it can sometimes go unnoticed by those at the corporate level if the system is not working correctly or used properly. Because most large corporations realize this could become a problem, systems consultants are often hired to keep close tabs on the branch office computer systems so they may answer any questions the staff may have, and correct any problems that may arise in the system.

Making sure that each office is getting the most out of its computer system can involve numerous tasks, such as visiting and evaluating each facility, training staff members to use the equipment or software, installing software, and even writing some programs that will better meet the needs at the facilities.

salary: Someone starting out in this industry could expect to make a salary in the mid $20,000s. As you gain experience, your salary will increase, but in order to make a salary above $40,000 a year you would need to move into a managerial position.

prospects: The availability of these jobs will vary from region to region. They are more likely to be found in larger cities where corporate offices are headquartered.

qualifications: A bachelor's degree in management of information systems or computer science is often a requirement for systems consultants. It would also be helpful to take some business courses in addition to your computer course work.

characteristics: People working in this industry are generally friendly and knowledgeable about computers. They are also very energetic and are willing to share any information that may be helpful to others.

Ella Moore *is a systems consultant.*

How did you get the job?

As a sophomore in college, Ella Moore found that she was bored by her business courses. Upon a friend's suggestion, she took a computer programming class and found it to be something she was not only interested in, but something she enjoyed. Ella's professor recognized her interest and, as a result, he took time out to show her some of the computer systems on campus and talk to her about the computer science degree. It didn't take too much persuading for Ella to change her major to computer science.

"I liked the problem solving. You would program something, and you would run it through to debug it, and there would be one line of code that would catch. Then you would know what the problem was. It could take you anywhere from two to 20 hours."

Although Ella enjoyed the programming courses she took in college, she decided after graduation that she wanted to

> CLASSIFIED ADS IN MAJOR METROPOLITAN AREAS WOULD BE A GOOD SOURCE OF INFORMATION WHEN SEARCHING FOR WORK AS A SYSTEMS CONSULTANT. IT IS ALSO HELPFUL TO CONTACT THE HUMAN RESOURCES DEPARTMENT OF A COMPANY YOU MAY BE INTERESTED IN WORKING FOR.

be in a field where there was more interaction with people.

"When I got out of college I realized I'd been in the lab until 4 in the morning for the past three years, and I decided that I wanted to be with some people too," she says. "I interviewed with companies to be a programmer, and I saw where I would have to work in a cubicle. The programmers didn't really do anything but sit there and I didn't want to do that."

When Ella interviewed for the systems consultant position at Beverly Enterprises, a conglomeration of nursing homes, she saw it as a perfect opportunity to use her computer skills, and yet still interact with people.

What do you do all day?

An average day for Ella usually involves some sort of travel, either by plane or car. Once she arrives at a facility, she usually starts by meeting with the facility's administrator to discuss any problems with the computer systems or software. If there are problems, Ella will begin to work toward finding a solution. This may require that she troubleshoot the software in order to discover the cause of a glitch, or rewire some portions of the facility's system. If a facility reports no problems in its computer system, Ella will usually print out reports from the previous business day and review them to make sure that everything is running smoothly.

When new employees are hired at one of the facilities Ella is assigned to, Ella may be called in to conduct training on the company's equipment and software. She also leads training seminars on a monthly basis for groups of new employees.

It is not unusual for Ella to spend an entire workweek out of town, but ideally she will spend one day a week at her home office where she will have time to put together expense reports to be sent to the corporate office. Also while she is in the home office, she will be called upon to help out with computer problems there.

Where do you see this job leading you?

From this job, Ella could move up into a management position. She could also use the skills that she has developed as a systems consultant to secure a job in computer training or in technical sales.

88. Systems Engineer

description: High-tech sales typically work like this: A salesperson makes contact with a potential customer, sets up an appointment to talk, gets a feel for the customer's needs, and reports back to the systems engineer. The systems engineer then takes over, providing technical demonstrations, working with the customer to put together a specific package, and overseeing the sales process.

Because systems engineers are the technical "brains" of the sale, they have to know their company's technology backwards and forwards. If a company is leaning toward your product but not sold, you might arrange a trial period. You also have got to understand your competition's products, because your customers will want to know how they differ. Systems engineers say the best part of this job is that while the product stays the same, every customer's problem has a new twist. That means no two deals, or days, are the same. On the downside, there's always the risk of becoming a "demo dolly" who does nothing but demonstrations. The way to avoid that trap is to carve out your own areas of expertise.

salary: Systems engineers often earn a salary plus commission. Someone new to the field could expect to start at $30,000 to $40,000 a year, depending on the size of the company. With several years experience, that increases to $40,000 to $80,000 a year. Commission can add anywhere from $10,000 to $40,000 to your annual salary.

prospects: Almost all high-tech vendors rely on systems engineers to sell their products. As companies grow, this is one of the first places they add jobs. Companies of all sizes frequently have openings.

qualifications: Computer programming skills are important, as is an understanding of the industry in which you hope to work. You also need to be outgoing and to feel comfortable speaking to groups. It is helpful to have a few years' experience working for a high-tech company, because the experience helps you empathize with your customers' needs. Many companies are willing to hire inexperienced people if they show promise.

characteristics: This isn't a 9-to-5 job, so you've got to be the kind of person who doesn't mind working late and traveling. To be successful in sales, you need to be self-confident, persuasive, and unwilling to take no for an answer—at least for the first ten times.

Meryl Surgan *is a systems engineering coordination manager for a software start-up company in Paramus, New Jersey.*

How did you get the job?

"I wanted to be a teacher from the time I was five years old, and I was a jock, so physical education seemed like a good major," Meryl Surgan says. After graduating from college, she worked as a P.E. and classroom teacher for a couple of years. "I got bored with teaching. It was the same thing over and over."

That was in the 1970s, when the Equal Employment Opportunities Commission was pushing a national insurance company to hire more women. "They were looking for teachers because they thought they thought logically," she says. Meryl got a job writing software documentation. "One day, I said, 'I can't write this unless I understand how it works,' so they taught me to program software." She went on to work there as a software programmer, and went on to work at several other companies doing programming.

She ended up working for a large company that was not exactly employee-friendly. She turned to a search firm to find a new job. "I knew I wanted to get out of there, and I was willing to take a pay cut for the right thing," she says. The search firm came up with the perfect match—a start-up company that needed a systems engineer. Meryl could work out of her home, and she could set her own hours. "I had that mixture of sales and technical skills they needed," she says. "They needed senior people who could take on leadership roles as the company grew."

Meryl has made it a priority to find her own challenges to avoid becoming burned out on demos. "I started studying the competition, and became known as the competitive maven," she says. "Now when anyone has a question about another company they come to me. Whether you get bored in your job is up to you." Meryl has been promoted twice in two years, most recently becoming product engineer manager.

What do you do all day?

Working out of her home has a lot of advantages. Meryl is at her desk at 6:45 A.M. She works until 8 A.M., when her seven-year-old son wakes up. She helps him get ready, and walks him to school. When she gets home it's back to work until about 5:30 P.M.

A lot of her day is spent talking by phone with salespeople about deals in the works. She also gets ready for upcoming presentations. At least twice a week she's out of the house on the road doing a presentation of some sort. "Yesterday I was in Toronto, next week it's New York." Customers look to her for examples of how her product will help solve their problems and an explanation of how it stacks up against the competition.

When she's not working on a demonstration, Meryl spends as much time as she can reading. "I'm always scouring the trade magazines. I tear out leads and give them to our salespeople."

If a salesperson has a question about the competition that Meryl can't answer off the top of her head, she logs onto the Internet, where she searches for background information.

> WOMAN-OWNED BUSINESSES OFTEN GIVE FEMALE GRADUATES THE CHANCE TO LEARN THE ROPES IN A SUPPORTIVE ENVIRONMENT. CHECK YOUR COLLEGE'S CAREER COUNSELING CENTER FOR INFORMATION ON WOMEN'S ASSOCIATIONS IN YOUR FIELD OF INTEREST.

Where do you see this job leading you?

"The next step at this company would be technical manager, which I would like to work my way into," Meryl says. She is committed to her company, which is woman-owned and has a lot of women managers. "It's a different environment than most businesses," she says.

89. Technical Sales Representative

description: A sales representative for a cosmetic or book company peddles products that are stored in a warehouse awaiting purchase, but a technical sales representative sells products that have not yet been produced.

In order to make a sale, a technical sales representative first goes to the customer to find out what is needed. For example, he or she may travel to a power plant and learn that the plant wants to generate a specific amount of power using a certain quantity of coal, and it needs special equipment. The technical sales rep will find out the quantity of coal being used to produce this power as well as its chemical makeup, and will also make note of the ancillary machinery being used, as well as other parameters of the plant. The sales representative will then relay this information to the manufacturing company he or she represents. The company, in turn, will put together a technical proposal for the equipment. The sales rep will then travel back to the plant and explain to the company why this manufacturer's equipment would be not only suitable but superior to any other equipment for making enough steam to produce their power. They work together to develop a sales plan, and hopefully a sale will be made.

salary: Technical sales representatives generally make somewhere in the neighborhood of $50,000 a year, but because their salaries are drawn from sales commissions, the sky is the limit.

prospects: Currently, the job market for technical sales reps is very good, because with the numerous changes in technology—especially the computerization of controls—there are a lot of new products to be created and sold.

qualifications: A bachelor's degree, preferably in engineering, is required for this type of work. It would also be advantageous for anyone going into this field to have some experience working for an operating company so that they can become familiar with the equipment from an operating standpoint.

characteristics: These salespeople must be personable, knowledgeable, and motivated. But perhaps more importantly, they must be able to overcome rejection. This job is not for the faint of heart.

Martin Block *is the president of a manufacturers' representative agency in Texas.*

How did you get the job?

Martin Block received his engineering degree from the United States Naval Academy. After release from active duty, he immediately went to work as a sales engineer at a large industrial manufacturing company. While he was manning a booth for the company at a trade show, he met an elderly gentleman who told him about an Italian-based manufacturing company that was looking for representation in the United States. Nineteen years later, Martin is still representing the Italian company, along with various American companies. Among the companies Martin represents in the United States are a boiler company, a company specializing in the fabrication of industrial equipment, and an industrial water treatment company.

What do you do all day?

A lot of Martin's day is spent in the office tracking down leads on potential clients and customer development. If he hears of a new plant or the expansion of an old one, he will start making phone calls to see what kind of equipment will be needed. If he determines that any of the manufacturing companies he represents could fill the new business' needs, he will get the wheels in motion for a proposal.

When Martin's not out taking care of old business, he goes out to see current clients to discuss their future needs. He also spends a lot of time on the

ANYONE INTERESTED IN FINDING WORK AS A MANUFACTURERS' SALES REPRESENTATIVE SHOULD LOOK TO THE TRADE JOURNALS TO FIND OUT ABOUT JOB OPENINGS IN THE INDUSTRY. LISTINGS CAN BE FOUND IN THE BACK OF MANUFACTURING AGENTS NATIONAL ASSOCIATION MAGAZINE AND IN THE BACK OF POWER MAGAZINE AND CHEMICAL ENGINEERING.

phone with the manufacturing companies discussing outstanding proposals and current orders.

As an independent businessman, Martin must also spend a great deal of time doing administrative work, which encompasses everything from the payroll to insurance and retirement planning.

Where do you see this job leading you?

Martin doesn't have a desire to make any future changes in his career; he intends to retire from this job. "I have the independence, I have the income, and I have the satisfaction and fulfillment that I want."

90. Technical Support Engineer

description: Technical support engineers are the ones who receive calls from panicked customers when a new or newly updated system crashes or is otherwise making a general nuisance of itself. You will be required to do a lot of telephone technical support on both software to hardware issues. You could be working with a variety of computer systems such as UNIX workstations and servers, PCs, Macs, or on mainframes and supercomputers. Additional responsibilities include on-site troubleshooting and installations, assembling equipment, and pre-sales technical support to in-house staff, as well as technical writing of installation procedures and operating instructions. Depending on the company, you may be involved in international correspondence. The basic skills involved in being a technical support engineer can be applied to both simple individual systems and more complex networked systems such as those found in universities and government sites.

salary: A technical support engineer can make anywhere from $18,000 to $60,000 a year. "It's simple economics," says technical support engineer Sue Conway. "You acquire more responsibilities as you gain more skills, which increases your value to the company—and they pay you more money."

prospects: With the trend toward making more technical support people available to their clients, companies are building up their support staff. "Technical knowledge of computers will continue to be quite marketable in the long-term foreseeable future," says Sue.

qualifications: The software and hardware background required to be a technical support engineer can typically be gleaned from a two-year computer technology degree. If you also have programming and electronics experience, doors will open for you.

characteristics: Technical support engineers need to be able to prioritize and work well under pressure. "Somewhat like triage in a war zone," says Sue, "I'm often putting out four to five fires at any given time." You need to develop good rapport with people, especially on the telephone. It also helps to be a quick study and to keep up or keep ahead of the current trends and technology.

Susan Conway *is a technical support engineer.*

How did you get the job?

Susan Conway has a two-year degree in computer technology. While in school, she worked for the computer department at the community college she attended—overseeing labs, wiring networks, and replacing broken equipment. "I didn't get paid much, but it looked great on my resume and gave me practical experience," says Sue.

Her first job after college was as a technician doing component-level repair (replacing chips on boards) and system integration. "After the initial training period, I was expected to work very independently, which often meant figuring out how something was *supposed* to work before figuring out how to fix it," Sue groans. "That usually involved deciphering piles of manuals in search of one tiny bit of pertinent information."

The first company chose her due in part to her age (early 30s at the time) and experience.

The college's department chair recommended her without hesitation, due to her work for the school. She had great grades—a 4.0 GPA—and good interview skills.

Sue's previous computer job also involved increasing amounts of customer interaction, which increased her qualifications as technical support engineer. "And, believe it or not, the many years that I spent waiting tables and tending bar contributed greatly to my communication skills and my ability to multitask," Sue says with a smile.

What do you do all day?

Susan's very full days usually consist of a mix of customer support (problem solving) and system integration and testing. "I start my day by answering e-mail from customers who've had problems after hours, and continue through the day helping customers either on the phone or by e-mail," says Sue. Problems can range from configuration issues—which usually means that hardware or software changes have to be made to their systems to allow her company's equipment to work—to faulty equipment.

Sue's skills are invaluable to her company. "I wanted 'Techno Goddess' on my business card, but it didn't pass the powers that be," she teases. In addition to technical support, Sue builds the more complex, custom systems that her company sells, or tests equipment that's been returned as defective. She also provides pre-sales support to her company's sales staff, to help ensure that the equipment they sell works.

She has the additional responsibility of system administrator, which means that she deals with the computer network for the whole company. "I

> **GET INVOLVED WITH LOCAL COMPUTER USER GROUPS, AND CRUISE THE NET, WHICH IS OFTEN A GREAT PLACE TO GAIN EXPOSURE.**

have an interrupt-driven day," she smirks.

"The best part about my job is that every day is different and challenging," exclaims Sue. "The time flies."

Where do you see this job leading you?

Sue is really happy with her job right now, so plans for change are a long way off. She would like eventually to move into a full-time system administration position or to do consulting either for a group or on her own.

Sue views the technical support engineer position as a good stepping-stone to anywhere in the computer world. "The position provides good exposure to many facets of the computer industry, and is a good way to find out which area you may want to pursue," says Sue. Those areas could include, among other things, software development, hardware development, or system administration.

91. Technical Writer

description: Technical writers are responsible for the manuals that accompany new computers, the text that appears on your computer screen when you install a new software program, and the troubleshooting guide that comes with your new color printer. Technical writers also research and write bids for government contracts, document the companies' manufacturing processes, and develop in-house marketing materials for company employees. In addition to excellent writing skills, technical writers need to understand how the technology works. Technical writers' schedules are predictable in that the hours are always long: sixty-hour workweeks are not uncommon.

salary: A beginning writer working full-time starts at about $25,000 to $30,000 a year. With three to four years of experience, it increases to $40,000, and with five to seven years, $50,000 to $55,000. It is not unusual for a senior contract writer to earn $66,000 to $70,000. It can increase from there, depending on how many assignments the writer chooses to take on.

prospects: The explosion of technology products in the past ten years has given this field a major boost. Another plus is that growth is not limited to certain geographic regions. Software start-ups from Omaha to Idaho need technical writers. Contract writers can live just about anywhere, since they simply transmit their work by modem.

qualifications: Most companies require a bachelor's degree, preferably with an emphasis on technical writing, but it is still possible to break in with a liberal arts degree and no experience in technical writing as long as that is coupled with superior writing skills. The amount of technical expertise needed depends on the product line. Writing instructions for using children's software programs doesn't demand as much technical experience as working for a company that designs computer semiconductors.

characteristics: You can't be easily intimidated or afraid to ask questions. You will be working with people who hold Ph.D.s in engineering and are experts in their field. If you don't understand something, it's up to you to keep asking until you get it. Engineers and programmers aren't always the most patient individuals, so you've got to be persistent.

Jeanne Mehan *is a technical publications site supervisor at a software company in Bellevue, Washington.*

How did you get the job?

Jeanne Mehan earned a degree in English literature from the University of Oregon and set out to become a poet. "I got a lot of poetry published, and that was good, but when it came time to have a family I realized I was out of money," she says. Her husband, a musical instrument repairman and self-described hippie, wasn't exactly earning big bucks either.

"Then I discovered Boeing was hiring contract editors for some big proposal, and I got a job working behind barbed wire writing government proposals," she says.

The hours were long—7:30 A.M. to midnight. "People just worked around the clock. It wasn't necessarily driven by management, it was just that people got so wired doing it they couldn't stop."

> **FOR MORE INFORMATION ON TECHNICAL WRITING, YOU CAN CONTACT THE SOCIETY FOR TECHNICAL COMMUNICATIONS. (SEE RESOURCES, PAGE 213).**

From writing proposals, she went on to documenting procedures, researching and writing technical reports, and mapping information. Then the economy took a turn, and Jeanne's group was notified they were going to be laid off. "Then a guy from a software company called and offered me a spectacular salary, but it was a risk because I didn't know squat about software," she says. Jeanne took the job, and spent the first month living in fear of being found out.

But she caught on quickly to the work, which involves writing on-line help material. "I had to vamp for a little bit, but I learned fast, and it turned out to be something I was really good at."

What do you do all day?

Jeanne arrives at work at 6:30 A.M. "It seems like every day I come in and the network has been disconnected, and I can't get in and finish what I was doing yesterday," she says. "It's 'what can I do' because I can't do my work." When the network comes back up, Jeanne deals with e-mail messages and loose ends from the day before.

At 9 A.M. she and her staff of writers sit down and discuss project schedules. "Some mornings there is nothing new, other mornings I've just gotten word that a new product is in that I didn't even know about." On those days, she and her staff shift gears and jump into writing for the new product.

As a supervisor, Jeanne is in charge of scheduling and hiring writers, and her previous work experience has influenced her decision making. "I insist that every person work a normal workday," she says. "I try not to hire abnormal people who yearn to work until the dead of night. I don't want a staff that's fried and completely burned out."

Where do you see this job leading you?

"I love the people I work with, but I look at that contractor's wage and I ask myself what in the world am I doing losing $30,000 a year," she says. "I wouldn't mind earning more and leaving the office politics behind, and that's what I think I'll end up doing."

92. Turnaround Expert

description: A turnaround expert specializes in finding small start-ups that are struggling financially, investing in them, and helping turn them around. Although the financial risk is high, if the company makes a comeback, the return can be enormous. Turnaround experts often work with a team of several people who oversee various aspects of the process, from evaluating a company's potential, to studying the market, to analyzing what's wrong and how to fix it. A company must have an excellent technology, but be owned by a high-tech genius who knows nothing about business or marketing. Or, as is often the case, it might be that a product looks good from the outside, but upon closer inspection is in the wrong market at the wrong time.

Turning a company around is a long-term project. After working with lawyers, accountants, and headhunters to find a promising venture, it's time to raise private financing. When the investment is complete, your team steps in and begins reorganizing. If the company has a weak management team, it might be replaced, with the turnaround team acting in its place. That can involve overseeing everything from the accounting books to manufacturing.

Once the company becomes profitable—which can take years—the turnaround team might sell it and split the return.

salary: You have to go in expecting nothing and be willing to wait it out. When successful, turnaround experts invest a couple of years working with the company and walk away with a million dollars. But when the business fails, you leave with empty pockets, or worse, a major debt. An entry-level position doing market research and finance usually starts at about $35,000 a year.

prospects: With more software and hardware start-ups popping up, the opportunities to help a struggling company turn around are increasing. But financing can be difficult, especially if you don't have any previous experience.

qualifications: Heading up a turnaround group requires an extensive background in technology and finance. But some turnaround groups hire entry-level staffers to join the team and help with market research, customer analysis, and overseeing the business, in return for equity.

characteristics: You definitely have to have an entrepreneurial spirit and be willing to take risks. And you have to be patient; this is not an overnight project.

Al Coob *is a turnaround expert who is working with a software start-up in Portland, Oregon.*

How did you get the job?

Al Coob has a bachelor's degree in accounting and an M.B.A. He got the idea of working with turnarounds while serving as the chief financial officer for a struggling software start-up in California. Al helped turn the company into a successful venture. "I felt like I was really using my skills. And out of that I realized I would like to do it again," he says.

Al teamed up with two other people and began looking for a company to invest in. It didn't happen quickly. "If you go in worrying where the next paycheck is going to come from, it's going to be hard to do," he says.

After a year spent looking closely at 50 businesses, and getting close to final negotiations

> **IF YOU'RE GOING TO HELP TURNAROUND COMPANIES, YOU'VE GOT TO KNOW HOW TO RUN THEM YOURSELF. GET EXPERIENCE IN MANAGEMENT AND FINANCE, AND OBSERVE ALL YOU CAN ABOUT OPERATING A BUSINESS. RESEARCH VENTURE CAPITAL FIRMS AND TURNAROUND COMPANIES TO SEE WHAT THE POSSIBILTIES ARE. BE WILLING TO START AS A GOPHER AND WORK YOUR WAY UP.**

on four, Al and a partner found a software start-up in Portland, Oregon, that they wanted to help turn around. (One of his partners had gone on to invest in another turnaround.)

Although it took a while to find the right business, Al is glad they didn't rush into anything. "You have to be willing to walk away, no matter how close it is, when you realize it's not right," he says. "We came close several times, but looking back I know we were right to pass them up."

What do you do all day?

Al is in the process of assessing the company's management and organization. He's also studying the company's technology and deciding which markets and which products are viable. That involves testing products, talking to customers about what they like and don't like about the software, and reading everything he can about the industry. He also spends time listening to developers and other employees, who have a lot of insight about the company to share.

It's not an easy process. "This is harder than running a brand-new company," Al says. "This is running a sick company."

Employees are understandably nervous about their futures, and there's the danger that the top talent, which Al needs the most, will find other jobs. "When you go through something like this, there's tons of uncertainty," he says. "It's hard on everyone."

But he believes the transition will be worth it. "This is a company that wouldn't have made it, and now it has the chance to be a success," Al says. "It's a good feeling to know you are keeping some very promising technology from going under."

Where do you see this job leading you?

After he turns around the software company, Al wants to try it again. "I'm going to keep looking for opportunities," he says.

93. University Computer Operations Coordinator

description: As a computer operations coordinator on a college campus, you will deal with issues that could be as complicated as reviving a crashed system or as simple as teaching one of the system's users how to change the colors on a monitor. Maintaining the computer system is the main focus of your job, but training the users how to operate the system can become the bulk of your work.

This job can be stressful. You are in charge of keeping the system running, and when something goes wrong, all eyes turn to you. Sometimes even when things are going right, you have demands from people using the system. But working in an academic setting has its advantages. The resources you will have at your fingers will be vast, and the opportunity to learn is always there.

salary: Someone just starting out in the field can expect to make around $38,000 annually. This amount will increase with experience.

prospects: As every other area of the technology field, this area is growing and the job prospects are good.

qualifications: Most universities will require that someone filling this position hold a bachelor's degree. While it is not required to have a background in computer science, you must have a strong knowledge of computers and networking systems.

characteristics: People working in this field are generally inquisitive. They are also usually very thorough and persistent, as they will spend much time sifting through manuals in order to solve a problem on the computer. Since you may find yourself working in a training capacity, it would also help you to be a patient communicator.

Greg Sherr *is a computer operations coordinator at a university in New York City.*

How did you get the job?

Greg Sherr says he got his job by taking a chance at doing something that nobody else knew how to do.

While Greg was working on his bachelor's degree in French and Spanish at Columbia University, he took on a part-time job working as an administrative assistant in the school of architecture. One of the school's departments wanted to put together a small computer lab, but no one in the department was sure where to start. Greg volunteered to set it up, and in the process learned a great deal.

"It's surprising how much you can learn on your own, and how much latitude people will give you, especially for something that is daunting and they don't want to deal with," he says. Greg later took on a full-time administrative position in the graduate school. While he was working there, the coordinator of computer operations for the graduate school of arts and sciences resigned. Greg volunteered to fill in, and was eventually hired on permanently.

What do you do all day?

Greg is responsible for about 40 to 50 administrators who do everything from packaging people's financial aid and requesting transcripts to writing letters on their computers. He must ensure that these administrators are able to access the information they need and accomplish daily tasks on the computer system.

On an average day, he may start out by installing a new computer or software for one of the administrators, and then instruct them in how to use it. He may spend time later installing an ethernet card that will allow an administrator access to the Internet, or conducting some high-level programming against mainframe records.

Another aspect of Greg's job involves security. Because this computer system can access statistical information about students' grades and financial aid, Greg has to develop and install numerous passwords to guarantee security of the information.

Where do you see this job leading you?

Greg doesn't plan to continue his work with computers for the long term. His next plan is to go to medical school. However, he says that if he were to further

> THE BEST WAY TO GO ABOUT GETTING A JOB IN UNIVERSITY COMPUTER OPERATIONS IS TO LOOK AT YOUR OWN UNIVERSITY WHILE YOU ARE STILL ENROLLED. OFTENTIMES, JUST WORKING IN A WORK-STUDY POSITION CAN LEAD TO SOMETHING FULL-TIME.

his career in computers, his experience at Columbia University could prepare him to manage local area networks in the private sector.

94. Value-Added Reseller Liaison

description: A value-added reseller (VAR) buys computer equipment directly from vendors, packages it, and resells it to customers. A VAR works with customers to figure out their needs, bundles up the right hardware and software, installs it, and provides training and support.

Many tech companies sell their products through VARs. A company that develops accounting software, for instance, might sell its program to a VAR who would then load it onto computers and install it at a chain of retail stores.

To sell to VARs, companies need a VAR liaison. VAR liaisons look for VARs to partner with, and work together to incorporate their product into the resale packages. They also go on sales calls with VARs, where the two work together to sell their products as a single solution. This job requires top-notch sales skills because VARs see dozens of similar products, and you have to convince them to choose yours. You also must sell the end user on the VAR package.

salary: Representing a company to VARs is a senior position. Salaries average about $100,000 a year. Large companies usually offer the highest pay and most comprehensive benefits.

prospects: More high-tech companies are turning to VARs to sell their products because it's so much cheaper than direct sales. That shift has been a boon to VAR liaisons. At many companies, they are considered a key part of a company's sales strategy. The best opportunities are in large- and medium-size businesses, because small companies usually can't afford a full-time VAR representative.

qualifications: You need a strong business background, because when you're putting together deals that combine your product and someone else's, you've got to make sure that the deal is a profitable one for your company. Technical skills are also important because you'll be running a lot of demonstrations and training courses. If you don't understand the product inside and out, it will be obvious to VARs and buyers.

characteristics: You need to be good at the art of persuasion because a lot of this job involves getting VARs' and customers' attention and convincing them that your product is the right one for their needs. The ability to handle rejection is also a must.

Mark Chamberlin *is regional VAR development manager for a leading voice mail company in Irvine, California.*

How did you get the job?

As a student at the University of California at Santa Barbara, Mark Chamberlin liked communications classes best but figured a business background would get him a job. So he majored in both. His first job was in marketing, where he traveled to 14 trade shows a year and learned the ins and outs of marketing. His next job was at a telecommunications manufacturer, in sales. The job involved selling telephone and voice mail systems through cold calls. While a lot of people cringe at the thought of calling strangers and trying to sell them something, Mark enjoyed it. "I really enjoyed working with customers, and making things happen and making money," he says.

He worked his way up to national sales manager. He left to work for another company when an interesting offer came his way. A headhunter recruited him to join a software start-up as director of sales. "I thought, 'Here's my chance to make the big bucks,'" he says. "I really thought I could make my mil-

lion dollars." Alas, it was not meant to be. "It was a very fun job, but we just ran out of money," he says. Mark left and joined a voice mail company as its VAR development manager. Why did he get the job? "My background was a lot more interesting than the average Joe's," he says. "I had the corporate background, I understood distribution, direct sales, and how the products work, and that's what they needed.

He had also learned a thing

> **BECOME FAMILIAR WITH COMPANIES SPECIALIZING IN VALUE-ADDED RESALE AND BE WILLING TO TAKE AN ENTRY-LEVEL JOB. THIS WILL GET YOU INSIDE, WHERE YOU CAN LEARN THE BUSINESS. BE SURE TO SEIZE ANY OPPORTUNITIES THAT COULD PROVIDE YOU WITH MANAGEMENT EXPERIENCE.**

or two about dealing with difficult people. "I've worked with some tough, tough people, and I was still able to make things happen," he says. "In this field, you have to be able to deal with all kinds of people."

What do you do all day?

Mark spends about 40 percent of his time on the road meeting with VARs. He sits down with company officials to discuss product and marketing strategies for pursuing new business. He talks with the company's accountants and financial specialists about the business end of the deals, and works with salespeople to make sure they're up to speed on his company's products.

During a recent trip to an Albuquerque business telephone system provider, Mark met with sales engineers and account managers to talk about how to promote his company's new voice mail products along with the VAR's phone system. He also made sales calls to help the local salespeople close a deal that involved selling his company's voice mail system to be installed by the VAR. "The

most fun part of the job is going out with them to their customers and trying to win the business," he says. "It's like being live on stage for an hour."

As the liaison between his company and its VARs, Mark does some of his most important work while socializing with the VAR's chief executive officer. "The personal bonds that I form are what will help us last through the downturns," he says. "I always try to find areas of common ground. I'm not a golfer like a lot of them are, so I find other connections, like books we've read or our children." He is an avid reader of *The Wall Street Journal* to keep up with workplace issues affecting CEOs. "They want to know what I think about certain topics, and it's important that I be tuned in."

Where do you see this job leading you?

"I'm still hoping to run my own business one day," Mark says. "I think I've got the right skill set. It's a matter of finding the right opportunity. I think that's my next step."

95. Venture Capitalist

SPECIALIZING IN HIGH-TECH COMPANIES

description: Venture capitalists obtain money from investors and then invest it in start-up companies. Deciding which company to invest in involves looking closely at the start-up's financial records and studying the market and the company's products to determine their potential. After choosing a company, a VC works closely with company officials to help them manage growth and develop and market new products.

Venture capital firms that specialize in high-tech companies are usually located near high-tech centers such as the Silicon Valley, Boston, and New York. This is a very competitive field. In many cases, it all comes down to your contacts, so you need to be well connected. The pressure to find winners is also great. Investing in a company that goes belly-up can cost your firm's investors millions. By the same token, finding a winner can mean a big financial payoff.

salary: Someone just starting out can expect to earn $75,000 to $85,000 a year. With a few years of experience and a good track record, that can increase to more than $100,000. Bonuses are given based on performance.

prospects: Getting your foot in the door of a venture capital firm isn't easy, but it can be done. Firms do hire associates right out of business school. But because most have fewer than 12 people on staff, there usually isn't a lot of hiring going on. It helps to know someone involved in the firm who can help get you an interview. Even knowing someone who knows someone can help. Venture capitalists like to say that everybody has a story about how they got their job. And it never involves sending in a resume and getting a call back.

qualifications: An M.B.A. is usually required. You need to be able to size up a company by looking at its numbers and its market. Taking a chance on a company also involves a certain amount of intuition, and you've got to trust yours. If you are too optimistic, you'll lose a lot of money and possibly your job. If you are too negative, you'll never make a deal. A technical background is also favored because it's important that you understand the technology in which you are investing.

characteristics: You get no hand-holding in this job. You have got to be self-driven and competitive, and willing to jump in and figure out what to do yourself. No one is going to tell you that you're doing a good job either. That's where self-confidence comes in.

Jeffrey Feldman *is a venture capitalist specializing in high-tech companies in Connecticut.*

How did you get the job?

After earning a Ph.D. in polymer science, Jeffrey Feldman went to work for a chemical company. After four and a half years, he decided that what he really wanted to do was work in a start-up environment as a venture capitalist. He enrolled in the business graduate program at Yale University. During the second year, as his friends began pursuing jobs with corporations, Jeffrey began calling VC firms. "I had no idea how hard it would be," he says. No one called him back. He began to feel less optimistic.

Then he got lucky. "I was at my wife's sister's wedding, and somebody knew somebody who worked at this venture capital firm. They wrote down a name on a napkin, I called, and I got an interview." But although he got an interview, he didn't get a job. "I told them I would work for free," he says. That they agreed to. After three months, they hired Jeffrey on permanently.

What do you do all day?

If the firm's partners are working on a deal, Jeffrey does due diligence work. That involves studying the company's financials and its overall track record.

He also spends a lot of time

pursuing his own deals. He meets with officials from area high-tech companies that are seeking financing, and talks by phone to companies across the country. He relies heavily on the industry contacts he is building to give him leads on promising companies that

CONNECTIONS ARE IMPORTANT IN THE VENTURE CAPITAL BUSINESS. START BY MAKING CALLS AND SENDING RESUMES TO VENTURE FIRMS TO SET UP INFORMATIONAL INTERVIEWS, AND BE SURE TO SPREAD THE WORD THAT YOU'RE LOOKING. YOU NEVER KNOW WHO MIGHT KNOW SOMEONE WHO CAN HELP YOU.

might make good investments.

Jeffrey also works with companies his firm is already backing. He attends board meetings and sits down with company officials to discuss their growth strategies.

When he's not in meetings, he reads. Newspapers from across the country, trade magazines, industry newsletters. "I'm always looking for leads, and that's the only way to keep up with what's going on in the high-tech industry," he says.

His days vary based on how many meetings he has set up and how much time he needs to spend tracking down leads. "The day has no official start or end," he says. "It's up to me."

Where do you see this job leading you?

"Becoming a partner here or somewhere else would be great," he says.

96. Video Tape News Editor

description: Evening news reports flash from one scene to the next in a seamless motion of digital images, but some shots may actually be taken hours or even days before they are paired with recent footage shot for television. It takes the hand of an experienced video tape news editor to massage choppy footage into a smooth chain of images.

Video tape news editors take footage brought in by reporters and work it into a story, coordinating sound and action, as well as adding any special effects necessary. To say the least, this job is fast paced and unpredictable. News reporters sometimes can bring in their stories with only minutes to spare before a news broadcast. On the other hand, some stories may come in hours before they are to air.

Though this position can often be stressful, video tape news editors often thrive on the barrage of last-minute tasks this challenging job presents them with daily.

salary: The salary for a video tape news editor will vary, depending on the size of the market you are working in and the amount of experience you have. In the television news industry, a market's size is determined by its viewing audience size. In the smaller markets, salaries could range anywhere from $17,000 to $22,000 a year. As you gain experience and move on to larger markets your salary could be anything from $40,000 to $70,000 a year.

prospects: These jobs are hard to get, but they do exist. In order to find them, you will most likely have to start working in a small town and work your way up to a larger market.

qualifications: Although there are veterans in this business who worked their way up the ranks without a college degree, a bachelor's degree, usually in communications, is now a requirement. It is also important to have experience in order to be taken seriously as a potential candidate for a job, and this is usually most easily gained through a summer internship.

characteristics: Video tape news editors are generally sociable people who are motivated by the thrill of racing the clock. These editors must have the patience to sit in a room all day in front of a television, but they must also be able to work well with people in intense situations.

Holly Fontana *is a video tape news editor for an independent television station in New York City.*

How did you get the job?

When Holly Fontana and her family toured Universal Studios and Hollywood, they saw the filming of a sitcom. "I saw all the men walking around with their cameras, and I decided that was what I wanted to do. It just looked so exciting. I had never realized before how much went on behind the scenes."

When Holly went to college, the memory of the cameramen was still alive. She pursued a degree in communications. By the time Holly was a senior in college, she had begun freelancing as a photographer and editor at a cable news station on Long Island. Shortly after graduation, she got a full-time position there.

After having worked two years for the cable station, she began working weekends as a freelancer for Channel 11 News in New York City. After spending a year doubling her work at the cable station with her free-lance jobs at the larger station, a full-time position opened up at Channel 11. Holly took it.

What do you do all day?

Holly spends all of her workday in an editing room. While most of her time is spent editing tape, some is also spent anticipating the arrival of a reporter with a story. Once a reporter comes in with script in hand Holly will immediately start looking at the material on tape.

Holly works on beta video tape, the industry standard. All of the tapes are coded with a special signal that allows Holly to call up a particular sound bite or picture by number, rather than blindly fast forwarding and rewinding through tape. Ideally, a reporter's script will have numbers noted so that Holly can begin to quickly pull footage from the source tapes and record them onto a tape for air. However, there are times when a reporter doesn't always have time to prepare a script, and Holly will have to sort through the tape, with help from the reporter, to quickly find the right image.

There are times when Holly has more time to spend with a story and she can add some special effects such as a wipe, which gives the effect that one image is "wiping" another off the screen as it takes over, or a dissolve, which allows one image to fade away while another comes into focus. More realistically, Holly says, she will be called upon to create a special effect for reasons other than aesthetic.

Although Holly enjoys the creative aspect of adding special effects, she says it is the thrill of putting together a story on deadline that she loves most. "Just to make that accomplishment. To have it make air and for everybody to say, 'Wow that was great, how'd you do that?' That's the best part of it for me."

Where do you see this leading you?

Holly hopes that her experience in video tape news editing will lead her to something with more freedom for creativity, such as working for a video production house, or editing music videos, documentary films, or commercials.

> PERHAPS THE BEST RESOURCE FOR SOMEONE LOOKING FOR JOBS IN TELEVISION NEWS IS <u>THE BROADCASTING AND CABLE YEARBOOK</u>. THIS SOURCE BOOK HAS A COMPLETE LISTING OF ALL THE TELEVISION NEWS STATIONS, AND ALSO PROVIDES YOU WITH THE NAMES OF PEOPLE AT EACH STATION, SO YOU WILL KNOW TO WHOM TO DIRECT YOUR RESUME. <u>BROADCASTING AND CABLE MAGAZINE</u> ALSO PUBLISHES JOB LISTINGS. (SEE RESOURCES, PAGE 212.)

97. Virtual Reality Developer

description: Virtual reality is a simulated environment created by a computer. Wearing headgear, goggles, and data gloves, the user "sees" and "feels" images and " hears" sounds as if they were real instead of computer-generated. More than 200 companies, most of them small start-ups, are developing equipment and software. Virtual reality has a wide range of applications with computer gaming companies, corporations, and the military all using it in different ways. But this is still a field that has generated more ideas than actual products, and many small virtual reality development houses are feeling increasing pressure from investors to deliver groundbreaking equipment.

Virtual reality developers create the hardware and software that together provides a "virtual" experience. Creating a single product can take months or even years. The payoff can be big, but many companies don't last that long. Many engineers are happy to take that risk because the opportunity to develop such revolutionary technology is the reward.

salary: A programmer with no previous experience can expect to start at $27,000 to $29,000 a year. Skilled hardware and software engineers with expertise in virtual reality can earn two to three times that a year.

prospects: Virtual reality is still a hot field, but jobs are very competitive. Most companies are small start-ups that don't have time or money to train programmers. Getting hired without experience is difficult. At the same time, the demand for talented programmers is great, and there are a lot of opportunities for those who have the skills. The Internet is a good place to look for job postings.

qualifications: Virtual reality developers usually have a degree in computer science or some type of engineering. Software programmers are most in demand, with hardware engineers in second place. A couple of years' experience is what most companies like to see, although some are willing to hire talented programmers right out of school.

characteristics: A lot of development is done by teams, so you have to be able to work closely with other people. You have also got to be a logical thinker and a risk taker, since many development houses fold before they release a product.

Mark Dobbrow *is a software programmer at a virtual reality development company in Redwood City, California.*

How did you get the job?

Mark Dobbrow studied aerospace engineering at Syracuse University before getting an engineering job at a helicopter company. "Then I started getting heavily into computers, and decided that's what I wanted to focus on," he says. That meant going back to school, so Mark enrolled in graduate school in computer sciences at Stanford University.

When he got his degree, Mark heard that a local virtual reality company was hiring programmers. "It started out as a short-term contract, and I was going to be there for two weeks," he says. "It turned into three months, and then they offered me a full-time job."

After developing virtual reality programs, it's hard for Mark to imagine doing anything else. "When you finish a project you

> COMPUTER TRADE MAGAZINES ARE ONE OF THE BEST WAYS TO FIND OUT ABOUT HOT COMPANIES DOING INTERESTING THINGS. IF THE COMPANY IS GROWING, CHANCES ARE THEY ARE HIRING, AND THIS WILL PRESENT YOU WITH A REASON TO INTRODUCE YOURSELF.

can go interact with it and play with it," he says. "I personally wouldn't find it that interesting to play around with a database program."

What do you do all day?

Mark's company develops virtual reality technology used to train employees, to demonstrate products at trade shows, and to simulate certain processes. A car company, for example, might want a virtual reality system that shows the interior of a car and simulates driving down a highway. When a "driver" steps in, it feels like he or she is driving a real car. For architects, a virtual reality version of a house allows them to show exactly where the light will fall at a certain time of day or how a view might vary depending on where windows are built. Mark's job involves customizing his company's virtual reality systems for customers.

He spends a lot of his day programming virtual environments. He also fields calls from customers who have questions or problems. About once a month he travels to a customer site to help install a new system or discuss new projects.

And then there's testing. Mark spent much of last summer testing new releases. "I'd spend days at a time testing and reporting bugs," he says. Spending the day in a computer environment was a bit strange. "It's kind of like being forced to walk around in reality with a fogged scuba mask and a snorkel all day," he says. "If you're in a virtual house, you walk around it as if you were in a real house, and it does seem like you're exploring a real house."

Where do you see this job leading you?

Mark would like to get more involved in programming the bottom layer of virtual reality technology, rather than reconfiguring existing systems. "It's more challenging to be in on that level," he says. Mark has no hankering to work in any area but virtual reality. "After doing this, it would be hard to go back and do something dry," he says. "It's an exciting time to be here, and I think new technology is only going to make it more so."

98. Virtual Reality Entertainment Center Operator

description: This job involves taking your customers to a different dimension. Visitors don helmetlike headgear and step onto a circular platform that mimics their movements. The equipment lets them enter a simulated three-dimensional world. Arcades and nightclubs featuring virtual reality games are popping up in high-tech centers around the country.

Although virtual reality centers draw big crowds, launching such a venture isn't an easy—or an inexpensive—proposition. The games cost between $25,000 and $40,000 apiece.

In addition to a major investment, you've got to be willing to devote a lot of time to the business.

salary: As with any retail venture, it can take a couple of years to make any money. But it's possible for a successful virtual arcade nightclub to bring in more than $1 million in annual revenues.

prospects: A lot depends on your market—cities that have a combination of techies and college students are ripest for this type of business. Virtual reality offers far more possibilities than traditional arcade games, and that keeps customers coming back. But only time will tell whether this is a niche with staying power, or just another short-lived fad.

qualifications: Running a virtual reality center requires multiple talents. You will need technical skills to keep the equipment running and business skills to keep the operation running. Effective advertising has a lot to do with whether a center sinks or swims, making the ability to carry out a public relations campaign crucial.

characteristics: Starting your own business is always a risk, so you've got to be willing to take a big chance. Leadership skills and the ability to motivate others are important, since everyone on your team will be looking to you for guidance. And a consuming passion for technology will help keep you wanting to come back and introduce customers to the world of virtual reality day after day.

Paul Kavuma *is co-owner of a virtual reality bar in Miami Beach.*

How did you get the job?

Paul Kavuma and his partner, Joseph Sabga, researched their concept while M.B.A. students at Cornell University. They even wrote a business plan for a high-tech nightclub while in college. But after graduating, they went their separate ways. Paul became a financial analyst in Florida, and Joseph moved to Washington, D.C., where he worked as a financial analyst for a national accounting firm.

"I never forgot about the business plan, and living in south Florida, I saw the perfect demographics," Paul says. "It's very tourist oriented, and South Beach has an international reputation." Paul and Joseph decided the time was right to pursue their idea. They quit their jobs and raised $500,000 for the club by pooling their savings and by finding private investors. The hardest part of the process wasn't finding money—it was finding a place to set up shop.

"Convincing a landlord to give us a chance was very, very difficult," Paul says. "We were just two guys out of grad school talking about virtual reality, which they had never heard of." They eventually found a 3,200-square-foot spot in Miami Beach. "It's not a perfect spot, but we were just happy to find a place."

What do you do all day?

Virtual Cafe is open from 5 P.M. to 3 A.M. on weekdays and 5 P.M. to 5 A.M. on weekends, but Paul keeps more regular hours. Much of his day is spent handling the day-to-day business operations of the cafe, which sells beer, wine, and liquor and offers a full menu, including Cyber Skins and Cyberwiches. Dealing with city regulations is a particularly consuming activity. "It seems like from the day you open, their goal is to shut you down," Paul says. "We discover new taxes monthly. And today we got a notice of violation because our sign doesn't meet code. One letter is supposedly an inch too tall."

There's also the matter of maintaining the club. "Some guy last night graffitied the bathroom, so I've got to deal with that," he says. "And we have the additional worry of all the technology. Right now I'm looking out for a FedEx package with parts for one of our machines."

He and Joseph are hoping to open three more cafes in south Florida in the next two years, and are meeting with investors to raise financing. They update their business plan every two months, and are constantly reediting promotional videotapes to add new clips of recent press coverage. He and Joseph frequently invite potential investors to meetings at their office, which is within walking distance of the club. They offer a tour of the operations and explain their long-term goals in detail. "We get a lot of questions," Paul says, "and we have to be prepared to answer every one."

Where do you see this job leading you?

Opening new clubs is Paul's priority. He also wants to relocate the Miami Beach club to another building. Paul and Joseph are also planning a line of retail products including T-shirts, caps, and cups.

> WHEN STARTING UP A BUSINESS, BE PREPARED TO DEAL WITH UPS AND DOWNS ON A DAILY BASIS. ALSO REALIZE THAT IT COULD TAKE SEVERAL YEARS BEFORE THE BUSINESS TURNS A PROFIT. YOUR LIFE WILL BE ANYTHING BUT STABLE.

99. Web Master

description: Web masters develop and oversee a company's presence on the Internet. That often means designing a Web site from scratch that has information on the company, job openings, new products, and technical support. In addition to computer-programming skills, Web masters need to be good graphic designers, as they're the ones who determine the look and feel of the site.

Web masters constantly update their sites with new information and record how many people are visiting the site every day. They are always on call in case the system goes haywire.

This is a job that didn't exist until recently. But as more companies promote themselves on the Net, there is a need for someone to manage the electronic storefront and keep it new and interesting. If a company doesn't change the look of its Web site, Net surfers will lose interest and move on to more dynamic sites.

salary: Pay varies with the size of the company and how extensive the Web site is. Entry-level jobs start in the low $20,000 range. Experienced Web designers with extensive programming skills who manage large Web sites can earn more than $50,000 a year.

prospects: This is a fast-growing field. Companies rely on their sites to educate customers about products, recruit new employees, take orders, and provide technical assistance. But operating a Web site takes work, and many companies are responding by making it a full-time job. Getting hired from the outside can be difficult, however. Because this is such a new job, many companies hire from within. They often end up making an employee—in many cases, the programmer who helped set up the site—Web master. As those people move on to other jobs, presumably breaking into it will become easier.

qualifications: A college degree isn't required for this job. But broad computer hardware and software expertise, programming, and graphic design skills are. Experience in systems administration is also helpful, since you'll also be responsible for reviving the system if the server crashes or a computer virus immobilizes it.

characteristics: In addition to technical skills, you need to work well with non-techies because you'll be dealing with people from all over the company, including public relations staffers, investor relations people, technical support teams, and department managers.

Fred Armer *is the Web master at a computer company in Round Rock, Texas.*

How did you get the job?

Fred Armer, who studied electronic engineering, first started work as a telephone support technician. "You had to talk to a minimum of 40 customers a day, and they all had broken computers," he says. "They

> GET AS MUCH
> HANDS-ON
> EXPERIENCE AS
> YOU CAN IN
> PROGRAMMING AND
> GRAPHIC DESIGN,
> AND AS MUCH
> KNOWLEDGE AS YOU
> CAN OF HARDWARE
> AND SOFTWARE.

weren't in a very good mood by the time they got through to me."

Fred was interested in computer networking, and when a temporary job opened in the Web server group, he was put "on loan" to the department for an unspecified period of time. The job involved working for the Web master doing graphical design for the Web site. When the Web master left the company, Fred took over. Deciding whether to take the job was a no-brainer. "I like the fact that I don't have to talk with customers," he says. "Dealing with

internal people, rather than external, is really nice." As a longtime Internet user, Fred finds the job fits him in another way. "I've always spent time on the Internet, and now I'm getting paid for it."

What do you do all day?

There is never a shortage of items on Fred's long-running to-do list. "I keep my own list of things I need to get done, and my boss has a tendency to drop by and give me large tasks," Fred says. On an average day, the work includes updating computer servers, adding product information and changing prices for equipment listed on the Web site, adding news releases to the site, and fixing any software bugs that pop up.

He gathers the updates from people in public relations and investor relations and posts them on a staging server, where the legal department checks them to make sure everything is satisfactory. When legal gives its

OK, Fred moves the updates to the Web server, which makes the information available to Internet users all over the world.

He also spends time checking out the competition. "I like to look at other Web sites to get ideas and see what everyone else is doing," he says. "Technology changes so fast, it's good to keep up with what features other sites are offering."

Fred gets together with other programmers and marketing staffers to brainstorm about new ideas for the company's site. "We talk about what we want to be in the future, and what we can do to get there," he says. "It's open to anyone who has good ideas. We just bounce around thoughts."

Where do you see this job leading you?

Fred would like eventually to move to more advanced network administration work. But for now, he's happy spending his days in cyberspace.

100. Worldwide Supply Base Administrator

description: Years ago, quality inspection was standard operating procedure. Parts, or completed pieces, from suppliers would be inspected at your company's site and the rejects returned.

Then came quality control, the next step in quality inspection. Quality control took place when items were in the *process* of being built. Suppliers set up their own systems, and your company came in during production to accept or reject parts before they were shipped.

Quality assurance is the new title given to this process.

The worldwide supply base administrator achieves quality assurance by setting up inspection systems with the suppliers at the beginning of a project, and ensuring that the suppliers institute their own quality control.

salary: Average salary is $30,000 to $60,000 per year, depending on the nature of the company and its location.

prospects: Supply base administration is growing rapidly as many companies subcontract their manufacturing. Efficiency and quality control are being built into the initial processes and systems from the beginning instead of waiting for problems and fixing them later.

qualifications: A supply base administrator will have some of the following: a four-year degree in systems, mechanical, or process engineering; work experience in quality control; knowledge of the technical aspects of quality systems; a background in procurement purchasing; and/or a fluency with computers, charts, reports, and statistics.

characteristics: Traits to pull from your bag of tricks could include a second language, good problem solving and communication skills, diplomacy—especially in foreign countries—and good judgment and discretionary skills.

Becky Clemens *is a worldwide supply base administrator at Microsoft.*

How did you get the job?

Before working at Microsoft, Becky Clemens was inspecting printed circuit boards. As her skills became honed, she was promoted to Pacific Circuit's highest level of quality control. From there, her skills and experience took her to Microsoft.

She worked her way up into her current position. Early on, Microsoft was just evolving from incoming inspection to setting up inspections at the supplier. Becky first taught the supplier how to inspect components and raw materials, report that data to Microsoft, and improve the quality of their raw materials. Quality engineer was her next job title. "When the company made the final step to supply base administrator, I was right there boarding a plane to Brazil to help set up Brazil's system," Becky says proudly. She then adds, "I attribute my success to being a very detail-oriented perfectionist."

What do you do all day?

Becky has her own suppliers and is in charge of several sites worldwide. She interfaces with the regional manufacturing management group (the Microsoft group who is in charge of a region) and the supplier or subcontractor, to help them meet the needs of the manufacturer's management group.

One of her main suppliers has multiple sites around the world, including Brazil, China, Australia, and Singapore. They each supply all the software packaging for that country—including the materials, the printing—even duplicating the disks. "This is all part of the efficiency of manufacturing on location and building up the local economy in that country," Becky explains.

Becky spends a lot of her time on location with her suppliers, looking at their systems and giving them feedback on how to improve those systems. She helps them assess if their suppliers have systems and processes in place.

THE AMERICAN SOCIETY FOR QUALITY CONTROL IS A GOOD RESOURCE FOR TRENDS OF SYSTEMS AND PROCESSES, AND QUALITY IMPROVEMENT—BOTH NATIONALLY AND INTERNATIONALLY. THEY ALSO HAVE NATIONAL AND REGIONAL MEETINGS. (SEE RESOURCES, PAGE 212).

When she's back stateside, she is in constant contact with her foreign sites, helping support them, evaluating their performance data, and reporting it all to management.

She works about 50 hours a week, with a somewhat flexible schedule, including lots of travel time.

Where do you see this job leading you?

Advancements for Becky could be to expand into the procurement field—getting more into negotiating contracts with the suppliers. "Procurement involves determining whether to make it or buy off the shelf," Becky explains. She may get into subcontract management—a position that is higher up in the decision making—and more involved in corporate-level communication, as opposed to site-level communication.

Becky could easily be a site-base administrator for many other kinds of manufacturing companies. "My personal aim at this point is to expand my experience and knowledge in the growing procurement field," she says. "The trend is that worldwide, everybody is already setting up their own basic systems." She sees procurement as being the next place to help drive those quality expectations and improvements when setting up initial relationships with the suppliers.

RESOURCES

American Association of University Professors (AAUP), 1012 14th St. NW, Washington, DC 20005; (800) 424-2973.

American Institute of Chemical Engineers (AICHE), 345 E. 47th St., New York, NY 10017; (800) 242-4363.
AICHE has inexpensive student memberships, offers employment services, and publishes a monthly newsletter.

American Library Association, 50 E. Huron St., Chicago, IL 60611; (312) 944-6780.
Contact the association for information on cyberlibrarians.

American Management Association, 135 W. 50th St., New York, NY 10020-1201; (212) 586-8100.

American Society of Heating, Refrigeration, and Air Conditioning (ASHRACE), 1791 Tullie Circle NE, Atlanta, GA 30329; (800) ASHRACE.
ASHRACE develops technical manuals, provides training, and has local chapters across the country.

American Society for Quality Control, ASQC, P.O. Box 3005, Milwaukee, WI 53201-3005; (800) 248-1946.
ASQC can provide you with information on supplier quality engineers and on ISO 9000.

Association for Computing Machinery, 1515 Broadway, New York, NY 10036; (212) 869-7440.
Contact the association for more information on graphical user interface design.

Cahners Publishing Company, 245 W. 17th St., New York, NY 10011; (212) 645-0067.
Cahners publishes Broadcasting and Cable Magazine, *which has job listings for those interested in television news.*

Human Factors and Ergonomics Society, P.O. Box 1369, Santa Monica, CA 90406; (310) 394-1811.
The society can provide you with information on graphical user interface design.

Institute for Electrical and Electronic Engineers, Inc., 345 E. 47th St., New York, NY 10017; (212) 705-7900.

International Association of Exposition Management, P.O. Box 802425, Dallas, TX 75380; (214) 458-8002.
Contact the association for more information on the trade show industry.

National Public Telecomputing Network, 50680 Bainbridge Rd., Cleveland, OH 44139; (216) 498-4050.
Contact NPTP for information on freenets.

New York Marketing Association 60 E. 42nd St., New York, NY 10165; (212) 687-3280.
The association can provide you with information on sales and marketing.

Society of Automotive Engineers, 400 Commonwealth Dr., Warrendale, PA 15096-0001; (412) 776-4841.
The society distributes a monthly newsletter that advertises employment opportunities in the engineering field.

Society for Technical Communications, 901 N. Stuart St., Suite 904, Arlington, VA 22203; (703) 522-4114.
Contact the society for information on technical writing.

ABOUT THE AUTHORS

Lori Hawkins grew up in Albuquerque, New Mexico, and studied journalism at the University of Arizona in Tucson. After graduating, she covered politics and business for Reuters News Service in Mexico City and Central America. She went on to report on Mexico and international trade for the now-defunct San Antonio Light *newspaper and on small business issues for the* Houston Business Journal. *She is married and lives in Austin, Texas, where she is a business reporter covering the software industry at the* Austin American-Statesman.

Betsy Dowling is an award-winning journalist from Texas who has recently relocated to New York City. While working as a newspaper reporter in Odessa, Texas, Betsy received the 1994 Anson Jones award for excellence in medical writing and a 1993 Texas State Teachers Association School Bell Award for outstanding education reporting. She is a graduate of Southwest Texas State University.

NOTES

NOTES

NOTES

NOTES

NOTES

NOTES

CAREERS   U.S. $14.95/CAN $19.95

- Are you eager to redefine the way we look at the world?
- Do you prefer programming languages to your native tongue?
- Is reality only real when it's virtual?
- Do you find the information superhighway more thrilling than the Indianapolis speedway?

If you answered "yes" to any of these questions, then one of the many jobs available in technology may be just right for you.

Spanning corporate, nonprofit, and freelance careers, *100 Jobs in Technology* provides all the basics needed—including brief descriptions of each job, typical salary levels, prospects for finding work, and qualifications and characteristics you should possess—to flourish in a chosen line of work. Along with each entry, there is an insightful profile of a person from each field that describes a typical day on the job and details the steps each took to rise to his or her current position.

Among the many careers and jobs, you'll find:

- **On-line Services,** with jobs including Freenet Director, Internet Access Provider, Web Page Designer, and Web Page Master;
- **Science,** including Genetic Research Technician, Biotechnology Researcher, Environmental Engineer, and Physicist;
- **Business and Marketing,** including Interactive Advertising Creative Director, Computer Sales Representative, Cyber Cafe Owner, and Computer Sales Representative;
- **Computer Hardware and Software,** including CD-ROM Producer, Computer Game Animator, Computer Chip Designer, and Virtual Reality Developer;
- **Publishing,** including Computer Book Author, Computer Trade Magazine Reporter, Technical Writer, and Book Designer;

and more!

If the boundaries of your imagination are as limitless as the possibilities the world of technology holds, then *100 Jobs in Technology* is the perfect tool to help you find and fulfill your dreams.

A Macmillan Reference Book
Macmillan • USA

another idea from becker&mayer!

ISBN 0-02-861431-3